KNOW YOUR
RELIGIONS

VOLUME 1

KNOW YOUR RELIGIONS

VOLUME 1

ॐ

A COMPARATIVE LOOK AT MORMONISM AND CATHOLICISM

Alonzo L. Gaskill

FOREWORD BY
Father Patrick L. LaBelle, O.P.

Millennial Press

Millennial Press, Inc.
P.O. Box 1741
Orem, UT 84059

ISBN: 1-932597-40-9

Cover design and typesetting by Adam Riggs
Production Editing By Martha Parker

To Professor Phillip A. Allred—a scholar, gifted teacher, and friend. In memory of our eye-opening time at the University of Notre Dame.

"These were days never to be forgotten . . ." (JS—H 1:75)

TABLE OF CONTENTS

ACKNOWLEDGMENTS...IX

FOREWORD...XI

INTRODUCTION...1

A BRIEF HISTORY OF CATHOLICISM..7

THE ONLY "TRUE" CHURCH..25

THE NATURE OF GOD..35

THE ROLE OF GRACE AND WORKS IN SALVATION..45

HEAVEN AND HELL...51

PURGATORY AND THE SPIRIT WORLD...59

LIMBO AND THE 67

SALVATION OF LITTLE CHILDREN..67

SACRAMENTS...71

THE SALE OF INDULGENCES..93

POPES AND PROPHETS...99

SCRIPTURE...109

THE GREAT APOSTASY 117

THE GREATAND ABOMINABLE CHURCH...121

SAINTS..129

MARY...139

ORIGINAL SIN..147

THE CROSS..153

CREEDS..161

LITURGY AND RITUAL..167

VESTMENTS, CLERICAL CLOTHING,AND TEMPLE GARMENTS........171

CHALLENGES FOR THE CATHOLIC CHURCH...175

CONCLUSION..183

APPENDIX:..189

CURRENT DEMOGRAPHICS..189

BIBLIOGRAPHY...193

Acknowledgments

I wish to acknowledge the invaluable contributions of several Roman Catholics who took time out of their busy schedules to read drafts of this book and to offer suggestions that have greatly improved the manuscript, namely, Father Joseph S. Rooney, S.J. of San Andres Catholic Church; Jorge de Azevedo, a practicing Roman Catholic from Brazil; and Father Patrick LaBelle, O.P. of Stanford University.

In addition, I express my appreciation to Tom Evans, a budding scholar of Roman Catholicism, and Florcita Cordobesa, who was a practicing Argentine Roman Catholic for some twenty-one years. Both provided a number of suggestions that improved the text.

I am ever grateful to Jan Nyholm, whose keen eye and editorial assistance have always improved my manuscripts.

I also express my appreciation to the staff at Millennial Press for their invitation to me to write this book and for their efforts in preparing this manuscript for publication. They have been wonderful to work with and have offered me great latitude in both style and content.

Finally, I remind the reader that this book is not a publication of The Church of Jesus Christ of Latter-day Saints or of Brigham Young University. While I believe the content to be accurate, I bear sole responsibility for what follows.

FOREWORD

In my many years of campus interfaith work at various universities, I am not sure if there has ever been a single local LDS institute of religion where I have not been asked to visit and give a presentation on Roman Catholicism. What I always found was an attempt, honest and sincere, by the directors of the institute to "show" the LDS students what Catholics were all about and then to, once again, "show" them a bona fide Catholic priest.

What was the setting like? Most often the institute directors would display pictures of various takes on what Jesus looked like and depictions of Mary and a few of the saints accompanied by rosaries, plastic statues, and the like. But I also always found a room full of very bright and inquiring young people. Every one of these students would be a most attractive missionary to Catholic students wherever they were sent to serve. They were also well cared for by the institute staff. Of course, in these LDS buildings there was always a gym, offices, decent reading rooms, etc., which were a part of the traditional environment of any LDS institute of religion, and, perhaps the most important of all, there was parking! I must admit that when I served as the president of the Dominican Theological School in Berkeley, I entered into an agreement with the director of the LDS institute to help him complete a work on some Catholic issue or other in exchange for the chance to "rent" a few parking places. That little exchange gave me the chance to get to know my colleague as well as park my car. The scene rarely changed.

One more aspect of my LDS experience has been finding many young people from the Mormon institute ever-present at the beginning of each academic year, helping with move-in problems and the like on campus, and then doing a little evangelizing on the side. I came to expect this whole picture at the five or six universities where I worked in an interfaith ministry, and I have heard of similar situations in other programs wherein the Catholic bishop had given my Dominican colleagues the pastoral care of the Catholic students at the local university.

When I arrived at Stanford University to take up the Catholic chaplaincy there, I presumed some things, learned many things, and was surprised by others. One of the things that came to me as a wonderful surprise was seeing how the Mormons dealt with other faiths. The very intelligent young LDS people were given serious scholarly materials to digest regarding what other people believe. The adults in the LDS community exhibited a fine example of hospitality and cooperation, and there was a wonderful respect for the beliefs and practices of others outside the Mormon family.

The energetic contacting of students gradually, but quite certainly, evolved into a friendly and genuine expression of religious respect. I was invited to speak to a number of the classes given at the institute of religion, and there I found myself a wonderful colleague in the author of this book, and later I found others in his successors. Thankfully, I did not find the Catholic "trinkets" that so often in the past had identified Roman Catholics in my prior experiences.

Having said all of that, I turn to this very thoughtful and carefully researched work by Dr. Alonzo L. Gaskill. I found in this work, *Know Your Religions: A Comparative Look at Mormonism and Catholicism*, the product of a man of faith, a man of learning and, once again, a man with his hand outstretched in friendship. His understanding of the structure, the customs, and the teachings of Catholicism all join together to make this a good read and good teaching. I found insights presented that are often omitted in many similar works written by and for Catholics. Often the material written for the university student and presented by Catholic writers is burdened by trivia, superstition, simplistic solutions to poorly asked questions, and an arrogance that has no place in Catholic teaching based as it is on the holy scriptures. This work, however, is theologically sound, expresses a clear understanding of Catholic thought and practice, points the serious student to additional information and resources, and opens the door to genuine dialogue for any who choose to engage in such a practice.

When the Winter Olympics came to Salt Lake City some years ago, many discussions arose among students who expressed a critical and unfounded distrust for what the Mormon family would do as the center of such an international spotlight. What the LDS Church and its leaders did was reach down deep into their tradition, which teaches that Mormons should try to be the best kind of persons possible, and offer that tradition to a surprised world. I believe that Dr. Gaskill has shown us in this work how such a negative perception is possible when discussions are so often clouded by prejudice and ignorance. He has shown us—especially those of us who are students of religion—how to understand the faith of another tradition with precision and accuracy, and, at the same time, he has allowed his readers to learn more about their own faith in the process. I believe that it would be a good idea to make this a regular text for Catholics who want to learn more about their own church. I cannot think of a better way to introduce this important work to university students and others who will grow in wisdom and grace as they walk with the author through the forest of Catholic tradition and thought.

Rev. Patrick L. LaBelle, O.P.
Director, The Catholic Community at Stanford University

INTRODUCTION

Because of our united belief in Jesus Christ's divine mission and ministry, *all* Christian denominations have their similarities. Most believe in baptism and the sacrament of the Lord's Supper.[1] The majority believes in the Bible as the word of God.[2] A belief in resurrection from the dead and a glorious afterlife for the faithful are common.[3] And, of course, central to all Christian faiths is the sacrifice of the Lord Jesus Christ. Certainly numerous other similarities could be cited.

It is no surprise that many would be more inclined to notice parallels between Protestantism and Mormonism than between Latter-day Saints and Catholics, and while many protestant faiths do have their parallels with Mormonism, the reader may well be surprised at how much Latter-day Saint Christians and Catholic Christians have in common. This book will examine some of the most famous and the most foundational ideas in Roman Catholicism, how they are similar to LDS theology, and in what ways they differ.

As a preface to this work, I remind Latter-day Saint readers of how they have felt when their faith has been misunderstood—when their doctrines, history, or beliefs have been inaccurately represented. Such

---

1   Some Christians see these rites, ordinances, or sacraments as necessary for salvation, while others see them as simply outward signs of inward commitment to Christ.

2   Some faiths see it as more of a symbolic message, while others take the biblical text more literally.

3   Some traditions believe the Resurrection to be physical, while others expect only a spiritual resurrection.

an experience is at best disappointing and in many cases offensive and even hurtful. Because we know well what it feels like to be misunderstood, we should never be guilty of misrepresenting any other faith. Latter-day Saints should be kind, caring, and loving toward their non-LDS neighbors. We should be sincerely interested in what is truly important to those of other faiths—particularly those who live among us. Elder M. Russell Ballard counseled the Saints: "Get to know your neighbors. Learn about . . . their views. . . . Our pioneer ancestors were driven from place to place by uninformed and intolerant neighbors. They experienced extraordinary hardship and persecution because they thought, acted, and believed differently from others. If our history teaches us nothing else, it should teach us to respect the rights of all people."[4] President Brigham Young taught, "It matters not what a man's creed is, whether it be Catholic or Episcopalian, Presbyterian, Methodist, Baptist, Quaker, or Jew, he will receive kindness and friendship from us."[5] Again, from Elder Ballard we read:

> If we are truly disciples of the Lord Jesus Christ, we will reach out with love and understanding to all of our neighbors at all times. . . . Perceptions and assumptions can be very dangerous and unfair. There are some of our members who may fail to reach out with friendly smiles, warm handshakes, and loving service to all of their neighbors. At the same time, there may be those who move into our neighborhoods who are not of our faith who come with negative preconceptions about the Church and its members. Surely good neighbors should put forth every effort to understand each other and to be kind to one another regardless of religion, nationality, race, or culture.[6]

Like Elder Ballard, time and again President Gordon B. Hinckley preached the importance of Latter-day Saints having forbearance and understanding for their non-LDS neighbors and friends. He taught that Mormons must recognize the good those of other faiths do, and the goodness of those who actively follow other religious traditions.

---

4   M. Russell Ballard, "The Doctrine of Inclusion," *Ensign* (November 2001): 37–38.
5   B. H. Roberts, *A Comprehensive History of The Church of Jesus Christ of Latter-day Saints, Century One*, 6 vols. (Orem, Utah: Sonos Publishing, 1991), 5:213.
6   Ballard, "The Doctrine of Inclusion," 36.

He urged the Saints to seek to understand other people's points of view without taking offense or being offensive.[7] Setting an example for the Saints to emulate, the Prophet Joseph Smith once stated:

> If it has been demonstrated that I have been willing to die for a "Mormon," I am bold to declare before Heaven that I am just as ready to die in defending the rights of a Presbyterian, a Baptist, or a good man of any other denomination; for the same principle which would trample upon the rights of the Latter-day Saints would trample upon the rights of the Roman Catholics, or of any other denomination who may be unpopular and too weak to defend themselves.[8]

There is much good in the various religious traditions of the world, and many good people in all denominations. Just as we have sometimes been misunderstood or misrepresented by others not of our faith, perhaps some of us have been guilty of misunderstanding our Catholic brothers and sisters. As the modern prophets and apostles have testified, this should not be. Thus, were I to pick one word to describe the purpose of this book, it would probably be *understanding*. Some one half of all of the earth's Christians are Roman Catholic. Latter-day Saints, regardless of where they live, will, at some point in their lives, likely have the opportunity to meet and interact with good, faithful Catholics. This book has been written not to criticize or condemn Catholics, but rather to inform Latter-day Saints of the basic beliefs of their Catholic brothers and sisters—and to set straight some of the common misconceptions Mormons might have about Catholics.

Throughout the text we will look at what Catholics believe and how it relates to LDS thinking on the same subject. While we will seek for common ground on those subjects where common ground indeed exists, we will also point out areas where Catholics and Mormons dif-

---

7   See, for example, Gordon B. Hinckley, "Remarks at Pioneer Day Commemoration Concert," *Ensign* (October 2001): 70; Gordon B. Hinckley, "Excerpts from Recent Addresses of President Gordon B. Hinckley," *Ensign* (August 1996): 60–61; Gordon B. Hinckley, "Words of the Living Prophet," *Liahona* (June 1997): 32; Gordon B. Hinckley, *Teachings of Gordon B. Hinckley* (Salt Lake City: Deseret Book, 1997), 662–67; and Gordon B. Hinckley, *Discourses of Gordon B. Hinckley, Volume 1: 1995–1999* (Salt Lake City: Deseret Book, 2005), 1:200, 201, 271, 294, and 496.

8   Joseph Smith Jr., *History of The Church of Jesus Christ of Latter-day Saints,* ed. B. H. Roberts, 2d ed., rev., 8 vols. (Salt Lake City: Deseret Book, 1978), 5:498.

fer on major issues. In many cases, the Latter-day Saint reader will be surprised by how much these two faiths are alike in many important areas.

It would be helpful for the reader to keep in mind that in both Catholicism and Mormonism, there are sometimes distinctions between what the laity believe to be doctrinal, and what the Church says is its official position on any given subject. This may be more prevalent in contemporary Catholicism than it is in Mormonism, specifically because the current Catholic Church allows its members a great deal of autonomy in what they believe, teach, write, or espouse. Mormonism, on the other hand, tends to stress unanimity among its members and congregations—certainly in teachings and writings but even more particularly in the style or nature of worship services. Thus there is a sameness about LDS worship services and classes throughout the world. Although Catholic texts, such as *The Order of Prayer in the Celebration of the Eucharist*, ensure that basically the same passages are read in each Catholic congregation on a given day,[9] the hierarchy of the Catholic Church does not seek to staunchly dictate things such as the style of worship in its congregations or the doctrines taught in meetings outside of the Mass, although there is perhaps a bit more doctrinal control than liturgical control. Thus, some Catholic congregations have a very high or formal liturgy, while others are much more casual in their approach to the Mass, including flexibility in the type of music used and even in the content of the priest's homily or sermon. Conversely, the style of worship in any Latter-day Saint congregation on any given Sunday would be nearly identical because there is a strict uniformity worldwide—a uniformity in doctrine and liturgy that is dictated by the leadership of the Church.[10]

---

9   Remember, Catholics don't celebrate the Mass (i.e., their version of what Latter-day Saints call "sacrament meeting") only on Sundays. The Mass is celebrated in many Catholic congregations on a daily basis.

10   Again, this is not to suggest that Catholics have no uniformity in doctrine. However, as a number of Catholics read this manuscript, I received one consistent message—a statement akin to this: "While this is the official doctrine of the Catholic church, many lay Catholics will not know about this teaching." Thus, in Catholicism it is not uncommon for the members to hold beliefs that are different from the official doctrinal position of the Church. While this also happens in Mormonism, it seems more common in Catholicism, in part because the Catholic Church exercises less control

Additionally, the reader should keep in mind that there are approximately one billion Catholics worldwide. There is no way to state, in a publication of any length, exactly what *all* Catholics believe. Just as lay Mormons might have their own personal beliefs about various gospel subjects, so it is within Catholicism. Not all Catholics think alike on all subjects. This is particularly true of Catholics in the United States when compared to Catholics in countries like Mexico. Thus, my intent in this book will be to examine the official Catholic and LDS positions where possible and to avoid discussing the many possible personal interpretations of Catholic or LDS doctrine, including those that may be culturally conditioned. Hence, you may meet a Catholic who sees things differently than I have presented them in this book. Nonetheless, I have earnestly sought to be as accurate as possible, and I have diligently endeavored to consult reputable Catholic scholars, practitioners, and publications in an effort to present what current Catholic teaching is on any given subject. If a Catholic disagrees with what I have said, it will not be because I have misrepresented their faith, but rather because I have sought to represent the Church's position instead of the multiplicity of positions held by lay Catholics.

Again, the goal of this book is to inform Latter-day Saint readers about the basic beliefs of their Catholic brothers and sisters. It is in *no way* intended as a polemic against Catholics or their faith. On the contrary, this small work is intended to be a step toward understanding, mutual respect, and friendship.[11] As similarities between these two faiths are highlighted in this book, it is my hope that Latter-day Saints and Catholics will see the good in each other and the common ground

---

over what is taught in classes, such as Sunday School, and perhaps also because Roman Catholics tend to feel more autonomy than Latter-day Saints when it comes to what they write or espouse. Thus, doctrinal uniformity is not as consistent in Catholicism as in Mormonism.

11   On a related note, Latter-day Saint scholar Robert L. Millet once noted, "While there are, to be sure, major doctrinal differences between us, there are a striking number of similarities once those involved in [the] discussion are able to put away arrogance and pettiness and defensiveness, once the participants are more concerned with coming to a deeper understanding of the truth than they are with proving the other to be wrong-headed." See Robert L. Millet, "Where Did the Cross Go?" (lecture presented to the BYU Religious Education Faculty, Brigham Young University, Provo, Utah, September 16, 2005). Transcript of this lecture in author's possession.

we hold by virtue of our mutual testimony that Jesus is the Christ, the
Son of the Living God.

A Brief History of Catholicism

Of all Christian denominations, Catholicism, being the oldest, arguably has the most detailed and complex history of any faith tracing its origins back to Jesus the Christ.[1] To give a recounting of that history in only a few short pages will seem to some a pointless exercise. Nevertheless, realizing that many Latter-day Saints may be unfamiliar with the history and development of Catholicism, I will attempt to highlight a few of the most significant events in that faith's history.

While Catholicism is believed by its adherents to be the faith established by Jesus in the Bible, the seminal event usually seen as the official beginning of the movement is more often than not Christ's commission of Peter. In the Gospel of Matthew we find this: "Blessed art thou, Simon Barjona . . . And I say also unto thee, That thou art Peter, and upon this rock I will build my church; and the gates of hell shall not prevail against it. And I will give unto thee the keys of the kingdom of heaven: and whatsoever thou shalt bind on earth shall be bound in heaven: and whatsoever thou shalt loose on earth shall be loosed in heaven" (Matthew 16:17–19). Faithful Catholics see this event, more than any other, as the beginning of their faith.

---

1   Catholicism sees itself as the Church that Jesus established in the New Testament; thus it is a tradition with some two millennia of history under its belt. Mormonism, on the other hand, holds that it is the faith introduced to the spirit sons and daughters of God in the pre-mortal world—a faith that has been revealed in every gospel dispensation, including the dispensations of the meridian of times and fullness of times. Thus, like Catholicism, Mormonism boasts of a multi-millennia history.

During the first century after the death of Christ, Catholics see the Church developing both doctrinally and ecclesiastically. Catholic scholars argue that during that crucial period, Christians began to interpret the significance of Jesus' life and teachings. During the second half of the first century, leaders of the Church, such as the Apostle Paul, helped the Christian community begin to see the Jesus of history as the Messiah of this new faith. It is also during this period that the Church began its transition from the unstructured, Jesus-centered movement, to a more ecclesiastically organized church with leaders of different levels of authority (e.g., popes, bishops, pastors, evangelists, and deacons).[2]

Catholic historians indicate that during the second through fifth centuries, the Church was confronted with the challenge of translating its decidedly Judaeo-Christian teachings into more Hellenistic categories that would be palatable to the large number of Gentile converts to Christianity. As Pope John Paul II put it, the Church "progressively entered into Greek culture and more clearly realized the need for ways of presenting her doctrine which would be adequate and convincing in that cultural context."[3] Because of this doctrinal transition, Catholicism has been criticized by some for its systematic "contamination of the gospel with Hellenism" during that period. However, Catholic scholars argue that these were not "contaminations," but rather natural, cultural developments. Historians also stress that the gospel cannot exist outside of its "cultural matrix"—which, at that time, was the Hellenized Greco-Roman culture.[4] Regardless, it is fair to say that during that era, the doctrines of the Church, and, to some degree, its general appearance, greatly evolved from the faith of the New Testament to an organization and theology with a much more Catholic feel.[5]

---

2   While lay Catholics might say that Peter was the first pope, and the Twelve and their successors were the bishops of the New Testament church, Roman Catholic scholars traditionally note that the current ecclesiastical structure of the Catholic Church was a later development. See, for example, Frederick J. Cwiekowski, *The Beginnings of the Church* (New York: Paulist Press, 1988), 185.

3   John Paul II, *Crossing the Threshold of Hope* (New York: Alfred A. Knopf, 1994), 46.

4   See John C. Cavadini, "Hellenism," in *Harper Collins Encyclopedia of Catholicism*, ed. Richard P. McBrien (San Francisco, Calif.: HarperSanFrancisco, 1995), 608–9.

5   This is not a criticism of Catholicism. Rather, it is simply a frank acknowledgment that the theological and Christological controversies of the first six centuries of Christianity

A major development of the third century was the beginning of the monastic movement. The founder of Christian monasticism was a man by the name of Anthony of Egypt (AD 251–356). Anthony retired to the desert to live the solitary life, but he soon attracted a following. From that point onward, monasticism was part of Catholicism—many would take vows of poverty, chastity, and obedience in an effort to draw closer to God and to bless the Church and the world through their examples and service. While Anthony is considered the founder of Catholic monasticism, to a great extent the movement gained its real momentum when the persecution of Christians became illegal under the Emperor Constantine. Monastics began to flee into the desert to get away from the rise of complacency, affluence, and corruption, or worldliness, within the Church.[6] When Constantine's conversion to Christianity made the religion both acceptable and popular, people began to flock to the Church for social or economic reasons—but not always out of true conversion. Church leaders often lived in costly homes and enjoyed a luxurious lifestyle, rather than apostolic poverty. Martyrdom was no longer feared, and for those who desired to lay down their lives for Christ, it was no longer an option. So Monasticism became a new form of "self-sacrifice" on behalf of Christ. Monks were the new martyrs who sought to get away from what appeared to be a church filled with corruption and hypocritical members. Church historian Bruce Shelley put it this way: "The hermit often fled . . . not so much from the world as from the world in the church."[7]

The fourth century saw a number of developments significant in the history of Catholicism. Constantine, who called for the First Coun-

provided a great deal of evolution and formalization, which has been acknowledged by Catholic scholars. In addition, one need only to read the writings of the Ante-Nicene Fathers to see this process of evolution and reorientation documented. Certainly early Christianity went through such a process, as did early Mormonism. As the various revelations of the Restoration came to Joseph Smith, he learned many things that he did not initially understand after receiving the First Vision. God and angels revealed to Joseph "line upon line" (Isaiah 28:10), and through that process, the Church developed and solidified its doctrinal positions.

6   See Justo L. González, *The Story of Christianity*, 2 vols. in 1 (Peabody, Mass.: Prince Press, 2001), 1:124, 1:136–37.

7   Bruce L. Shelley, *Church History in Plain Language*, 2d ed. (Nashville, Tenn.: Thomas Nelson Publishers, 1995), 118.

cil of Nicaea (AD 325), was converted in the fourth century. In AD 313, he signed the Edict of Milan, which ended the legal persecution of Christians. Augustine was also converted during the fourth century. He left an indelible mark on the doctrines of Catholicism through his teachings on the subjects of grace, original sin, the Trinity, and human sexuality, to name a few. In AD 330, construction was begun on Catholicism's principal church, Saint Peter's Basilica.

But perhaps one of the most important events of the fourth century was Constantine's convening of the First Council of Nicaea. Nicaea I was the first ecumenical (or worldwide) council of the Catholic Church, and it lasted from late May until late August of AD 325. While this council addressed a number of things, the most important was a discussion regarding the Arian controversy.

Arius was a very popular priest in Alexandria, Egypt, who had been teaching that God must be unique and above all things. According to Arius, Jesus was certainly the son of God. However, He could not be God or be equal to God. He had to be subordinate to the Father because (1) He was created by God,[8] thus "there was [a time] when He was not,"[9] and (2) if Jesus was equal to God the Father, then Christians were polytheists.[10] So, according to Arius' thinking, the Father and Son must be of "*like* substance" rather than of "*one* substance."[11]

Arianism had several vocal opponents, including Alexander and Athanasius of Alexandria. Alexander was Arius' bishop, and he argued that Arius was wrong because a being that is anything less than fully God would be incapable of saving His creations.[12] Thus, according to Alexander, Jesus could not have been created by God. Alexander had

---

8   This was one of the sticky parts of Arius' position: namely, that he claimed that since Jesus was a created being, "unlike the Father, he was capable of change." See A. Kenneth Curtis, J. Stephen Lang, and Randy Petersen, *The 100 Most Important Events in Christian History* (Grand Rapids, Mich.: Fleming H. Revell, 1998), 35. This was heretical in the eyes of most—anciently and today.

9   See González, *Story of Christianity*, 1:161; and Samuel Wells, "Trinity," in *Encyclopedia of Christianity*, ed. John Bowden (New York: Oxford University Press, 2005), 1209.

10   See González, *Story of Christianity*, 1:161.

11   See Roger Keller, "Christianity," in Spencer J. Palmer, Roger R. Keller, Dong Sull Choi, and James A. Toronto, *Religions of the World: A Latter-day Saint View* (Provo, Utah: Brigham Young University, 1997), 189.

12   Curtis, Lang, and Petersen, *100 Most Important Events in Christian History*, 35; See González, *Story of Christianity*, 1:161.

Arius condemned.[13] But this only added fuel to the fire. Riots erupted over the controversy and the two alternate positions. To deal with this controversy—and to settle the question as to who was actually right—Constantine called the First Council of Nicea (AD 325). More than 300 bishops attended. In the end, the question was this: Are the members of the Godhead of the "same substance," or are they of "like substance"? The council decided that they were of the "same substance." Arius, and two bishops who sided with him, were exiled, and the "official" beginnings of the doctrine of the Trinity were born. The famous "Nicene Creed" was specifically calculated to combat the Arian heresy[14] with phrases like: Jesus is "true God of true God," or Jesus was "begotten, not made," and Jesus was "from the substance of the Father." Each of these creedal statements implied that Arius was heretical in his teachings. Thus, the fourth century Nicene Creed was less a statement about what Christianity believed, but rather more of a statement about what Christianity rejected—namely Arianism.

The fourth century also saw the First Council of Constantinople. This council, held from May to July of AD 381, reiterated Nicaea I's stance on the Trinity (in opposition to Arianism). It also declared the full humanity of Jesus, in opposition to Apollinarianism, which claimed that Jesus had no human soul, but rather had an entirely divine soul that had replaced His human soul.[15] Constantinople I also taught the divinity of the Holy Ghost, contra the "Macedonians" or "Pneumatomachians," who rejected the Spirit's divinity. The Nicene-Constantinopolian Creed—a longer version of the Nicene Creed—is traditionally associated with the First Council of Constantinople, although it was not formulated until decades after the council.

In the fifth century, the councils of Ephesus (AD 431) and Chalcedon (AD 451) were held. The Council of Ephesus dealt primarily with the question as to whether Mary was the mother of God (*Theotokos* in Greek), or simply the mother of Jesus' human body. At this council,

---

13   Curtis, Lang, and Petersen, *100 Most Important Events in Christian History,* 35; See González, *Story of Christianity,* 1:162.

14   See González, *Story of Christianity,* 1:165–66; and Wells, "Trinity," in *Encyclopedia of Christianity,* 1209.

15   See Richard P. McBrien, *Catholicism,* rev. ed. (San Francisco, Calif.: HarperSanFrancisco, 1994), 471, 489.

Nestorianism, which taught that Jesus had a "human person" and a "divine person" within Him, was condemned as heretical. The Council of Chalcedon's focus was related to that of Ephesus in that it highlighted the Catholic belief that Jesus was one person with two natures—one human and the other divine. Thus, according to Chalcedon, Jesus had dual natures but not dual personhood.

Perhaps the most important event in the sixth century was the Second Council of Constantinople (held May through June of AD 553). This council, called by the emperor (Justinian I) and not attended by the pope, posthumously condemned the teachings of three prominent theologians whose dogmas seemed on the surface to be related to Nestorianism.[16] The pope reluctantly accepted the council's decision to condemn these three men.

In the seventh century, the Catholic Church held its sixth ecumenical council, known as the Third Council of Constantinople (November AD 680 through September AD 681). This council declared that Jesus had both a human will and a divine will. The council reiterated Chalcedon's teaching that Jesus had two natures and argued that His dual nature established that He had two wills, which functioned together in perfect harmony.

One of the most interesting events of the eighth century was the beginning of the Iconoclast Controversy (AD 726–780 and AD 815–843). The world "Iconoclast" means "icon smasher," and the controversy centered on a debate as to whether icons, or religious art, should be allowed in Christian worship. In AD 726, Emperor Leo III condemned the use of icons, but in time their use was reinstituted within the Church. However, in AD 815–843 the controversy surrounding their use arose again. While the controversy was brewing, significant physical damage was done to religious art in the churches in the Byzantine Empire. Mosaics were gouged from the walls, and icons were painted over with whitewash. Iconophile monks were heavily persecut-

---

16   The three condemned theologians were Theodore of Mopsuestia (d. AD 428), Ibas of Edessa (d. AD 457), and Theodoret of Cyrrhus (d. circa AD 458).

ed for their practices and in some cases were punished by being forced to marry against their will or by having their eyes gouged out.[17]

During this same century, the papal states officially began. These states were portions of France and central Italy that acknowledged the temporal sovereignty of the pope. While various popes had claimed temporal power over certain parts of Italy as early as the fourth century, it was not until the eighth century that the Catholic Church actually assumed administrative control over these states. In 1870, when France withdrew its protection, these states ceased to belong to the Church and fell under the kingdom of Italy.

In AD 787, the Byzantine empress, Irene—with the support of Pope Hadrian I—convened the three-week long Second Council of Nicaea. It responded to the first Iconoclast Controversy by reinstituting the veneration of icons in worship.[18] It also affirmed the belief in the power of saints to intercede on behalf of the living—although it cautioned Catholics that God alone is worthy of our worship and adoration. The Second Council of Nicaea is the last of the ecumenical councils of Catholicism to be acknowledged by the Eastern Orthodox faith.

From October of AD 869 through February of AD 870, the Catholic Church held the Fourth Council of Constantinople. The council was convened to resolve what has become known as the "Photian Schism" between the East and the West. Without the sanction of a Church council or the pope, a layman named Photius had been appointed to replace the exiled patriarch of Constantinople. When the exiled patriarch (Ignatius) complained that he had been deprived of a position rightfully his, Pope Nicholas I refused to acknowledge Photius as patriarch. This began the schism, which lasted for some thirty years. Constantinople IV was held to resolve this issue, although the council was never acknowledged as authoritative by the Eastern side of the Church, which would eventually break off and become the Eastern Orthodox Church.

---

17   See John C. Cavadini, "Iconoclasm," in *Harper Collins Encyclopedia of Catholicism*, ed. Richard P. McBrien (San Francisco, Calif.: HarperSanFrancisco, 1995), 650.

18   This does not mean that Catholics or Eastern Orthodox "worship" images. Both faiths emphatically forbid their members to do so.

It was during the tenth century (in AD 993) that the Catholic Church declared its first "saint," a man by the name of Ulric, bishop of Augsburg.[19] It is true that others were perceived as "saints" much earlier than the tenth century. Indeed, from about the fifth century onward, local bishops were basically canonizing individuals whom they were convinced had lived holy lives. However, it wasn't until nearly the eleventh century that the Catholic Church took control of the matter in an effort to end a number of abuses and customs that had arisen because such declarations of sainthood had, previous to this time, been made by local leaders.

Midway through the eleventh century, the "Great Schism" of the Catholic Church took place. From the year AD 1054 onward, the Catholic Church was officially and permanently divided between East and West. Problems between the two sides had been evident as early as the First Council of Nicaea, however, what happened in 1054 caused more than a simple theological debate. It literally severed a portion of the Church, thereby giving birth to the Eastern Orthodox Church.

CRUSADER KNIGHT SWORD AND SHIELD

One author described the event as follows:

> One summer afternoon in the year 1054, as a service was about to begin in the Church of the Holy Wisdom at Constantinople, Cardinal Humbert and two other legates of the Pope entered the building and made their way up to the sanctuary. They had not come to pray. They placed a bull of Excommunication upon the altar and marched out once more. As he passed through the western door, the Cardinal shook the dust from his feet with the words: "Let God look and judge." A deacon ran out after

---

19   See Richard P. McBrien, *Lives of the Saints* (San Francisco, Calif.: HarperSanFrancisco, 2001), 7.

him in great distress and begged him to take back the Bull. Humbert refused; and it was dropped in the street.[20]

While attempts at unification were made, the Great Schism of the eleventh century would never be healed. To this day, the two faiths—Eastern Orthodoxy and Roman Catholicism—exist as separate churches that are fairly similar in their doctrines, but significantly different in their modes of worship.

During the eleventh century, the Catholic Church also began the first of several "crusades" against the expanding influence of Islam. The "people's crusade" (AD 1095), a precursor to the seven major crusades, was led by a man named Peter the Hermit, and it sought to liberate Jerusalem from the Muslims. Like the "people's crusade," the first crusade (AD 1096–1099), comprised primarily of knights from France, Germany, and Southern Italy, also sought to free Jerusalem from Muslim hands. The second crusade (circa AD 1146–1149) was called for because the pope's popularity was waning due to his excessive lifestyle. A revolt took place in Rome. The laity stormed the Vatican and turned it (and St. Peter's Basilica) into a "people's palace." The pope needed a distraction, so he employed the charismatic monk, Bernard of Clairvaux, to travel about telling the people that the Church was in peril because of the advancement of Islam. The people believed, and crusade number two was on! Crusade number three (AD 1189–1192) is the most romanticized of them all. King Richard the Lion-Hearted fought Saladin, the sultan of Egypt and Syria, in an attempt to regain access to the Christian holy sites of Palestine. The fourth crusade (circa AD 1199–1204) was initially bound for Egypt—to free it from Muslim hands. However, the Byzantine emperor had been ousted, blinded, tortured, and imprisoned by his corrupt brother. The son of the imprisoned emperor begged the pope to send the crusaders to his aid. They came and successfully retook the empire. However, after ravaging the city, the crusaders set up a Latin empire in Constantinople. This officially made any attempts at reunification be-

---

20   Robert Pollock, *The Everything World's Religions Book* (Avon, Mass.: Adams Media Corporation, 2002), 65.

tween the Eastern and Western churches fruitless. The fifth crusade (AD 1217–1221) instituted heavy taxes upon Christians in order to finance the Church's attack on Egyptian Muslims. According to one source, 20 percent of all income and revenues was required as a "crusade tax." However, when that did not provide enough revenue, the Church created another tax called "Peter's Pence," which consisted of 20 percent on top of the previous 20 percent for any who did not enlist in the "holy army."[21] The sixth crusade (AD 1228) was led by the excommunicated Roman Emperor Frederick II, known as *stupor mundi* or "the stupor of the world." Frederick made friends with the Muslim emperor—the man he was supposed to be fighting to regain the Holy Land. They struck a deal that the Christians would be allies with the Muslims against Genghis Khan, and in return they would be given Jerusalem (and many other sites in Palestine). Frederick agreed, and thus never had to fight a single battle in order to gain access to the Holy Land. However, some fifteen years later, the Muslims owned the city once again. Like during the fifth crusade, during the seventh (AD 1248–1252) money was tight. Taxes doubled to pay for the ongoing—but unproductive— crusades. Beyond the taxation, homes, properties, and possessions were subject to confiscation in order to finance the war. Like each of its predecessors, crusade number seven did not return Jerusalem to the hands of the Christians permanently.

The twelfth century saw three different ecumenical councils. The First Lateran Council (AD 1123) was held to ratify an agreement that lay political figures (such as kings or emperors) would no longer seek to choose candidates to become bishops. This council also issued prohibitions against simony (the purchasing of priesthood offices), and clerical marriage. Although the Second Lateran Council (AD 1139) addressed issues such as the inappropriateness of usury and the monastic study of law, its primary purpose was to heal a schism within the Church that had arisen over the questionable election of Pope Innocent II. Because of scandals like the election of Innocent II, Lateran III was called to promote unity within

---

21   See Paul L. Williams, *The Complete Idiot's Guide to The Crusades* (Indianapolis, Ind.: Alpha Books, 2002), 243–44.

the Church, to address abuses, and to establish a requirement of a two-thirds majority in the election of any pope.

The twelfth century saw the second and third crusades, and the beginnings of scholasticism, but it was also the century in which St. Francis of Assisi was born. Assisi is known for his compassion for people and love for all of God's creations. He is the patron saint of the environment and has been called by some the first environmentalist.

The thirteenth century saw four crusades, three Catholic ecumenical councils, and two major thinkers—Aquinas and Dante. St. Thomas Aquinas (AD 1225–1274) is considered the greatest of medieval theologians. He sought to reconcile Christian doctrine with the philosophy of Aristotle, as the philosopher's teachings were perceived as a great threat to Christianity. Dante Alighieri (AD 1265–1321) was Italy's greatest poet and the author of the famous *Divine Comedy*, which chronicles a journey through the three realms of the dead common in medieval Catholic thought: hell, purgatory, and paradise.

The Fourth Lateran Council lasted two weeks and was held in AD 1215. It was not only the most important of the Lateran Councils, but probably also the most important council of the Middle Ages. Among other things, it condemned the teachings of several heretical sects and addressed the place of non-believers in society. It ordered Muslims and Jews to wear identifiable clothing and was directly responsible for the beginnings of the papal inquisition. It also affirmed the doctrine of transubstantiation, and made annual confession and annual partaking of Holy Communion mandatory for all Catholics. The First Council of Lyons (June through July of AD 1245) addressed a number of issues, most notably the persecution and seizure of papal lands by the Roman Emperor Frederick II. The council also addressed clerical abuses, the Mongol threat to eastern Europe, the Latin Empire of Constantinople, and the liberation of Jerusalem from Muslim hands. The Second Council of Lyons (AD 1274) was primarily focused on the reunion of Catholicism and Eastern Orthodoxy. It also discussed the liberation of the Holy Land and the need for church reform within Catholicism.

The fourteenth century was one of controversy. From AD 1309 until AD 1377 the "Avignon Papacy" or "Babylonian Captivity" of the Church took place. During this period, the Church moved its headquarters from Rome to Avignon, France. For the two centuries prior to this, popes had held unrivaled power both politically and religiously. However, during the Avignon years the government was more powerful than the Church, and that forever changed the degree of power future popes would have over the word and over Catholic Christians. It was also during the fourteenth century that the "Great Western Schism" of the Church took place (AD 1378–1417). During this period, Catholicism had two and then three popes simultaneously claiming authority over the Church.

Finally, the Council of Vienne was held in AD 1311–1312. While it condemned a number of rogue groups, such as the Beguines and Beghards, it examined, but did not condemn, the Order of the Knights Templar. Among other things, this council also placed restrictions on the inquisition.

During the fifteenth century, the Catholic Church held two ecumenical councils and saw the beginning of the longest running inquisition ever—the Spanish Inquisition (AD 1479–1834)—initiated in an effort to ferret out heretics and those whose conversions to Christianity were feigned. The Council of Constance (AD 1414–1418) was called to resolve the Great Western Schism by abdicating all three popes, and then calling a singular pope to replace them. This council also condemned the teachings of protestant reformers John Wycliffe and John Huss. Huss was arrested and burned at the stake for heresy. The Council of Basel, the Catholic Church's seventeenth ecumenical council, lasted from AD 1431 until AD 1449. It sought to resolve the authority crises caused by the Great Schism. The Council of Basel, however, was fraught with its own authority issues. While the goal was to end the questions of papal authority, because of internal dissensions, this council served only to highlight the lack of a clear and recognized authority in the Church.

The sixteenth century is one of the most famous in Catholic history, as it saw what many scholars consider to be the beginning of the Protestant Reformation.[22] Not surprisingly, as the reformation movement began to gain momentum, the Catholic Church began its "Index of Forbidden Books"—a list of texts Catholics were forbidden to possess or read (except under specified circumstances).[23] The index was established in AD 1557 and was regularly updated until the Church abolished it in 1966.

In AD 1512, the Fifth Lateran Council opened, and it continued until AD 1517. This particular council has been called the "missed opportunity," in that it made only some minor, albeit useful, changes in how the Church was being run. Had major, and much needed, changes taken place, Lateran V may have avoided Luther's reformation movement. Its changes were small, however, and only a few months after it closed, Luther posted his "Ninety-five Theses" on the doors of the Wittenberg Chapel.[24] The Council of Trent (AD

---

22   One historian noted, "The date that is usually given as the beginning of the Reformation is 1517, when Luther posted his famous 95 theses." Justo L. González, *Church History: An Essential Guide* (Nashville, Tenn.: Abingdon Press, 1996), 69. Luther was obviously not the first Reformer. Men like John Wycliffe (AD 1320–1384) and John Huss (AD 1374–1415) predate Luther by nearly 200 years. However, it was Luther and his followers that gave the Reformation the momentum it needed to have a lasting effect upon Christianity.

23   Some notable authors, whose writings were placed upon the "Index of Forbidden Books," were Calvin, Luther, Copernicus, Descartes, Galileo, Machiavelli, Milton, Pascal, Spinoza, Voltair, Zwingli, Victor Hugo, David Hume, and Immanuel Kant. Of course, there were many, many others. Each individual placed in the "Index" was guilty of teaching or writing things that were considered contrary to the faith and/or morals of the Church.

24   Some of Martin Luther's major concerns included his belief that the Catholic Church was placing too much emphasis on personal works, and not enough on God's grace. He believed that salvation was *sola gratia*—by "grace alone" through one's faith in Christ. He didn't reject righteousness. Indeed, he held that "good works do not make a man good, but a good man does good works." Yet he felt that God's grace was unmerited and unearned, and that no amount of good works on our part would make us more acceptable to God. Luther saw indulgences as problematic, as they seemed to suggest that one could purchase "grace"—not by faith, but by money, or an act of some kind. Luther also held that if salvation comes from faith alone, the intercession of priests must be superfluous. Sinners don't need confession before a priest or assigned penance from a priest. Like the reformers Wycliffe and Huss who preceded him, Luther saw scripture as supreme, something to be trusted over tradition or church practice. He didn't reject *all* traditions, but he measured everything against the Bible. Luther rejected the Catholic doctrine of transubstantiation. He felt Christ was somehow physically present in the sacrament of the Lord's Supper, but he didn't believe the bread and wine became Jesus' body and blood (as transubstantiation teaches). He rejected the idea that Jesus was actually being repeatedly offered on Calvary's cross every time a Mass was held, and he didn't believe that, when

1545–1563) was called specifically in response to the Reformation. It tackled numerous major issues dividing Catholics and Protestants, and a number of minor issues also.[25] Because so many of the decrees of Trent were decidedly anti-Protestant, it has been suggested that the Council of Trent ensured that the growing chasm between Catholicism and the reformers would never again be closed.

Compared to the sixteenth century, the seventeenth century was relatively quiet for Catholics. It was less a period of controversy and more one of development. Not only was St. Peter's Basilica consecrated in AD 1626, but the Baroque Catholic moment also began. The Church began to go new directions in its theology, its authority, its monasticism, etc. The laity began to seek a more intense spiritual connection with God—something previously associated with the monastics. A number of these same lay Catholics recounted miracles or visionary experiences they were having. For many, religion became a strongly emotional thing during the Catholic Baroque period.[26]

The eighteenth century saw Catholicism's expansion into the United States. In AD 1790, Jesuit priest John Caroll was consecrated as the first Catholic bishop in the United States. Caroll started the first Catholic seminary (St Mary's) and the first Catholic university (Georgetown College) in the United States. While very ecumenical, he nevertheless took the role of apologist in an effort to clarify Catholic beliefs to U.S. Protestants.

Mass was over, the bread and wine continued to have Jesus' literal presence in them. He felt that the common life—the life of the laity—should be holy, so he rejected monasteries and convents as purposeless. He preached a "priesthood of all believers," in that all the faithful were God's priests. Luther felt that the Church was *not* the hierarchy, but rather the united laity. He also felt that the majority of the sacraments of the Catholic Church were not scriptural (baptism and the Lord's Supper being the only exceptions). He rejected infant baptism. There were other concerns, but these were some of Luther's major ones.

25   Some of the major declarations of Trent were the equal reverence due to scripture and tradition, the rejection of justification by faith alone, the salvific nature of the sacraments independent of the recipient's faith (or lack thereof), and the doctrine of transubstantiation (or the real presence of Christ in the Eucharist)—declared in opposition to Luther's doctrine of consubstantiation.

26   While the Baroque period is traditionally dated from about 1580 until around 1680, the Catholic Baroque era lasted until the late nineteenth century. See Thomas F. O'Meara, "Baroque Catholicism," in *Harper Collins Encyclopedia of Catholicism*, 140.

Three of the most significant events in nineteenth-century Catholicism were the Church's official articulation of the dogma of the immaculate conception of Mary (AD 1854), the creation of the "Syllabus of Errors" (AD 1864), and the convening of the First Vatican Council (December AD 1869 through October AD 1870).

The immaculate conception of Mary is the belief that she, unlike each of us, was born free from the stain of original sin. While the belief began to arise centuries earlier, it did not become an official teaching until the nineteenth century.

The "Syllabus of Errors" listed eighty previously condemned theses. Most fell into the categories of pantheism, naturalism, rationalism, or political liberalism, and all appeared to threaten the Church's autonomy.[27]

Although it had lofty goals, the First Vatican Council only approved two dogmatic constitutions (or declarations).[28] It made a declaration on the relationship of reason and faith, and it declared the pope infallible on matters of morals and doctrine. The doctrine of papal infallibility was controversial at the time of its declaration, and it has remained so in contemporary Catholicism.[29]

Some of the most dramatic changes in Catholicism's nearly two thousand year history took place during the last third of the twentieth century. It is universally agreed

STATUE OF A ROMAN CATHOLIC BISHOP

---

27   See Richard R. Gaillardetz, "Syllabus of Errors," in *Harper Collins Encyclopedia of Catholicism*, 1233.

28   The council had fifty-one schemas or proposed decrees, of which only six were discussed, and of those six only two were acted on. See Herman J. Pottmeyer, "Vatican Council I," in *Harper Collins Encyclopedia of Catholicism*, 1297.

29   The controversy is not so much among the laity, but rather among Roman Catholic scholars who often challenge the validity of the declaration—in part because it was the pope who declared himself infallible, rather than being declared such by other members of the magisterium (or hierarchy).

that the most important Catholic event of the last century was the Second Vatican Council (October AD 1962 through December AD 1965). It was the twenty-first ecumenical council of the Church and has been called, by Catholic scholars, the most important religious event since the Protestant Reformation. While most of the previous councils had been called to combat heresy, Vatican II's purpose was decidedly different. Pope John XXIII, who called the council, was an optimist. In his opening remarks, he criticized the "prophets of gloom" who "regard the modern era as worse than others and getting worse all the time, and who are 'always forecasting disaster.'"[30] John XXIII's stated goal of Vatican II was "to promote peace and the unity of all humankind"[31] and to bring "the church up to date."[32] A year after the opening of Vatican II, John XXIII died, and Paul VI became the new pope. Pope Paul VI listed four aims of the council: (1) "The development of a clearer idea of [what constitutes] the Church," (2) the Church's "renewal," (3) "the unity of all Christians," and (4) a "dialogue between the Church and the world."[33] While there is no question that the council met goals one and four, more conservative Catholics question the propriety of those goals. In addition, some conservatives in the Church believe that goals two and three have not been realized.

The twenty-first century is young, and it is perhaps too early to tell where the Catholic Church will head during the next hundred years. One major Catholic decision of this century is relevant to Mormonism. On the June 5, 2001, the Congregation for the Doctrine of the Faith—a Catholic "watchdog office . . . that constantly surveys the theologians and teachers and their published work"[34]—issued a ruling that baptisms performed by The Church of Jesus Christ of Latter-day

---

30   Richard P. McBrien, "Vatican Council II," in *Harper Collins Encyclopedia of Catholicism*, 1302.

31   John XXIII in his opening address, given October 11, 1962, cited in McBrien, "Vatican Council II," in *Harper Collins Encyclopedia of Catholicism*, 1301.

32   See Curtis, Lang, and Petersen, *100 Most Important Events in Christian History*, 198; Shelley, *Church History in Plain Language*, 453.

33   See McBrien, "Vatican Council II," in *Harper Collins Encyclopedia of Catholicism*, 1304.

34   Bob O'Gorman and Mary Faulkner, *The Complete Idiot's Guide to Understanding Catholicism*, 2d ed. (Indianapolis, Ind.: Alpha Books, 2003), 255. See also 277.

Saints were invalid in the eyes of the Roman Catholic Church.[35] As non-ecumenical as such a declaration might seem, Mormons would do well to remember that, like Catholics, we too expect converts to the LDS Church to be rebaptized.

---

35   See Alonzo L. Gaskill, "Maximus Nothus Decretum: A Look at the Recent Catholic Declaration Regarding Latter-day Saint Baptisms" in *FARMS Review of Books* 13, no. 2 (2001): 175–96.

THE ONLY "TRUE" CHURCH

Both Catholicism and Mormonism have at some time in their history claimed to be the only "true" church. Certainly first-century Christianity saw itself as the *only* "true" branch of Judaism, though the Jews rejected this declaration. What do Catholics and Mormons mean by the phrase "true church"? Is such a declaration intended to imply that other faiths have no truth? Is the current position of these two faiths any different today than it was in their respective histories?

LATTER-DAY SAINTS

Mormons are known to use, with some frequency, the phrase "the only *true* church." By this we mean that ours is a living faith with living prophets and apostles and with a strong belief in continuing revelation akin to that which is described in the Holy Bible.

It is true that some, when they hear us say we are members of the "only *true* church," suppose we are saying that no one else has *any* truth—that all are in utter apostasy! Yet this has never been our position. Latter-day Saints acknowledge that many peoples and many faiths contain truths given of God and revealed from heaven. The Prophet Joseph said, "One of the grand fundamental principles of 'Mormonism' is to receive truth, let it come from whence it may."[1] And from whence might it come? President Brigham Young stated:

---

1   Joseph Fielding Smith, comp., *Teachings of the Prophet Joseph Smith* (Salt Lake City: Deseret Book, 1976), 313.

For me, the plan of salvation must . . . circumscribe [all] the knowledge that is upon the face of the earth, or it is not from God. Such a plan incorporates every system of true doctrine on the earth, whether it be ecclesiastical, moral, philosophical, or civil: it incorporates all good laws that have been made from the days of Adam until now; it swallows up the laws of nations, for it exceeds them all in knowledge and purity; it circumscribes the doctrines of the day, and takes from the right and the left, and brings all truth together in one system, and leaves the chaff to be scattered hither and thither.[2]

Elder Orson F. Whitney of the Quorum of the Twelve reminded Latter-day Saints:

[God] is using not only his covenant people, but other peoples as well, to consummate a work, stupendous, magnificent, and altogether too arduous for this little handful of Saints to accomplish by and of themselves. . . . All down the ages men bearing the authority of the Holy Priesthood— patriarchs, prophets, apostles and others, have officiated in the name of the Lord, doing the things that he required of them; and outside the pale of their activities other good and great men, not bearing the [Mormon] Priesthood, but possessing profundity of thought, great wisdom, and a desire to uplift their fellows, have been sent by the Almighty into many nations, to give them, not the fulness of the Gospel, but that portion of truth that they were able to receive and wisely use. Such men as Confucius, the Chinese philosopher; Zoroaster, the Persian sage; Gautama or Buddha, of the Hindus; Socrates and Plato, of the Greeks; these all had some of the light that is universally diffused, and concerning which we have this day heard. They were servants of the Lord in a lesser sense, and were sent to those pagan or heathen nations to give them the measure of truth that a wise Providence had allotted to them.[3]

---

2   Brigham Young, in *Journal of Discourses*, 26 vols. (Liverpool: F. D. Richards, 1855–86), 7:148.

3   Orson F. Whitney, *Conference Report*, April 1921, 32–33. On February 15, 1978, the First Presidency of the Church (under the signatures of Spencer W. Kimball, N. Eldon Tanner, and Marion G. Romney) released the following declaration: "The great religious leaders of the world such as Mohammed, Confucius, and the Reformers,

Thus, the use of the phrase "only *true* church" for Latter-day Saints has reference to both the expectation and acceptance of continued modern-day revelation, and also to the belief in restored authority, doctrines, and ordinances necessary for salvation, but generally rejected by the rest of the world. It is a statement about our openness to the Father's will over man's traditions. It is a claim that we believe, aside from the majority of the world, that there are living apostles and prophets upon the face of the earth still revealing (in a scriptural sense) God's will for mankind. It is not, however, a statement that no one else has *any* truth—religious or secular. Nor is it a claim that no other faith enjoys the love of God or promptings of His Holy Spirit.[4]

Thus, from a Latter-day Saint perspective, the "true" church is not the only place "saved" beings can be found. It is, however, the "authorized" church and the church fully "open" to God's continued revelations.

---

as well as philosophers including Socrates, Plato, and others, received a portion of God's light. Moral truths were given to them by God to enlighten whole nations and to bring a higher level of understanding to individuals." Cited in Spencer J. Palmer, "World Religions (Non-Christian) and Mormonism," in *Encyclopedia of Mormonism*, ed. Daniel H. Ludlow, 4 vols. (New York: Macmillan, 1992), 4:1589. The *Encyclopedia of Mormonism* states, "Latter-day Saints believe . . . God inspires not only Latter-day Saints but also founders, teachers, philosophers, and reformers of other Christian and non-Christian religions." Palmer, "World Religions (Non-Christian) and Mormonism," in *Encyclopedia of Mormonism*, 4:1589. The thirteenth article of faith clearly states, "If there is anything virtuous, lovely, or of good report or praiseworthy, we seek after these things."

4   The Prophet Joseph Smith taught, "There is a difference between the Holy Ghost and the gift of the Holy Ghost. Cornelius received the Holy Ghost before he was baptized, which was the convincing power of God unto him of the truth of the Gospel, but he could not receive the gift of the Holy Ghost until after he was baptized." Smith, *Teachings of the Prophet Joseph Smith*, 199. President Joseph Fielding Smith wrote:

> The Holy Ghost will manifest himself to any individual who asks for the truth, just as he did to Cornelius. . . . Every man can receive a manifestation of the Holy Ghost, even when he is out of the Church, if he is earnestly seeking for the light and for the truth. The Holy Ghost will come and give the man the testimony he is seeking, and then withdraw. . . . He may have the constant guidance of that other Spirit, the Spirit of Christ. Every man may receive such a manifestation from the Holy Ghost when he is seeking for the truth, but not the power to call upon the Holy Ghost whenever he feels he needs the help, as a man does who is a member of the Church. (Joseph Fielding Smith, *Doctrines of Salvation*, 3 vols. [Salt Lake City: Bookcraft, 1998] 1:42)

CATHOLICS

But what of Catholicism? While it is common to recite Cyprian of Carthage's axiom, "No Salvation Outside the Church,"[5] when speaking of the Catholic view of other religions—and even other Christian churches—this would not be an accurate depiction of modern Catholic thought. While it is true that for many centuries the Catholic Church took the position that salvation could only be had by those who were members of the Roman Catholic faith, such is certainly not the Church's position today. The *Encyclopedia of Catholicism* notes:

> The most severe interpretation of this doctrine stated that salvation was possible only for visibly incorporated members of the Catholic Church, excluding from salvation Jews, Muslims, pagans, apostates, and members of Christian Churches not in union with Rome. This interpretation was repeatedly rejected by Pius IX as invalid for those 'invincibly ignorant of the true religion (1854, 1863), and condemned by the Holy Office in *Suprema Haec Sacra* (1949). Pius XII in *Mystici Corporis* (1943) taught that non-Catholics can be saved by being "ordained to the mystical body of the Redeemer by some kind of unconscious desire or longing."[6]

The "Decree on Ecumenism," an official document from the Second Vatican Council that specifically defines the Church's position on this matter, makes several important points regarding other faiths. Among other things, it informs us:

- Christ's true church "subsists in" Catholicism, but is not coextensive with it. Indeed, outside of the "visible boundaries" of the true church are other Christians and their communions, in which exist

---

5   See Cyprian of Carthage, "The Epistles of Cyprian," epistle 61, verse 4, in Alexander Roberts and James Donaldson, eds., *Ante-Nicene Fathers*, 10 vols. (Peabody, Mass.: Hendrickson Publishers, 1994), 5:358. While the axiom predates Cyprian (finding support in the teachings of Irenaeus and Origin), it finds its classic expression in Cyprian. See also Francis X. Clooney, "Salvation Outside the Church," in *Harper Collins Encyclopedia of Catholicism,* ed. Richard P. McBrien (San Francisco, Calif.: HarperSanFrancisco, 1995), 1159.

6   See Clooney, "Salvation Outside the Church," in *Harper Collins Encyclopedia of Catholicism,* 1159.

divine "endowments" that "give life to" the true church.[7]

- In the history of man, "large communities" of faithful children of God have become "separated from full communion" with Catholicism. "One cannot charge with the sin of the separation those who at present are born into these communities and in them are brought up in the faith of Christ, and the Catholic Church accepts them with respect and affection as brothers."

- Those outside of Catholicism can have "gifts of the Holy Spirit," which "come from Christ and lead back to him."

- "Those who have been justified by faith in baptism are incorporated into Christ; they therefore have a right to be called Christians, and with good reason are accepted as brothers by the children of the Catholic Church."

- "Separated Churches and communities . . . have been by no means deprived of significance and importance in the mystery of salvation. For the Spirit of Christ has not refrained from using them as means of salvation which derive their efficacy from the very fullness of grace and truth entrusted to the Catholic Church."[8]

---

7   On June 29, 2007, the current pontiff, Benedict XVI, ratified and confirmed a document produced by the Congregation for the Doctrine of the Faith, under the title "Responses to Some Questions Regarding Certain Aspects of the Doctrine on the Church." This text reemphasizes the fact that the Catholic Church holds itself to be the "true church," but that this does not mean that other faiths do not have truth or that they do not play a significant role as instruments in the salvation of those outside of Catholicism. Thus, as recently as June of 2007, the Catholic Church reminded the world that other faiths are used by "the Spirit of Christ . . . as instruments of salvation." See William Cardinal Levada, "Responses to Some Questions Regarding Certain Aspects of the Doctrine on the Church" (Rome: Congregation for the Doctrine of the Faith, June 29, 2007).

8   "Decree on Ecumenism," section 3, in Austin Flannery, ed., *Vatican Council II: The Conciliar and Post Conciliar Documents*, new rev. ed. (New York: Costello Publishing, 1992), 455–56.

Thus, today the Catholic Church holds that the "saved" can exist outside of communion with Roman Catholicism, and many who are in other faiths, including other Christian faiths, have been used by God, are accepted by God, and have spiritual endowments from God.

For a number of years the Catholic Church has taught something known as "baptism of desire." The principle is a response to the dilemma posed by the fact that baptism is necessary for salvation, and yet most people will die having never received that salvific ordinance. From the Council of Trent (AD 1524) onward, the Catholic Church has held that "those who do not actually receive [baptism] can be saved by the 'desire' (*votum*) of baptism."[9] As one Catholic scholar wrote, "Baptism of desire (that of one preparing for baptism, or that of a person of goodwill who simply is unaware that God is calling the person to the Church) . . . may substitute in the case of water baptism."[10] Thus, if someone desired a valid baptism, but never received one (but perhaps thought that he or she had), in God's eyes it will be as though he or she had been baptized properly and authoritatively, and the individual will be allowed entrance into the kingdom of heaven.[11]

Connected to "baptism of desire" is the offshoot dogma of "anonymous Christianity." According to the Catholic Church, "anonymous Christians" are those who are saved via "implicit faith in Christ which is unrecognized to themselves."[12] In other words, one could be a non-Catholic Christian (such as a Mormon, Protestant, Jehovah's Witness, etc.) or even an atheist, and still go to heaven because of this unrecognized faith in God, which the Second Vatican Council described as "a sort of secret presence of God" dwelling in the heart and soul of

---

9   Edward J. Yarnold, "Theology of Baptism," in *The New Dictionary of Sacramental Worship* (Collegeville, Minn.: Liturgical Press, 1990), 119.

10   Anthony Sherman, "Baptism," in *Harper Collins Encyclopedia of Catholicism*, 138.

11   See D&C 137:7, which reads, "Thus came the voice of the Lord unto me, saying: All who have died without a knowledge of this gospel, who would have received it if they had been permitted to tarry, shall be heirs of the celestial kingdom of God."

12   Yarnold, "Theology of Baptism," in *New Dictionary of Sacramental Worship*, 119. It is worth noting that, although "baptism of desire" and "anonymous Christianity" are official doctrines of the Catholic Church, many, if not most, lay Catholics will know nothing of these teachings. They are official theological positions of the Church, and yet the laity of the Church seldom discusses them.

the nonbeliever.[13] As one highly influential twentieth-century Catholic scholar put it, "Even according to the teachings of the [Catholic] Church itself, a man may already possess the sanctifying grace, and may therefore be justified and sanctified, a child of God, heir of heaven, and mercifully and positively on his way towards his supernatural and eternal salvation even before he has accepted an explicitly Christian confession of faith and has been baptized."[14]

The position of contemporary Catholicism regarding being the "only *true* church" seems clear. While they would hold that Catholicism is likely a better way—a "truer" way—it is certainly not the *only* way, and those in other faiths—even those who reject a belief in religion and God—still have the ability to be used by God, to enjoy spiritual endowments from God, and to be saved in the kingdom of God.

SUMMARY

The Latter-day Saint and Catholic position on being the "true church" is somewhat similar. Both faiths hold that God works with willing individuals inside and outside of the faith, and both acknowledge that God has set up a plan, per se, to address the salvation of those who do not have access to the "truth" during their mortal sojourn. For Latter-day Saints the doctrine of a spirit world coupled with vicarious work for the dead provides the answer to the problem of what to do with those who have never heard the truth. For Catholics, the doctrines of "baptism of desire" and "anonymous Christianity" resolve the concern. In both faiths God neither ignores nor rejects those who are outside of the faith through no fault of their own, and in both faiths God is willing to prompt, direct, and inspire those who sincerely seek after truth, regardless of their religious affiliations.

---

13   *Ad Gentes Divinitus,* section 9, in *Vatican Council II: The Conciliar and Post Conciliar Documents,* 823; See also *Lumen Gentium,* section 17, in *Vatican Council II: The Conciliar and Post Conciliar Documents,* 368–69; Geffery B. Kelly, "'Unconscious Christianity' and the 'Anonymous Christian' in the Theology of Dietrich Bonhoeffer and Karly Rahner," in *Philosophy and Theology* 9 (Autumn/Winter 1995): 117–49; Karl Rahner, "Anonymous Christianity and the Missionary Task of the Church," in *IDOC Internazionale* 1 (April 4, 1970): 70–96; and Mourice Boutin, "Anonymous Christianity: A Paradigm for Interreligious Encounter?" in *Journal of Ecumenical Studies* 20 (Fall 1983): 602–29.

14   Rahner, "Anonymous Christianity and the Missionary Task of the Church," 76.

So, is there any divergence in our views? Certainly there is. First and foremost, Mormons still hold that everyone must accept their faith—either here or in the spirit world —in order to gain the highest reward God has to offer, namely exaltation in the celestial kingdom. Catholics, on the other hand, make no such claim regarding those who will be saved by "baptism of

INTERIOR OF 19TH CENTURY ROMAN CATHOLIC CHURCH

desire" or "anonymous Christianity." While their "desire" to do what is right is necessary, there is no suggestion that they will at some point in time have to acknowledge and accept that Catholicism was the "right" or "true" way back to God. Thus, in that sense, Mormonism emphatically declares itself to be the *only* "true" church and a requisite part of salvation for *all* of God's children (though it may be in the spirit world that one is first introduced to LDS beliefs).

Latter-day Saints also diverge when it comes to ordinances. Where Catholicism teaches that a "desire" to have a valid baptism is sufficient for salvation (in the case of those who did not have the opportunity to have a valid one), Mormonism requires that every human being that is to be saved in the kingdom of God be baptized by immersion by one holding valid priesthood authority—hence the LDS ordinance of "baptism for the dead" (1 Corinthians 15:29). Again, this implies that the LDS concept of an "only *true* church" is somewhat different than the Catholic understanding.

THE NATURE OF GOD

A primary or foundational definition of the word "religion" is the belief in and worship of God—a supreme being who, in some way incomprehensible to you and I, is responsible for the creation, preservation, and eventual salvation of humanity. While some non-Christian traditions may struggle with parts of this definition, Catholics and Mormons seem united on the point: we both have faith in and a testimony of God the Eternal Father, His Son Jesus Christ, and the Holy Ghost—even though the particulars of the Trinity and/or Godhead cause us to diverge.[1]

CATHOLICS

Discussions regarding the Trinity are often confusing and frequently inaccurate, whether those discussing the subject are Catholic, Eastern Orthodox, Protestant, or LDS. The Eastern Orthodox refer to the doctrine as "a mystery."[2] One Catholic theologian wrote:

---

1   Mormons are not the only Christian denomination to see the nature of God differently than Roman Catholics. For example, the Eastern Orthodox Church, the Universalists, and the Jehovah's Witnesses are all branches of Christianity, and yet each sees the Godhead or Trinity differently than Roman Catholics do.

2   Dean Timothy Andrews, *What is the Orthodox Church?* (New York: Greek Orthodox Archdiocese of North and South America, 1964), 11; emphasis added. When all of its various branches are combined (e.g., Albanian, Armenian, Bulgarian, Russian, Greek, Serbian, and Ukrainian), the Eastern Orthodox Church is the second largest Christian denomination in the world. Its practitioners consider it to be the least evolved or changed of all Christian denominations from the original New Testament church. In the year AD 1054, the Eastern Orthodox Church officially split from the

> Mystery [is] a term that refers to the infinite incomprehensibility of God. . . . God is essentially mystery; not just unknown, but unknowable, literally incomprehensible. While [the word] "mystery" is also used in Catholic theology to refer to those things that merely confound the finite intellect, [the term] mystery in its most fundamental sense refers to the permanent character of God's incomprehensibility.[3]

The "mysterious" nature of the triune God has escaped the understanding of many Christians, regardless of their tradition. As one scholar noted of the doctrine of the Trinity, "If it is explained so that you understand it, it hasn't been explained correctly."[4]

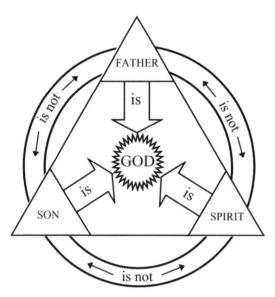

THIS DIAGRAM IS AN EXAMPLE OF STANDARD ATTEMPTS AT VISUALLY DEPICTING THE RELATIONSHIP BETWEEN THE THREE PERSONS OF THE TRINITY.

None of this is intended as a criticism of Catholics or their way of defining God. Indeed, early in the history of The Church of Jesus Christ of Latter-day Saints, the presiding Brethren occasionally used the term "trinity" when speaking of the Godhead.[5]

Roman Catholic Church. From that time forward it has "officially" existed as a separate denomination—even though divisions between Eastern and Western Christians predate AD 1054.

3   Nancy Dallavalle, "Mystery," in *Harper Collins Encyclopedia of Catholicism,* ed. Richard P. McBrien (San Francisco, Calif.: HarperSanFrancisco, 1995), 900.

4   R. J. Joynt, "Are Two Heads Better Than One?" quoted in Kathleen V. Wilkes, "Is Consciousness Important?" *British Journal of the Philosophy of Science* 35 (1984): 223.

5   See, for example, John A. Widtsoe, comp., *Discourses of Brigham Young* (Salt Lake City: Bookcraft, 1998), 30; John Taylor, *The Gospel Kingdom: Selections from the Writings and Discourses of John Taylor* (Salt Lake City: Bookcraft, 1998), 28; Joseph Smith Jr.,

Additionally, in Latter-day Saint theology we have numerous doctrines that are mysteries we do not fully understand or that have yet to be fully revealed. For example, President John Taylor and Elder James E. Talmage both referred to the "mysterious" and "incomprehensible" nature of the Atonement.[6] There are certain aspects of the Fall of Adam and Eve that have yet to be revealed, and thus remain a mystery.[7] We have no idea how many worlds are part of God's plan and Christ's Atonement.[8] We don't know the identity of certain scriptural angels such as Raphael.[9] The length of the "little season" at the end of the millennium remains an unrevealed mystery to Latter-day Saints.[10] Indeed, one commentary on the Book of Mormon states, "The doctrines of the incarnation, the birth, the death, the resurrection of Christ and, we may add, the salvation for the dead, are mysteries."[11] President Wilford Woodruff stated, "There are some things which have not been revealed to man, but are held in the bosom of God our Father."[12] He then added, "The whole of the dealings of God to man are a mystery."[13] I think most Latter-day Saints would admit that although we hold that we have a fuller understanding of God, His nature, and His plan, even we are aware that there is much about our Eternal Father, His creation of us, and the sacrifice of His Son that

History of The Church of Jesus Christ of Latter-day Saints, ed. B. H. Roberts, 2d ed., rev., 8 vols. (Salt Lake City: Deseret Book, 1978), 7:254.

6   See, for example, John Taylor, *Mediation and Atonement* (Salt Lake City: Deseret News Company, 1882), 148–49; and James E. Talmage, *A Study of the Articles of Faith* (Salt Lake City: The Church of Jesus Christ of Latter-day Saints, 1975), 76.

7   See, for example, Orson F. Whitney, *Saturday Night Thoughts* (Salt Lake City: Deseret News, 1921), 95; and Bruce R. McConkie, *Mormon Doctrine*, 2d ed. (Salt Lake City: Bookcraft, 1979), 289, s.v. "forbidden fruit."

8   Rodney Turner, "The Doctrine of the Firstborn and Only Begotten," in H. Donl Peterson and Charles D. Tate Jr., eds., *The Pearl of Great Price: Revelations from God* (Provo, Utah: Brigham Young University, Religious Studies Center, 1989), 108.

9   McConkie, *Mormon Doctrine*, 412, s.v. "keys of the kingdom." Elder McConkie added, "In reality, we know very little about the organization that exists among angelic beings; that a perfect, proper, and complex organization does exist is obvious, but the positions held by the various ministers in that celestial hierarchy have not been revealed in our day." McConkie, *Mormon Doctrine*, 51, s.v. "archangels."

10   McConkie, *Mormon Doctrine*, 486, s.v. "meridian of time."

11   George Reynolds and Janne M. Sjodahl, *Commentary on the Book of Mormon,* ed. Philip C. Reynolds, 7 vols. (Salt Lake City: Deseret Book, 1955–61), 1:6.

12   Wilford Woodruff, in *Journal of Discourses*, 26 vols. (Liverpool: F. D. Richards, 1855–86), 18:33. See also Joseph Fielding Smith, *Answers to Gospel Questions*, 5 vols. (Salt Lake City: Deseret Book, 1993), 2:147–48, 3:95.

13   Wilford Woodruff, in *Journal of Discourses*, 18:39.

we simply do not understand. Thus, our Catholic brothers and sisters are not alone in their acknowledgment that a full understanding of the Godhead by finite beings is utterly impossible.[14]

In the end, Catholics do have a reason for believing the Trinity, and it is primarily scripturally based. One text notes:

> Why do Christians believe the doctrine of the Trinity, that God is three Persons rather than only one? The doctrine sounds strange, even shocking, even after it is explained. . . . The Church gradually defined the doctrine of the Trinity, in her first six ecumenical councils, to explain her data in Scripture . . . Christ . . . called God his Father, prayed to him, loved him, taught his teaching, and obeyed his will. On the other hand, he claimed to be one with, and equal to, the Father. And he also promised to send the Spirit. The scriptural data from which the Church derives the doctrine of the Trinity are essentially:
>
>   a. that there is only one God (Deut 6:4);
>   b. that the Father is God (Jn 5:18);
>   c. that the Son is God (Jn 8:58);
>   d. that the Holy Spirit is God (Mt 28:18). . . .
>
> The doctrine of the Trinity surpasses human reason, but it does not contradict human reason.[15]

Thus, the Catholic reasoning behind a belief in the Trinity is hardly silly. It is just somewhat different than the reasoning of Latter-day Saints.

As we approach this subject, it is imperative that the reader understand that this topic is in many ways extremely complex. Entire tomes have been written on the subject of the Trinity.[16] The length of this text will not allow for an in-depth discussion of the "hows" and "whys."

---

14   See Peter J. Kreeft, *Catholic Christianity: A Complete Catechism of Catholic Beliefs based on the Catechism of the Catholic Church* (San Francisco, Calif.: Ignatius Press, 2001), 36, who states, "God is infinite; therefore he cannot be defined."

15   Kreeft, *Catholic Christianity*, 40–41. See also *United States Catholic Catechism for Adults* (Washington, D.C.: United States Conference of Catholic Bishops, 2006), 51–53.

16   See, for example, Catherine Mowry Lacugna, *God For Us: The Trinity and Christian Life* (San Francisco, Calif.: HarperSanFrancisco, 1991); Leonardo Boff, *Trinity and Society* (London: Burns and Oates, 1988); William G. Rusch, *The Trinitarian Controversy* (Philadelphia, Pa.: Fortress Press, 1980); Karl Rahner, *The Trinity* (New York: Herder and Herder, 1970); David Cunningham, *These Three are One* (Malden, Mass.: Black-

Thus, what I will present here is a very basic definition of the doctrine of the Trinity, rather than a detailed explanation of its controversies, development, and implications.

The doctrine of the Trinity holds that the Father, Son, and Holy Spirit are one God existing in three persons.[17] What exactly does that mean? It means that the three members of the Trinity are simultaneously united in their *substance*, but distinct in their *personhood*.[18] What exactly is the difference between *substance* and *personhood*? Basil of Caesarea, Gregory of Nyssa, and Gregory of Nazianzus—three influential Church fathers who are commonly referred to as the Cappadocians—explained the distinction as follows: *substance* refers to divine nature—thus, the Father, Son, and Holy Spirit have the same divine nature. *Personhood*, on the other hand, refers to individual roles or characteristics. Therefore, the callings, responsibilities, and activities of the Father, Son, and Holy Spirit are different.[19] So, though they share the same nature (e.g., goodness, mercy, love, compassion and perfection), their roles (e.g., Father = unbegottenness and unoriginate; Son = generation of the Father and redeemer; Holy Spirit = possession from the Father and Son and sanctifier) are different.

Analogies are often used to explain the oneness and yet distinctness of these three divine beings. A commonly utilized example is that of water, ice, and vapor. They are all forms of the same thing, H_2O, and yet each is decidedly different. One must be cautious about such examples, however, as they can be misleading. For example, the water/ice/vapor analogy implies "modalism," or the belief that the Trinity is really one God manifesting Himself in three different ways.[20] Modal-

---

well Publishers, 1998); and J. N. D. Kelly, *Early Christian Doctrines*, rev. ed. (New York: HarperSanFrancisco, 1978), 83–137.

17   Catherine Mowry LaCugna, "Trinity, Doctrine of the," in *Harper Collins Encyclopedia of Catholicism*, 1271.

18   LaCugna, "Trinity, Doctrine of the," in *Harper Collins Encyclopedia of Catholicism*, 1271.

19   Samuel Wells, "Trinity," *Encyclopedia of Christianity*, ed. John Bowden (New York: Oxford University Press, 2005), 1209.

20   *United States Catholic Catechism for Adults*, 52; Janice Poorman, "Modalism, in *Harper Collins Encyclopedia of Catholicism*, 876–77; and *Encyclopedia of Christianity*, 520–21 and 1211.

istic understandings of the Trinity, while common among lay Catholics, are, nevertheless, inaccurate. The God of the Trinity is not a God who functions under the pseudonyms of "Father," "Son," or "Holy Spirit," contingent upon the "saving act" He is currently performing. Additionally, "God the Father" of the Trinity did not leave heaven to become the "Jesus" of the Bible. Each of these assumptions misses the distinct "personhood" of the Father, Son, and Holy Spirit.

The opposite end of the spectrum would be "tritheism" (i.e., three utterly distinct Gods sharing one essence or nature).[21] This interpretation of the Trinity stems from the tendency to emphasize the "personhood" of the members of the Trinity so much that one turns them into three utterly separate Gods. As Elder M. Russell Ballard recently noted regarding the three persons of the Trinity, "We find that most people think they're separate and distinct. When you go door to door, as we did as young men, and talk to the average person—the theologians might have a different view—but people think of them as distinct."[22] Again, this is contrary to the actual doctrine of the Trinity—even if it is a commonly held view among some lay Catholics. To be fair, while many Catholics do view the Trinity much like Latter-day Saints do, many do not, believing instead in the official doctrine as taught by the Church.[23]

In official Catholic teaching, the three members of the Trinity are one God! And while Latter-day Saints—or Catholics, for that matter—may struggle to get that, such must be kept in mind when explaining this doctrine. While all analogies are, to some degree, flawed, one of the most coherent is that of an egg. It has three parts – shell, white, and yolk. All three parts are egg, yet all three parts are distinct. If you placed each part in separate containers, you would still have "egg" in each of the three containers. Yet, it requires all three parts to have, in the fullest sense, "one egg." Thus, the shell, white, and yolk are one in their

---

21   LaCugna, "Trinity, Doctrine of the," in *Harper Collins Encyclopedia of Catholicism*, 1271; and *Encyclopedia of Christianity*, 504.

22   M. Russell Ballard, cited in Jay Tolson, "QA: Elder M. Russell Ballard on the Mormon Way," in *U.S. News and World Report*, November 12, 2007, 28.

23   Exactly what percentage of Roman Catholics believe as Mormons do, and what percentage believe as the Roman Catholic Church officially teaches is anyone's guess. There simply is no way to tell.

substance or nature (i.e., "eggness"), and yet they are distinct in their personhood (i.e., the shell, which protects; the white, which nourishes; and the yolk, which is the embryo). While the analogy is imperfect, the principle is clear. One egg with three distinct but connected parts! One God with three distinct yet connected parts!

As the reader will no doubt be aware, the vast majority of all Christians accept the Trinity as the standard theological definition of the relationship between the three members of the Godhead. Having said that, there are a few differences of opinion on some details, primarily the equality of the Father and the Son, and the origins of the Holy Spirit. Eastern Orthodox Christians believe that Jesus and the Holy Spirit are subordinate to the Father, whereas Catholics hold that the Father and Son are equal. And where Eastern Orthodox hold that the Holy Spirit proceeds from the Father only, Roman Catholics believe that it comes from both the Father and the Son.

Before we turn our attention to the contrasting LDS understanding of the Godhead, we should acknowledge one or two other facets of the Catholic approach to the Trinity, namely what Catholics say the Bible teaches about the Trinity, and how dependant Catholics are upon the Bible for their doctrine of the Trinity. One Catholic scholar wrote:

> It was common in neo-scholastic manuals of dogmatic theology to cite texts such as Gen. 1:26, "Let us make humankind in our image, according to our likeness" (see Gen. 3:22; 11:7; Isaiah 6:2–3), as proof of a plurality in God. Today, however, scholars generally agree that there is no doctrine of the Trinity as such in either the OT or the NT. . . . It would go far beyond the intention and thought-forms of the OT to suppose that a late-fourth-century or thirteenth-century Christian doctrine can be found there. . . . Likewise, the NT does not contain an explicit doctrine of the Trinity. . . . It would be anachronistic to say that the NT necessarily implies what will later be expressed with metaphysical refinement as a Trinity of three coequal divine Persons who

share the same substance. . . . The vocabulary of metaphysics cannot be found in the scripture. Because of this, there are theologians who regard all postbiblical doctrinal developments as arbitrary or even aberrant. For them, one cannot go beyond the language and concepts of the Bible.[24]

Similarly, biblical exegete Phillip Harner noted that in "the first two centuries A.D. . . . the specific doctrine of the Trinity was not yet formulated" and the "early Christians . . . apparently believed in 'two powers' in heaven, i.e., Jesus and God."[25] In explaining this shift in thinking, Pope John Paul II indicated that the formulation of the Nicene-Constantinopolitan creed was a response to the Hellenization of the Church and its realized need for "ways of presenting her doctrine which would be adequate and convincing in that cultural context."[26]

Thus, Latter-day Saints should understand that it is common for modern Christian biblical scholars to acknowledge that the Trinity is neither a doctrine taught in the Bible[27] nor is it an approach to the doctrine of God that Jesus would have used or taught. The Catholic Church does not claim that its source for Trinitarian doctrine is primarily the Holy Bible. Rather, it would be more accurate to say that a Trinitarian approach to the Godhead grew out of post-biblical interpretations of scripture, which the Catholic Church sees as both inspired and authoritative.[28]

LATTER-DAY SAINTS

We've spoken of things Latter-day Saints do not understand, but what of that which we *do* understand? What of the Trinity and the

---

24   LaCugna, "Trinity, Doctrine of the," in *Harper Collins Encyclopedia of Catholicism*, 564–66.

25   Philip Harner, *The "I Am" of the Fourth Gospel: A Study in Johannine Usage and Thought* (Philadelphia, Pa.: Fortress Press, 1970), 24.

26   John Paul II, *Crossing the Threshold of Hope* (New York: Alfred A. Knopf, 1994), 46.

27   See, for example, Catherine Mowry LaCugna, *God For Us: The Trinity And Christian Life* (San Francisco, Calif.: HarperCollins Publishers, 1991), 102–3; and Rahner, *The Trinity*, 11. See also, LaCugna, *God For Us*, 6 and 8; Rusch, *Trinitarian Controversy*, 1–80; Kelly, *Early Christian Doctrines*, 83–137; Harner, *The "I Am" of the Fourth Gospel*, 24; John Paul II, *Crossing the Threshold of Hope*, 46; and LaCugna, "God," in *HarperCollins Encyclopedia of Catholicism*.

28   For a discussion of the role of extra canonical tradition in the formulation of Catholic doctrine, see chapter six of this book.

Godhead? How are our beliefs similar and in what ways are they different from those of our Catholic brothers and sisters? We'll now turn our attention to the Latter-day Saint understanding of the relationship between the three members of the Godhead.

Just as Catholic theologian Catherine Mowry LaCugna wrote, "there is no doctrine of the Trinity as such in either the [Old Testament] or the [New Testament],"[29] so also did Brigham Young teach:

> "I and my Father are one," says Jesus; what, one body? No, it never entered the Savior's mind that such a rendering of this saying would ever enter into the minds of persons holding the least claim to good sense. They are no more one person than I and one of my sons are one person. If my son receives my teaching, will walk in the path I mark out for him to walk in, if his faith is the same as mine, his purpose is the same, and he does the work of his father as Jesus did the work of his Father, then is my son one with me in the scriptural sense.[30]

While President Young spoke somewhat tongue in cheek, he does highlight a major difference between Catholics and Latter-day Saints. Like the Cappadocians we would say that the three members of the Godhead are one in *substance* and yet unique in their *personhood*. However, our take on *substance* is slightly different than contemporary Catholic understandings. We agree that *substance* refers to divine nature and that *personhood* refers to the individual roles or characteristics of the three members of the Godhead, but we part company with Catholic views when it comes to metaphysics. We reject the idea that by sharing *substance* (or divine nature) the three members of the Godhead become, wholly or in part, physiologically or metaphysically one. Rather, Latter-day Saints see the "oneness" of the members of the Godhead as being more akin to the following words from the *Encyclopedia of Catholicism*: "Persons are one with the triune God insofar as they accept the gift of divine grace, that is, the sanctifying presence of the Holy Spirit."[31] Just

---

29 LaCugna, "Trinity, Doctrine of the," in *Harper Collins Encyclopedia of Catholicism*, 564–66. See also Barbara A. Finan, "Holy Spirit," in *Harper Collins Encyclopedia of Catholicism*, 628.

30 Widtsoe, *Discourses of Brigham Young*, 28.

31 Finan, "Holy Spirit," in *Harper Collins Encyclopedia of Catholicism*, 630.

as we can become "one" with God through the Spirit, while still remaining physically separate from the Father, Son, and Holy Spirit, so also do Mormons hold that Jesus is one with the Father, yet He remains separate or individual in His "substance" or material makeup.

On a related note, when it comes to the Holy Spirit, Latter-day Saints are much closer to the Eastern Orthodox than to the Catholics in that we do not believe that the Holy Ghost, the third member of the Trinity or Godhead, proceeds forth from the Father *and* the Son. Rather, it is the LDS position that the Holy Spirit issues forth from the Father only.[32] Thus, unlike Catholics, Latter-day Saints could rightfully be called subordinationists, as were, incidentally, most Catholic Church fathers of the first three centuries: Hermas, Justin Martyr, Irenaeus, Tertullian, Clement of Alexandria, Origen, etc.[33] We hold that the Son and the Holy Spirit are both subordinate to the Father.

Summary

Catholics and Mormons believe that the heavenly hierarchy is made up of three divine persons: the Father, the Son, and the Holy Ghost. Both faiths believe that each divine person shares the same nature or divine attributes with the other two, and both Catholics and Mormons believe that, while the substance or nature of the Father, Son, and Holy Spirit are the same, the three are distinct in their personhood or roles.

The main areas of divergence between Catholic and Mormon approaches to the doctrine of God would be that (1) the LDS reject the metaphysical or physical oneness of the members of the Godhead, (2) we see the Son and the Holy Spirit as subordinate to the Father, and (3) we believe the Holy Ghost is the offspring of the Father.[34]

---

32   And why is such the case? Because in LDS belief the Holy Ghost is a spirit son of God. See, for example, Heber C. Kimball, in *Journal of Discourses*, 5:180; Joseph Fielding McConkie, "Holy Ghost," in *Encyclopedia of Mormonism*, ed. Daniel H. Ludlow, 4 vols. (New York: Macmillan, 1992), 2:649; and Stephen E. Robinson, "God the Father," in *Encyclopedia of Mormonism*, 2:548.

33   See "Subordinationism," *Harper Collins Encyclopedia of Catholicism*, 1227.

34   Heber C. Kimball, in *Journal of Discourses*, 5:180; McConkie, "Holy Ghost," in *Encyclopedia of Mormonism*, 2:649; and Stephen E. Robinson, "God the Father," in *Encyclopedia of Mormonism*, 2:548.

THE ROLE OF GRACE
AND WORKS IN SALVATION

Just as it is with Mormonism, the purpose of the Catholic Church is also to aid its parishioners in gaining salvation in the kingdom of God. For both faiths, salvation is realized through the Atonement of the Lord Jesus Christ, and the sacraments or ordinances play a large role in the believers' ability to access Christ's Atonement.

We will investigate the sacraments or ordinances of both faiths in a later chapter, but here we will focus our discussion on what Catholics and Mormons believe about the roles of grace and works in the salvation of believing Christians.

CATHOLICS

Every practicing Christian, regardless of his or her denomination, will at some point wonder "What must I do to be saved?" Of this question one scholar noted: "Sadly, though we have had the New Testament for almost twenty centuries, Christendom still gives an unclear answer to this question."[1] Definitions of grace and the exact role it plays in the salvation of Catholics are hard to nail down. Indeed, it seems fair to say that "grace" is a somewhat slippery term in contemporary Catholic thought.

---

1   Erwin Lutzer, *The Doctrines that Divide* (Grand Rapids, Mich.: Kregel Publications, 1998), 83.

As a theological term, Catholic understandings of what grace means have changed over the centuries.[2] The Eastern side of the early Church tended to interpret grace as the God-given opportunity to participate in the divine life of the Trinity (also referred to as "divinization" or "theosis"). The Western side, on the other hand, interpreted grace as God's power to save and heal us from sin. Catholics in the East saw death as the consequence of sin, whereas Catholics in the West saw guilt as the consequence. In the fourth century, Augustine saw grace as the divine force that could liberate humans from the bondage of sin. The Holy Spirit, in Augustine's mind, freed us from the damage done to us by original sin, all the while illuminating our minds and causing us to delight in righteousness. Centuries after Augustine, Thomas Aquinas suggested that grace heals our human nature (a standard Western approach), while elevating us to a level at which we can participate in the divine nature with the Trinity (a standard Eastern approach). Thus, in Aquinas, Eastern and Western ideas about grace were harmonized into a singular view. In wasn't until the twentieth century that Catholics began to see grace in broader terms, specifically as a gift offered by God, not only to baptized Catholics but also to those outside of the faith. Eventually Catholic theologians began to discuss grace in terms of God's "self-communication"[3] to all of His creations, human or otherwise, in this universe and beyond. Succinctly stated, one modern Catholic theologian defined it this way: "'Grace' is essentially God's self-communication to us, and, secondarily the effect(s) of that self-communication."[4]

While Catholics do use the term "grace" with some frequency, they do not traditionally refer to "works," as Protestants or Latter-day Saints might. However, for Catholics the "works" component of the "grace/works" duality would be the seven sacraments of the Church, with the heaviest emphasis being placed on the salvific sacraments of baptism, Holy Communion, the Eucharist, and penance. We will discuss these

---

2   For a discussion of the evolution of Catholic thought on the doctrine of grace, see Mary Katherine Hilkert, "Grace," in *Harper Collins Encyclopedia of Catholicism*, ed. Richard P. McBrien (San Francisco, Calif.: HarperSanFrancisco, 1995), 577–82.

3   See Karl Rahner, *Foundations of Christian Faith* (New York: Crossroad, 1993), 116.

4   Richard P. McBrien, *Catholicism*, rev. ed. (San Francisco, Calif.: HarperSanFrancisco, 1994), 180.

in more detail later, but suffice it to say that through participation in the saving sacraments, Catholics lay hold on God's grace.

LATTER-DAY SAINTS

For Latter-days Saints the relationship between grace and works is not much different than within Catholicism, and our definition of grace is not significantly different from current Catholic definitions, although the terminology we use to define it is somewhat different. The LDS Bible Dictionary defines grace as the:

> divine means of help or strength, given through the bounteous mercy and love of Jesus Christ. . . . It is through grace . . . that mankind will be raised in immortality. . . . It is likewise through grace . . . that individuals . . . receive strength and assistance to do good works that they otherwise would not be able to maintain if left to their own means. This grace is an enabling power that allows men and women to lay hold on eternal life and exaltation after they have expended their own best efforts.[5]

From a Latter-day Saint perspective, grace is the help we receive from God enabling us to keep commandments, do good to others, and eventually attain eternal life in the presence of God and Christ. Most contemporary Catholics would likely agree with this definition of grace, and technically Latter-day Saints would not disagree with the Catholic claim that grace is God's "self-communication" to His creations.

First Nephi chapter eleven speaks of the "condescension of God," or how His Only Begotten Son, as an act of grace, condescended to come to earth, take a body, live among men, and eventually suffer and die that all, through Him, might live again. Thus, from a Latter-day Saint perspective, an important manifestation of God's grace was His decision to send His Son as a "communication" to His creations of His nature (or "self"), His will, and His saving power (through the Atonement of Christ).

---

5   See LDS Bible Dictionary, "Grace" (Salt Lake City: The Church of Jesus Christ of Latter-day Saints, 1989), 697.

Like Catholics, Latter-day Saints see certain "works" as necessary components to attaining salvation. Contemporary Catholics and Mormons alike attest to the fact that no rite, ordinance, or sacrament can save. However, both faiths profess these acts to be part of God's commands or expectations for salvation.

Catholics and Latter-day Saints alike would likely accept a common early Christian view of the relationship between grace and works.[6] For example, Gregory of Nazianzen wrote, "Our salvation comes . . . both from ourselves and from God. If God's help is necessary for doing good and if the good will itself come from Him, it is equally true that the initiative rests with man's free will."[7] Similarly, John Chrysostom taught that "without God's aid we should be unable to accomplish good works; nevertheless, even if grace takes the lead, it cooperates with free will. We first of all begin to desire the good and to incline ourselves towards it, and then God steps in to strengthen that desire and render it effective."[8] Finally, Patristic scholar J. N. D. Kelley penned this: "So Ambrose states, 'In everything the Lord's power cooperates with man's efforts'; but he can also say, 'Our free will gives us either a propensity to virtue or an inclination to sin.' In numerous passages he lays it down that the grace of salvation will only come to those who make the effort to bestir themselves."[9]

Thus, grace and works cooperate with each other. God's grace gives us the power and drive to do what we should. Keeping the divinely commanded "works" enables us to lay hold on the rewards God freely gives. Therefore, like the Catholic sacraments, Mormons believe that participation in certain ordinances is necessary in order to access God's full grace and to return eternally to God's presence.

---

6   See Peter J. Kreeft, *Catholic Christianity: A Complete Catechism of Catholic Beliefs based on the Catechism of the Catholic Church* (San Francisco, Calif.: Ignatius Press, 2001), 126–27.

7   Cited in J. N. D. Kelley, *Early Christian Doctrines*, rev. ed. (San Francisco, Calif.: HarperSanFrancisco, 1978), 352.

8   See Kelley, *Early Christian Doctrines*, 352.

9   See Kelley, *Early Christian Doctrines*, 356.

SUMMARY

Catholics and Mormons both understand grace to be God's enabling power, God's changing and exalting influence, God's freely given gifts (both spiritual and temporal), and God's choice to reveal or manifest Himself to His creations. Each faith believes in the harmonious relationship of grace and works—that these two function in concert with each other to bring to pass the salvation of mankind. Both traditions hold that active participation in the sacraments, rites, ordinances, or commandments of one's respective faith is the primary means of attaining that grace.

Do we in any way differ on the role of grace and works? Perhaps in one small way; our understanding of the sacraments, rites, ordinances, or acts that provoke grace, and how they provoke grace, is somewhat different. We will explore those differences in a later chapter.

HEAVEN AND HELL

While both Catholics and Mormons would agree that the central doctrine of Christianity is the atoning sacrifice of the Lord Jesus Christ, it may be fair to say that during the last two thousand years thoughts of heaven and hell have occupied the minds of more Christians than have thoughts of the Atonement. Texts like *Hell on Trial: A Case for Eternal Punishment*[1] or *Heaven: A History*[2] show the fixation Christians sometimes have with potential rewards and dreaded punishments. It seems fair to say that both Catholics and Mormons would acknowledge that rewards and punishments should never be the motivating factor in living one's religion. Nevertheless, all Christians are aware that the judgment day is coming, and thus thoughts of heaven and hell are hard to ignore.

CATHOLICS

As with most any other Christian denomination, Catholics believe in an afterlife, which consists of a heavenly reward or divine punishment. Some Latter-day Saints might assume that Catholics simply believe in heaven and hell, with all of the bad going to hell and each of the good going to heaven. However, this is an oversimplified view of the Catholic understanding of the afterlife.

---

1   Robert A. Peterson, *Hell On Trial: The Case for Eternal Punishment* (Phillipsburg, N. J.: P & R Publishing, 1995).

2   Colleen McDannell and Bernhard Lang, *Heaven: A History* (New Haven, Conn.: Yale University Press, 1988).

First of all, what is heaven in Catholic thought? One Catholic scholar noted that "there is no definitive teaching of the magisterium [or hierarchy of the Church] that would give us a 'proper picture' of heaven."[3] While the Catholic Church has not officially defined its nature, scholars of that tradition speak of it in terms of a "celestial sphere that is the home of God."[4] One text states of the Catholic construct of heaven: "Whatever else it will be, whatever else it will feel like, it will feel like home."[5] For Catholics, heaven is the place where, as resurrected beings,[6] the just enjoy the "beatific vision," or, in other words, "the direct knowing and loving of God after death."[7] This means that the righteous deceased person enjoys "full personal participation in the trinitarian life of God"[8] through his or her acceptance of God's grace.

Catholic scholars sometimes refer to the forthcoming heavenly reward as "deification" or "divinization."[9] Catholics sometimes express concern that this doctrine might to some sound like pantheism. Thus, they highlight that our participation in the "Trinitarian life of God" is

---

3   Paul Crowley, "Heaven," in *Harper Collins Encyclopedia of Catholicism*, ed. Richard P. McBrien (San Francisco, Calif.: HarperSanFrancisco, 1995), 605.

4   Crowley, "Heaven," in *Harper Collins Encyclopedia of Catholicism*, 604.

5   Peter J. Kreeft, *Catholic Christianity: A Complete Catechism of Catholic Beliefs based on the Catechism of the Catholic Church* (San Francisco, Calif.: Ignatius Press, 2001), 150.

6   For Catholics the Resurrection consists of the raising of "the whole human person"—not simply one's spirit. While many Catholics perceive the Resurrection as physical, that "whole person" that is to be raised will be made up of new atoms or new matter but in the identity and continuity of what that person was physically in mortality. The resurrected being will be in a final state of being beyond anything mortal. See John R. Sachs, "Resurrection of the Body," in *Harper Collins Encyclopedia of Catholicism*, 1110–111. See also *United States Catholic Catechism for Adults* (Washington, D.C.: United States Conference of Catholic Bishops, 2006), 155–56.

7   Kreeft, *Catholic Christianity*, 150; and Paul Crowley, "Beatific Vision," in *Harper Collins Encyclopedia of Catholicism*, 146.

8   Crowley, "Beatific Vision," in *Harper Collins Encyclopedia of Catholicism*, 147.

9   See "Deification," in *Harper Collins Encyclopedia of Catholicism*, 405, where we find this: "Deification, a theological theme also known as divinization. Judaism emphasized the transcendence of God, but the Incarnation gave Christians an intimation of accessibility to the divine. Paul said: 'For in him we live and move and have our being' (Acts 17:28). Elsewhere in the NT it is said: 'You . . . may become participants of the divine nature' (2 Pet 1:4). Clement of Alexandria's words became a commonplace: 'The Word of God became man that you may learn from man how man may become God.' Eastern theology has been very much at home with this theme. . . . Contemporary [Catholic] theologians Karl Rahner and Hans Urs von Balthasar have come closer to the Eastern Language of deification" than many of their Catholic predecessors.

a gift from God to us, a gift from the divine. It does not mean we, of ourselves, are equal to God or worthy of such status. Rather, it implies that God has given the ultimate gift to those who do not of themselves merit it.

And what of hell in Catholic thought? Books, like Dante's *Inferno*, have given the world a perception of a Catholic hell that consists of the devil holding a pitchfork and flames licking up at the heals of the damned. Perhaps such a picture accurately represented the Catholic hell of an earlier generation. However, many Catholics today would reject such an image, and official teachings certainly have moved away from any such construct—if it ever did represent the general view.[10]

A SCENE FROM DANTE'S *INFERNO*

Most non-Catholics will be surprised by the following statement from one Catholic priest: "While the possibility of hell is a proper part of the gospel, it should not be viewed as an equal alternative to heaven. . . . While the Church has canonized many saints, affirming that there are human beings in heaven, it has never affirmed that there is, in fact, a single human being in hell."[11] Another Catholic source notes:

> Hell is the pain produced by our choice of utterly and deliberately refusing to live in relationship with God, *if such a choice is even possible*. . . . Speaking on the subject of hell, Pope John Paul II said not to consider it a place, but rather a state that the soul suffers when it denies itself access to God. . . . The pope went on to say that God has never revealed

10   Kreeft, *Catholic Christianity*, 147.
11   John R. Sachs, "Hell," in *Harper Collins Encyclopedia of Catholicism*, 608.

"whether or which human beings" are eternally damned. . . . The Church does not say this has ever happened to anyone.[12]

Thus, from a Catholic position, although heaven definitely exists as a reward for the righteous and many have gone there, hell, which apparently *does* exist, could quite possibly be uninhabited, specifically for two reasons. First, God loves all of His creations and desires the salvation of them all. As one source notes: "A good illustration occurs in the New Testament when Jesus does not condemn those who have participated in his crucifixion. Rather, he says, 'Father, forgive them, for they . . . know not what they are doing.' (Luke 23:34)."[13] Second, in Catholic thought, in order to go to hell, one must "deliberately" refuse God and then die in a state of "mortal sin."[14] But, as the *Encyclopedia of Catholicism* states, "the Church has never taught that anyone has, in fact, died in such a state."[15]

It may be helpful to note that Catholics make a distinction between "mortal sin"—which Mormons would refer to as the "denial of the Holy Ghost," an act that would make one a son of perdition—and "venial" sins, which are slight or minor sins committed by all human beings in the course of the mortal experience. In Catholic thought, "mortal sin" will send you to hell, or, as Latter-day Saints would say, make you a son of perdition. "Venial sins," on the other hand, are not "serious enough to rupture a person's relationship with God."[16] They are sins that are relatively easy to gain pardon for. Hence if one's life has "venial sins," but not "mortal sins," one will go to heaven rather than hell. In a nutshell, Catholic doctrine teaches that many have gone to heaven, but there have been few, if any, sons of perdition.[17]

---

12   Bob O'Gorman and Mary Faulkner, *The Complete Idiot's Guide to Understanding Catholicism*, 2d ed. (Indianapolis, Ind.: Alpha Books, 2003), 264–65; emphasis in original.

13   O'Gorman and Faulkner, *Complete Idiot's Guide to Understanding Catholicism*, 265.

14   Hence, the catechism states, "Freely chosen eternal separation from communion with God is called *hell*." *United States Catholic Catechism for Adults*, 155.

15   See Sachs, "Hell," in *Harper Collins Encyclopedia of Catholicism*, 607.

16   See "Venial sin," in *Harper Collins Encyclopedia of Catholicism*, 1307.

17   The Prophet Joseph Smith explained how one becomes perdition in the following way: "All sins shall be forgiven, except the sin against the Holy Ghost; for Jesus will save all except the sons of perdition. What must a man do to commit the unpardonable sin

LATTER-DAY SAINTS

We will now briefly look at the LDS constructs of heaven and hell. Like Catholics, Latter-day Saints would be very comfortable with heaven being defined as a "celestial sphere that is the home of God," which is not entirely capable of being comprehended by mortals. And like Catholics, Mormons hold that the heavenly reward of the faithful consists of a complete or full knowledge of God. The restored gospel[18] also teaches a doctrine of divinization or deification, and, like Catholics, acknowledges that this should not be taken as a statement that the exalted or deified somehow replace God or have earned godhood. In LDS thought, even the deified will always see the Father, Son, and Holy Spirit as the Godhead through whom mortals have received their exaltation as a gift stemming from God's grace. Finally, Latter-day Saints see resurrection of the dead as physical, consisting of the whole person—body and spirit—just as Catholics do.

The LDS idea of hell is surprisingly similar to the Catholic view, including the declaration that few mortals have likely gone there after this life. By that I mean that the Latter-day Saint concept of "outer darkness" is equivalent to the Catholic place called "hell." Just as Catholics say that "venial" or minor sins will not send you to hell, Mormons argue that minor sins won't send you to outer darkness. Both faiths hold that open rebellion against God, performed with full knowledge

---

[and thereby become a son of perdition]? He must receive the Holy Ghost, have the heavens opened unto him, and know God, and then sin against Him. After a man has sinned against the Holy Ghost, there is no repentance for him. He has got to say that the sun does not shine while he sees it; he has got to deny Jesus Christ when the heavens have been opened unto him, and to deny the plan of salvation with his eyes open to the truth of it; and from that time he begins to be an enemy. This is the case with many apostates of the Church of Jesus Christ of Latter-day Saints." See Joseph Fielding Smith, comp., *Teachings of the Prophet Joseph Smith* (Salt Lake City: Deseret Book, 1976), 358.

18   One Catholic reader of this text suggested that the phrase "restored gospel" made him feel that his gospel was not complete and was somehow corrupted. It should be noted that the word "restored" as used by Latter-day Saints is not intended pejoratively toward other faiths. By it we only mean to suggest that The Church of Jesus Christ of Latter-day Saints professes to be a restoration of the New Testament church, which we hold was lost from the earth through an apostasy—which, incidentally, we *do not* believe was caused by the Roman Catholic Church. Thus, the use of this term is only intended as a clarifier, and in no way as a statement of condescension to our Christian brothers and sisters in Catholicism who do not traditionally hold that there was an apostasy of New Testament Christianity.

of Him, is requisite to inherit that worst of all eternal abodes. Just as Catholics hold that all who do not commit a "mortal sin" will received a reward in heaven, so also does LDS belief teach that each of the three degrees of glory are a heavenly reward for those who did not merit the status of sons of perdition.

SUMMARY

LDS and Catholic takes on heaven and hell are similar in most regards. Both faiths believe that the vast majority of God's children will receive a reward in heaven, both faiths reject the idea that a significant number of people will inherit permanent spiritual death (in the form of "outer darkness") after this life, and both faiths acknowledge that part of the heavenly reward is deification.

Of course, there are differences in how we perceive each of these doctrines. Whereas Catholics see most people dwelling permanently in God's presence, Mormons acknowledge three degrees of heaven (see D&C 76), and thus a percentage of those inheriting a degree of glory will still be damned or excluded from the Father's presence throughout eternity. Because Catholics don't accept a doctrine of the premortal existence of the spirit of man, they expect very few to be confined to outer darkness or hell. Latter-day Saints, acknowledging the events of the grand council and war in heaven, might say few mortals will become sons of perdition,[19] but a third-part of the hosts of heaven qualified for such a punishment before any human stepped upon this earth.

Finally, the Catholic view of deification is decidedly different from the LDS view. Some Catholics see it as simply an implication that the saved will dwell in God's presence for eternity. Some see it as a sort of Christian nirvana, wherein the recipient does not retain individuality, but rather becomes one with the Trinity, just as Jesus prayed His disciples might during His great intercessory prayer (John 17:21).[20]

---

19   See, for example, Richard O. Cowan, *Answers to Your Questions About the Doctrine and Covenants* (Salt Lake City: Deseret Book, 1996), 74; Joseph Fielding Smith, *Church History and Modern Revelation,* 4 vols. (Salt Lake City: The Church of Jesus Christ of Latter-day Saints, 1946–49), 2:53; and Roy W. Doxey, *The Doctrine and Covenants and the Future* (Salt Lake City: Deseret Book, 1954), 127.

20   Father Joseph A. Fitzmyer, a distinguished Roman Catholic scholar, wrote, "It should be noted that deification does not mean absorption into God, since the deified creature remains itself and distinct. It is the whole human being, body and soul, who is

However, the Latter-day Saint view on deification tends to be more fully defined or developed. While the members of the Godhead will retain their position of respect and authority over those they have deified, the exalted saint is seen as becoming what God currently is and being empowered to then do what God does throughout eternity. Thus, from an LDS position, God quite literally intends to give each of us all that He has—power, knowledge, nature, stature, etc.

transfigured in the spirit into the likeness of the divine nature, and deification is the goal of every Christian." Joseph Fitzmyer, *Pauline Theology: A Brief Sketch* (Englewood Cliffs, N.J.: Prentice Hall, 1967), 42.

PURGATORY
AND THE SPIRIT WORLD

Curiously, while most Protestants tend to speak of the afterlife in terms of heaven and hell, both Catholics and Latter-day Saints hold that there is a bit more to our next stage of existence than that fine line. Catholics are wont to speak of "purgatory," and Mormons hold to a belief in a post-mortal "spirit world." In both traditions, these are but a stop along the path that leads to our eternal abode, and what happens there, in the opinion of these two faiths, seems curiously similar.

CATHOLICS

While the term "purgatory" is almost a household word in Catholicism, some Latter-day Saints may not know what it means. One Dominican priest defined it as:

> an intermediate state of purification between death and heaven that provides for the removal of remaining personal obstacles to the full enjoyment of eternal union with God. According to Catholic doctrine, such purification continues and completes the process of sanctification (or divinization) that makes intimate union with the triune God possible for persons justified and reconciled in Christ. The obstacles in view here are . . . venial [or minor] sins, unrepented [of] at the time of death. . . . Purgatory affords an interval of final

purification for erasing conditions that would prevent justified persons from enjoying full fellowship with God.[1]

In other words, purgatory is the stage of existence for the spirit of
a deceased person before they inherit their eternal reward. It is a place
where one bound for a heavenly glory resolves any outstanding issues,
such as unrepented of sins. Some Catholics perceive purgatory as an
actual place, while others suppose it to be nothing more than a state
of mind for those not entirely ready to enter God's presence.[2] In either
case, it is simply a stop on the way to one's heavenly reward—a stop
designed to take care of "un-
finished spiritual business."[3]

On a related note, Ca-
tholicism has had in times
past a formal doctrine of
"supererogation." This teaching has been defined as "an
immense treasury of good
works which holy men have
performed over and above
what duty required, and that
the Roman pontiff is the
keeper and the distributor
of this treasure; so that he is
able, out of his inexhaustible
fund, to give and transfer to
every one such an amount of
good works as his necessities

A SCENE FROM DANTE'S *PURGATORIO*

1   Joseph A. Di Noia, "Purgatory," in *The Harper Collins Encyclopedia of Catholicism,* ed.
     Richard P. McBrien (San Francisco, Calif.: HarperSanFrancisco, 1995), 1070.
2   See Bob O'Gorman and Mary Faulkner, *The Complete Idiot's Guide to Understanding
     Catholicism,* 2d ed. (Indianapolis, Ind.: Alpha Books, 2003), 20.
3   "'The Church gives the name *Purgatory* to [the] final purification of the elect, which
     is entirely different from the punishment of the damned.' Those who die in a state of
     friendship with God but who are not fully purified and perfected are assured of their
     eternal salvation. However, they must undergo a purification to obtain the perfection .
     . . to enter heaven. . . . This process is called Purgatory." See also *United States Catholic
     Catechism for Adults* (Washington, D.C.: United States Conference of Catholic Bish-
     ops, 2006), 154. See also 161.

require, or as will suffice to avert the punishment of his sins."[4] Elsewhere we read:

> According to the Catholic doctrine, the special merit of su-
> pererogatory acts accredited to their agent can be used both
> for that individual's own salvation and for the salvation of
> others. The "superabundant merit," most typically collect-
> ed by the actions of Jesus and the saints, who far exceeded
> what was required for their own salvation, is deposited in
> the Spiritual Treasury of the Church to be disposed by the
> Pope and the bishops for remitting the sins of other, ordi-
> nary believers.[5]

Thus, acts of supererogation are those that exceed the demands
of morality. From a Catholic perspective, in order to gain salvation
all of us must live the minimum moral requirements given by God
in scripture. However, one who lives a life beyond those minimum
requirements is said to be more fully imitating Christ. Monastics,
for example, take vows of poverty, chastity, and obedience, which
go far beyond the scriptural dictates for salvation. Therefore, their
lives go beyond that which is expected or required by the commandments, approaching the ideal standard. Any praiseworthy action that exceeds the minimal demands of morality would be super-
erogatory. For example, if a woman saves a child by pushing it out
of the path of an oncoming vehicle, knowingly sacrificing herself in
the process, she has performed a work of supererogation.[6] According to this teaching, the works (and associated merit) of individuals
like this aforementioned woman, or others who similarly lived lives
of holiness, can be "transferred," so to speak, to those whose lives
have *not* met the minimum standard of morality. This "transfer" of
merit would be at the discretion of the Church's clerical leadership,
and it would limit the length of (or negate entirely the need for)

---

4   John Lawrence Von Mosheim, *Institutes of Ecclesiastical History, Ancient and Modern,* 4
         vols. (New York: Harper and Brothers, 1847), 2:254.

5   David Heyd, "Supererogation," in *Stanford Encyclopedia of Philosophy,* http://plato.
         stanford.edu/entries/supererogation.

6   See "Supererogation, Works of," in *Harper Collins Encyclopedia of Catholicism,* 1231.
         See also "Counsels, Evangelical," in *Harper Collins Encyclopedia of Catholicism,*
         372–73.

the sinner's stay in purgatory. However, as famous as supererogation has become in anti-Catholic literature, this teaching has not had a significant place in Catholic teachings since the end of the sale of indulgences, and it is not a common teaching in contemporary Catholicism.

LATTER-DAY SAINTS

Latter-day Saints have a concept similar to purgatory, which we refer to as the spirit world. It is a location where all individuals go between their death and resurrection. As in Catholic thought, the LDS perceive the spirit world—specifically for those in spirit "prison" or spirit "hell"—as a place to "take care of" any unresolved issues prior to the receipt of one's heavenly reward.

Additionally, supererogation has some relationship to the Latter-day Saint practice of work for the dead. In both the Catholic doctrine of supererogation and the LDS practice of temple work for the dead, individuals are doing for others what they cannot do for themselves. In both cases it is the vicarious works of a living person that enables a deceased person to move from purgatory or the spirit world into a realm near or in the presence of God.[7]

SUMMARY

While some obvious parallels exist between Catholic and LDS understandings of the post-mortal and pre-reward stage of existence for the "soul" (as Catholics would call it) or "spirit" (as Mormons would call it), there are also a few significant differences.

First of all, Roman Catholics hold that there are two judgments, one taking place immediately upon death (known as the "particular judgment"), and one taking place at the Second Coming of Christ (known as the "general judgment"). Thus, Catholics see purgatory as a post-judgment location,[8] or, in other words, an "individual judgment"

---

7   The occasional LDS author has made mention of the idea of supererogation. See, for example, James E. Talmage, *The Great Apostasy* (Salt Lake City: Deseret Book, 1968), 135; and Bruce R. McConkie, *Doctrinal New Testament Commentary,* 3 vols. (Salt Lake City: Bookcraft, 1987–88), 1:366.

8   "Divine judgment of the moral character of a person's life [is] rendered immediately following death. . . . God assigns the person to heaven, hell, or purgatory on the

for all who have just died.[9] It determines what "remaining obstacles" exist in the life of the recently deceased that will keep them from "the full enjoyment of eternal union with God."[10] Thus, while this is not the "final judgment" (according to Catholic thinking), it is the judgment that is seen as coming out of God's informed examination of you at the instant that you died. The "general judgment," on the other hand, is the time when God pronounces a "definitive judgment upon the moral quality of each person's life"[11] after the individual has had time in purgatory to become purified and sanctified from those things that were deemed unacceptable to God at the "particular judgment." While Latter-day Saints certainly acknowledge death to be one of several "judgments"[12] and the spirit world as having a similar purpose as purgatory, they do not see the "final judgment day" as being at Christ's Second Coming, but rather as taking place after one's time in the spirit world has been completed, and after the Resurrection has been accomplished. The *Encyclopedia of Mormonism* states:

> The concept of a final judgment requires that it be deferred until the entire mortal experience is completed. The Plan of Salvation teaches of a partial judgment at the time of death, when the spirit leaves the mortal body and enters the world of spirits (Alma 40:11–14), of another partial judgment at the time of resurrection, when the spirit and the physical body are permanently resurrected and reunited (Alma 11:45); and of a final judgment (Rev. 20:12; D&C 38:5) that will consign individuals to an eternal status (D&C 29:27–29; 3 Ne. 26:4). Thus, this final judgment will take place following the reuniting of body and spirit in the resurrection (Alma 11:44; 12:12). By that time, every person will have been given an opportunity to receive an

---

basis of this judgment." See "Judgment, Particular," in *Harper Collins Encyclopedia of Catholicism*, 724. See also *United States Catholic Catechism for Adults*, 161.

9   See Di Noia, "Purgatory," in *Harper Collins Encyclopedia of Catholicism*, 1070.

10   See Di Noia, "Purgatory," in *Harper Collins Encyclopedia of Catholicism*, 1070.

11   See Donal Leader, "Judgment, Particular," in *Harper Collins Encyclopedia of Catholicism*, 723; and *United States Catholic Catechism for Adults*, 161.

12   E.g., temple recommend interviews, personal priesthood interviews, death, the Second Coming for those who are alive when Jesus returns, the Resurrection (for those brought forth prior to the final judgment day), and the final judgment day.

understanding of the gospel of Jesus Christ (1 Pet. 3:19–20; Luke 4:18; Isa. 42:7).[13]

Another difference between LDS views of the spirit world and Catholic constructs of purgatory has to do with conversion. In Catholic thinking purgatory cannot be a place for conversion or post-mortal acceptance of the gospel, namely because formal judgment takes place prior to one's consignment there.[14] As noted above, the Vatican II teaching that non-Catholics can go to heaven to some degree makes post-mortal conversion somewhat of a moot point. Unlike Catholics, Latter-day Saints see learning about the fullness of the gospel of Jesus Christ as a major part of what goes on in the spirit world—alongside repentance (something both Catholics and Mormons see as happening there).

Finally, where Catholics see purgatory as a singular place or singular state of being, Mormonism holds that the spirit world has basically three groups of spirits temporarily residing there: "paradise" is for those who accepted the fullness of the Gospel while in mortality, and then did their best to live up to it; "prison" is for those who did not receive the restored gospel in mortality, but otherwise lived good lives—while in "prison" they will be taught what they had not before or had not accepted; and "hell" is a temporary state for those who, whether they knew about the restoration or not, did not, as mortals, live up to what they knew (via the light of Christ, their conscience, or the Holy Ghost) to be right and good. They were, in a word, wicked.[15]

---

13   Donald N. Wright, "Judgement Day, Final," in *Encyclopedia of Mormonism,* ed. Daniel H. Ludlow, 4 vols. (New York: Macmillan, 1992), 2:774.

14   See Di Noia, "Purgatory," in *Harper Collins Encyclopedia of Catholicism*, 1070.

15   In the glossary of uniquely LDS terms found in the *Encyclopedia of Mormonism*, we are informed that the spirit world is "the place where the spirits of the dead await resurrection and judgment; it consists of paradise, prison, and hell." Glossary, in *Encyclopedia of Mormonism*, 4:1772, s.v. "spirit world." The entry under "spirit prison" informs us that it is "the place where the spirits of the dead, particularly the *untaught* and *nonrighteous*, await resurrection and judgment." Glossary, in *Encyclopedia of Mormonism*, 4:1772, s.v. "spirit prison," emphasis added. Paradise, we learn, is "the dwelling place of the spirits of the righteous dead who await resurrection and judgment." Glossary, in *Encyclopedia of Mormonism*, 4:1770, s.v. "spirit paradise." This refers to those righteous dead who have accepted the gospel in mortality. There is a second segment listed, which consists of "righteous dead" that are waiting in prison for the opportunity to be taught the gospel, which they didn't have a chance to hear in mortality. This

last category of spirits is not in spirit "prison" because of disobedience, rebellion, or unrighteousness. Finally, there is a segment of the prison populous that is awaiting forgiveness in the place the *Encyclopedia of Mormonism* terms "hell." Those found in this "temporary dwelling place," it states, are "the unrepentant." Glossary, in *Encyclopedia of Mormonism*, 4:1768, s.v. "hell." Thus, a distinction exists in Latter-day Saint theology between the degrees of conversion, states of being informed, and levels of righteousness in the post-mortal/pre-reward stage of existence.

LIMBO AND THE SALVATION OF LITTLE CHILDREN

Jesus said: "Suffer the little children to come unto me, and forbid them not: for of such is the kingdom of God" (Mark 10:14). Certainly implicit in this statement is the reality that God sees the inherent purity of little children. Nevertheless, for centuries the dogma of "limbo" has caused Catholic parents to live in fear of the consequences should one of their newborns die prior to being baptized.[1]

What is this doctrine that seems to provoke such distress? How does it relate to LDS beliefs? What is the Catholic Church's current position on the place called "limbo"? In this chapter we will examine this unique and controversial topic.

CATHOLICS

Limbo is the belief that a place is prepared as a post-mortal residence (outside of heaven) for all children who die unbaptized. St. Augustine (AD 354–430) contended that infants who die before baptism must go to hell. Medieval theologians, who found the Augustinian position unacceptable or offensive, sought to soften the Church's position by introducing the concept of limbo. It is a place of eternal happiness, but those dwelling there are denied the actual presence of God (i.e., the "beatific vision"). That's the

---

1   See David Van Biema, "Life After Limbo," in *Time*, January 9, 2006, 68.

bad news.[2] The good news is that "Limbo is in Limbo!"[3] In other words, it is all but rejected by the Church today. Pope Benedict XVI has referred to it as nothing more than a "theological hypothesis" and as "problematic."[4] One Catholic source noted that "this theological postulate plays no role in contemporary Cath-

FOR CENTURIES, CATHOLICS HELD THAT CHILDREN WHO DIED UNBAPTIZED WOULD SPEND ETERNITY IN A PLACE CALLED LIMBO.

olic theology."[5] The 2001 *Complete Catechism of Catholic Beliefs* and the 2006 *United States Catholic Catechism for Adults* don't even mention limbo.[6] Thus, while for centuries many Catholics may have lived in fear of the loss of a child to limbo, today no such worry should exist. Indeed, because of the Vatican II (1962–65) "Decree on Ecumenism," which stated, among other things, that the unbaptized, the non-Christian, and even the atheist can go to heaven, a theological construct like limbo is untenable. Most Catholics today would assume that any child who dies prior to baptism would simply go straight to heaven, as they are "not guilty of personal sin."[7] Through the centuries, Catholic reason has brought about a doctrinal position that is remarkably similar to LDS teachings.

---

2   Its worth noting that one of my Hispanic readers, raised outside of the U.S., indicated that in her experience, Spanish speaking Catholics typically do not make a distinction between limbo and purgatory, even though the Church in Rome has.

3   See Van Biema, "Life After Limbo," 68.

4   Cited in Van Biema, "Life After Limbo," 68.

5   "Limbo," in *Harper Collins Encyclopedia of Catholicism,* ed. Richard P. McBrien (San Francisco, Calif.: HarperSanFrancisco, 1995), 771.

6   See Peter J. Kreeft, *Catholic Christianity: A Complete Catechism of Catholic Beliefs based on the Catechism of the Catholic Church* (San Francisco, Calif.: Ignatius Press, 2001); and *United States Catholic Catechism for Adults* (Washington, D.C.: United States Conference of Catholic Bishops, 2006).

7   "Limbo," in *Harper Collins Encyclopedia of Catholicism,* 771.

LATTER-DAY SAINTS

Latter-day Saints have never had a doctrine of limbo. However, our belief in the terrestrial kingdom has some similarities. Just as Catholics once held that limbo was reserved for the unbaptized who did not deserve to go to hell, but who, because they did not receive the necessary ordinances, could not reside eternally in God's presence, so also do Mormons believe that the terrestrial kingdom exists for those who have lived good lives, but who have not fulfilled all God has requested of them in order to return to the fullness of His presence. From an LDS perspective, the residents of that kingdom are those who do not deserve to be sent to "hell"—i.e., the telestial kingdom or outer darkness—but because of their rejection of ordinances and the fullness of the gospel of Jesus Christ, they are consigned to a place of happiness that is outside of the presence of God the Father.

SUMMARY

Latter-day Saints have never held that little children will be kept out of the presence of God should they die unbaptized (see Moroni 8:8–12). Indeed, we believe "Little children . . . are all alive in [Christ] because of his mercy" (Moroni 8:19). Although it has not always been the case, contemporary Catholic teaching on this subject is basically in harmony with LDS doctrine. Little children who die unbaptized will be saved in heaven—what Mormons call the celestial kingdom of God (D&C 137:10).

SACRAMENTS

Latter-day Saints have a number of religious terms in common with other Christian denominations.[1] Certainly we use common theological words such as "repentance," "atonement," "forgiveness," or "ordinances."[2] However, in our past we have also used other descriptive words that might seem more Catholic than LDS. For example, it was once common to speak of some of our Church curriculum as our "catechism,"[3] and to refer to the members of the Godhead as the "Trinity."[4] While contemporary Mormons seldom use those terms, we

1   See, for example, Robert W. Blair, "Vocabulary, Latter-day Saint," in *Encyclopedia of Mormonism,* ed. Daniel H. Ludlow, 4 vols. (New York: Macmillan, 1992), 4:1537.

2   It should be noted that when we do use the same terminology, we do not always mean exactly the same thing as our non-LDS Christian brothers and sisters.

3   See, for example, John Jaques, *Catechism for Children: Exhibiting the Prominent Doctrines of the Church of Jesus Christ of Latter-day Saints* (Liverpool: F. D. Richards, 1854), footnote to the sixth lecture of the 1835 edition of the *Lectures on Faith.* See also Naomi M. Shumway, "Primary," in *Encyclopedia of Mormonism,* 3:1147; Paul H. Peterson, "Reformation (LDS) of 1856–1857," in *Encyclopedia of Mormonism,* 3:1197; B. Lloyd Poelman, "Sunday School," in *Encyclopedia of Mormonism,* 3:1425; Larry E. Dahl and Charles D. Tate Jr., eds., *The Lectures on Faith in Historical Perspective* (Provo, Utah: Religious Studies Center, 1990), 2, 13–14, 94, 227, and 241; and Larry E. Dahl, "Lectures on Faith," in Arnold K. Garr, Donald Q. Cannon, and Richard O. Cowan, eds., *Encyclopedia of Latter-day Saint History* (Salt Lake City: Deseret Book, 2000), 649.

4   See, for example, John A. Widtsoe, comp., *Discourses of Brigham Young* (Salt Lake City: Bookcraft, 1998), 30; John Taylor, *The Gospel Kingdom: Selections from the Writings and Discourses of John Taylor* (Salt Lake City: Bookcraft, 1998), 28; and Joseph Smith Jr., *History of The Church of Jesus Christ of Latter-day Saints,* ed. B. H. Roberts, 2d ed., rev., 8 vols. (Salt Lake City: Deseret Book, 1978), 8:254.

do have other theological words or phrases that we still hold in common with Roman Catholics. One such word is "sacrament," which comes from Latin, meaning to swear an oath of allegiance, to make something sacred, or to consecrate.[5] In both faiths, the word sacrament describes outward acts that lead to the receipt of God's grace or, in other words, that allow us to lay hold upon the saving power of Christ's Atonement.[6] Elder Jeffery R. Holland once offered this definition of sacraments:

> A sacrament could be any one of a number of gestures or acts or ordinances that unite us with God and his limitless powers. We are imperfect and mortal; he is perfect and immortal. But from time to time—indeed, as often as is possible and appropriate—we find ways and go to places and create circumstances where we can unite symbolically with him and, in so doing, gain access to his power. Those special moments of union with God are sacramental moments, such as kneeling at a marriage altar, or blessing a newborn baby, or partaking of the emblems of the Lord's Supper. This latter ordinance is the one we in the Church have come to associate most traditionally with the word *sacrament,* though it is technically only one of many such moments when we formally take the hand of God and feel his divine power.[7]

Since the Fourth Lateran Council (AD 1215), the Catholic Church has held that there are seven official "sacraments" that function as "an outward sign, instituted by Christ, to give grace."[8] These sacraments are (1) baptism, (2) confirmation, (3) the Eucharist, or Lord's Supper, (4)

---

5   See Jean L. McKechnie, ed., *Webster's New Twentieth Century Dictionary,* 2d ed. (N.p.: Collins World, 1978), 1593, s.v. "sacrament."

6   The *United States Catholic Catechism for Adults* defines a sacrament as: "An efficacious sign of grace, instituted by Christ and entrusted to the Church, by which divine life is dispensed to us by the work of the Holy Spirit." *United States Catholic Catechism for Adults,* 526. See also Peter J. Kreeft, *Catholic Christianity: A Complete Catechism of Catholic Beliefs based on the Catechism of the Catholic Church* (San Francisco, Calif.: Ignatius Press, 2001), 296.

7   Jeffrey R. Holland, "Of Souls, Symbols, and Sacraments," (devotional, Brigham Young University, Provo, Utah, January 12, 1988), cited in Jeffrey R. Holland and Patricia T. Holland, *On Earth As It Is in Heaven* (Salt Lake City: Deseret Book, 1989), 193.

8   Mark R. Francis, "Sacrament," in *Harper Collins Encyclopedia of Catholicism,* ed. Richard P. McBrien (San Francisco, Calif.: HarperSanFrancisco, 1995), 1147.

penance or reconciliation, (5) anointing of the sick, (6) marriage, and (7) holy orders. Other things are seen as "sacramentals"[9] in Catholicism, such as Jesus' incarnation, the Church, the rosary, the lighting of candles or incense, etc.[10] However, these are not seen as significant conveyors of grace to the degree that the standard seven sacraments are.

BAPTISM

Catholics

Baptism in Catholicism is most often performed on infants, by pouring water on the child, rather than immersing the infant in water. However, baptism by this mode and at this age is not required within Catholicism. One Catholic scholar noted, "The manner of administration of the sacrament [of baptism] today is either by immersion or the pouring of water, whichever seems to better ensure that the baptism is not a mere purification, but [rather] the sacrament of being joined to Christ."[11] The

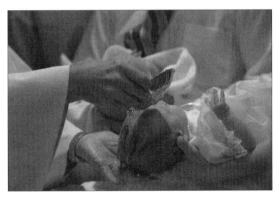

INFANT BAPTISM CONTINUES TO BE THE NORM IN ROMAN CATHOLICISM.

---

9   "Sacramentals are sacred signs which resemble the seven sacraments, but are not instituted by Christ. . . . Instead, they are instituted by the Church and symbolize spiritual effects which come about primarily through the prayer of the Church. They open us to God's grace if we use them with faith. . . . Sacramentals dispose us to receive the grace of the sacraments and sanctify various occasions in human life. Most sacramentals are related to the sacraments in some way. Holy water, for example . . . recalls our baptism. . . . Important sacramentals are prayers of blessing, blessed ashes, bells, candles, crosses, crucifixes, statues, sacred images, medals, oils, palms, and rosaries." Oscar Lukefahr, *"We Believe . . .": A Survey of the Catholic Faith*, rev. ed. (Liguori, Mo.: Liguori Publications, 1995), 100.

10   Francis, "Sacrament," in *Harper Collins Encyclopedia of Catholicism*, 1147; Bob O'Gorman and Mary Faulkner, *The Complete Idiot's Guide to Understanding Catholicism*, 2d ed. (Indianapolis, Ind.: Alpha Books, 2003), 133.

11   Anthony Sherman, "Baptism," in *Harper Collins Encyclopedia of Catholicism*, 137.

Catholic Church sees New Testament baptisms as being primarily by immersion, but it acknowledges that the rite or ordinance of baptism has gone through "deterioration" over the centuries.[12] According to the *Encyclopedia of Catholicism*, the sacrament of baptism has several purposes. First of all, "baptism is the sacrament by which one becomes a member of the Christian community."[13] Baptism also pardons sin and rescues recipients from the power of darkness.[14] Finally, for Catholics, baptism allows those submitting to the ordinance to become "new creations" and be called the "sons and daughters of God."[15]

LATTER-DAY SAINTS

For Latter-day Saints much of the Catholic construct of baptism will sound familiar. First of all, the purpose of baptism in Mormonism is not significantly different than it is in Catholicism. By it we officially become members of Christ's church[16]; we have our sins remitted, and we receive newly found power to resist evil[17]; Through it we hold that we may become new creations in Christ, being adopted as His spiritual

---

12   See Sherman, "Baptism," in *Harper Collins Encyclopedia of Catholicism*, 135–36.

13   Sherman, "Baptism," in *Harper Collins Encyclopedia of Catholicism*, 133. See also *United States Catholic Catechism for Adults*, 193.

14   Sherman, "Baptism," in *Harper Collins Encyclopedia of Catholicism*, 137. See also *United States Catholic Catechism for Adults*, 192; and Kreeft, *Catholic Christianity*, 308.

15   Sherman, "Baptism," in *Harper Collins Encyclopedia of Catholicism*, 137. See also *United States Catholic Catechism for Adults*, 193; and Kreeft, *Catholic Christianity*, 308.

16   The *Encyclopedia of Mormonism* states that for Latter-day Saint Christians, baptism enters them "into the fold of God." Carl S. Hawkins, "Baptism," in *Encyclopedia of Mormonism*, 1:92. LDS scholar John Gee wrote, "With baptism the individual witnesses that he has repented of his sins, takes on the name of Christ, and becomes *a member of the Christian community*, all at the same time." John Gee, "'La Trahison des Clercs: On the Language and Translation of the Book of Mormon,' A Review of Brent Lee Metcalfe's *New Approaches To the Book of Mormon: Explorations in Critical Methodology*," *FARMS Review of Books* 6, no. 1 (1994): 76; emphasis added.

17   Many Latter-day Saint leaders and passages within the LDS canon speak of the power repentance, baptism, and receipt of the Holy Ghost to remit sins and dispel the powers of darkness. See, for example, Joseph B. Wirthlin, "Christians in Belief and Action," *Ensign* (November 1996): 72; James E. Faust, "The Great Imitator," *Ensign* (November 1987): 36; Dallin H. Oaks, "The Aaronic Priesthood and the Sacrament," *Ensign* (November 1998): 39; Boyd K. Packer, "Washed Clean," *Ensign* (May 1997): 10; Mark 1:4; Luke 3:3; Moroni 8:11, 25; D&C 13:1, 19:31, 55:22, 84:27, 107:20, 138:33; JS—H 1:68–69; and the fourth article of faith.

sons and daughters.[18] Like Catholics, Latter-day Saints acknowledge that baptism in the New Testament was by immersion and that over the centuries the ordinance has seen much evolution. Although we do not baptize infants, as Catholics most often do, we do baptize young children, and, like Catholics, we expect that family members and other adults[19] will help guide the young initiate to a fuller understanding of the covenant made at the time the ordinance was performed.

Thus, for Catholics and Mormons alike, the ordinance or "sacrament" of baptism is a rite that God has commanded we participate in, that is necessary for salvation, and that makes us a member of Christ's church. Both faiths see it as saving and empowering. Both faiths encourage its performance at a young age—for Catholics, shortly after birth, and for Mormons, shortly after accountability begins.[20]

Unlike Catholics, Latter-day Saints reject the post-biblical developments that allow for baptism by "infusion" (or the pouring of water upon the person being baptized) and the baptizing of infants. However, it should be noted that the primary LDS concern about infant baptism surrounds the issue of accountability and the LDS belief that those unaccountable will not be damned should they die unbaptized (D&C 137:10; Moroni 8:8–12).

CONFIRMATION

CATHOLICS

Like the sacrament and the ordinance of baptism, confirmation has also evolved in its meaning and practice over the centuries. In general terms, Catholicism holds that while the term "confirmation" was not

---

18   Both the scriptures that Latter-day Saints have in common with Catholics and those unique to Mormonism speak of the converted and baptized as becoming "new creations" in Christ (2 Corinthians 5:17; Galatians 6:15; and Mosiah 27:26) and being adopted as His "sons and daughters." 2 Corinthians 6:18; Mosiah 27:25; D&C 25:1, and 76:24.

19   Catholics often have "godparents" to help them along. Latter-day Saints see this as primarily the role of parents, but they acknowledge the assistance of primary teachers, leaders in the young men and young women organizations, priesthood leaders, etc.

20   The LDS general church handbook of instructions states, "Children should be baptized on or as soon after their eighth birthday as reasonable." *Church Handbook of Instructions, Book 1: Stake Presidencies and Bishoprics* [leadership handbook] (Salt Lake City: The Church of Jesus Christ of Latter-day Saints, 2006), 32.

used until the forth or fifth century, the rite existed in New Testament times and was performed for receipt of the Holy Spirit.[21] It wasn't until the medieval period that theologians began to argue that the Spirit was received at baptism, and thus confirmation was a "separate" conferral "of the Spirit."[22]

Around the turn of the twentieth century, the sacrament or rite of confirmation in Catholicism experienced a transition in its meaning, becoming a "puberty rite" or "graduation exercise."[23] In 1910, Pope Pius X indicated that children should be baptized as infants, have their first confession, and then have their first partaking of the Eucharist at the age of accountability or "age of reason"—approximately seven or eight years of age[24]—and then be confirmed later, at about ten years of age.

In the minds of many Roman Catholics, confirmation is like a second baptism. Being baptized as an infant was decided for you by your parents. However, when you are confirmed (around the time you become a teenager), you are choosing to renew those covenants made in your infancy, and this time you are making this decision of your own free will and choice. This is an important decision for Catholics.

While this rite used to be performed exclusively by the imposition of hands, ideally by a bishop, today the bishop or priest performing the confirmation does not necessarily physically lay hands on individuals in order to give them the Holy Spirit.[25] Rather, the priest may simply extend his hands over those being confirmed. This rite performed in this manner is seen by Catholics as equivalent to the physical laying on of hands.

LATTER-DAY SAINTS

In Mormonism, confirmation has a dual purpose. It not only makes one an official member of The Church of Jesus Christ of Latter-

---

21   Mary Piil, "Confirmation," in *Harper Collins Encyclopedia of Catholicism*, 346. See also *United States Catholic Catechism for Adults*, 205.

22   See Piil, "Confirmation," in *Harper Collins Encyclopedia of Catholicism*, 347.

23   See Piil, "Confirmation," in *Harper Collins Encyclopedia of Catholicism*, 347.

24   See "Age of Reason," in *Harper Collins Encyclopedia of Catholicism*, 24–25.

25   See Piil, "Confirmation," in *Harper Collins Encyclopedia of Catholicism*, 350.

day Saints, but it also enables one to receive the right to the constant companionship of the Holy Spirit.

As with baptism, Latter-day Saints reject post-biblical developments in the ordinance of confirmation. Thus, Mormons today believe that the Holy Ghost is received, not at baptism, but by the laying on of hands at confirmation. Thus, the Prophet Joseph Smith taught:

> You might as well baptize a bag of sand as a man, if not done in view of the remission of sins and getting of the Holy Ghost. Baptism by water is but half a baptism, and is good for nothing without the other half—that is, the baptism of the Holy Ghost. . . . The baptism of water, without the baptism of fire and the Holy Ghost attending it, is of no use; they are necessarily and inseparably connected.[26]

From an LDS perspective, confirmation should take place immediately after baptism.[27]

Latter-day Saints and Catholics do not greatly differ in their understanding of the meaning of the sacrament or ordinance of confirmation. Both see it as connected to the receipt of the Holy Spirit. Both hold it to be a rite necessary for one's salvation. However, how the rite is performed, when it is performed, and the parameters of what it does are each areas where Catholics and Mormons disagree. Confirmation is an

AT APPROXIMATELY TEN YEARS OF AGE, MOST CATHOLIC CHILDREN PARTICIPATE IN THE RITE OF CONFIRMATION, THROUGH WHICH THEY RENEW THE COVENANTS MADE FOR THEM AT THEIR BAPTISM, AND BY WHICH THEY ALSO RECEIVE THE HOLY GHOST

---

26   Joseph Fielding Smith, comp., *Teachings of the Prophet Joseph Smith* (Salt Lake City: Deseret Book, 1976), 314, 360.

27   If it is an eight year old who is being baptized, the confirmation should take place the same day the baptism is performed. If the baptismal candidate is older than eight, the confirmation should take place after the baptism or in a sacrament meeting, as soon as is reasonable.

important part of Catholic practice, nevertheless, for most Catholics, one who has been baptized is seen as an official member of the Church prior to confirmation.[28] In other words, Catholics who were baptized in infancy but never confirmed members of the Church would still see themselves as Catholics. However, for Mormons one is not a member of the Church after baptism until after the ordinance of confirmation is performed.[29] Thus, while both rites are associated with the receipt of the Holy Spirit, their larger implications are quite different.

THE EUCHARIST

CATHOLICS

The Eucharist,[30] Lord's Supper, Holy Communion—these are but a few of the many names used in reference to this central rite of Christianity. For Catholics, when consecrated, the bread and wine are changed *substantially* (or in their essence) into the *real presence of Christ*, while the *accidents* (i.e., the appearance—color, shape, taste, etc.) of bread and wine remain.[31] In other words, while after being consecrated the bread and wine continue to look like bread and wine, they are in substance or reality the actual body and blood of Christ. Catholics call this doctrine "transubstantiation." While Catholics tend to disagree on how this takes place, there is general agreement on what has taken place.[32]

---

28   It is worth nothing that *Catholic Christianity: A Complete Catechism of Catholic Beliefs based on the Catechism of the Catholic Church*, states, "Confirmation is the completion of baptism." See Kreeft, *Catholic Christianity*, 316.

29   Thus the Prophet Joseph Smith taught, "You might as well baptize a bag of sand as a man, if not done in view of the remission of sins and getting of the Holy Ghost. Baptism by water is but half a baptism, and is good for nothing without the other half—that is, the baptism of the Holy Ghost. . . . The baptism of water, without the baptism of fire and the Holy Ghost attending it, is of no use; they are necessarily and inseparably connected." Smith, *Teachings of the Prophet Joseph Smith*, 314, 360.

30   The word "Eucharist" comes from Greek and means "thanksgiving," implying our need to give thanks to God for all that He has given to and done for us—specifically for the atonement He wrought on our behalf.

31   See Regis A. Duffy, "Eucharist," in *Harper Collins Encyclopedia of Catholicism*, 485; John J. Strynkowski, "Transubstantiation," in *Harper Collins Encyclopedia of Catholicism*, 1264; John J. Strynkowski, "Real Presence," in *Harper Collins Encyclopedia of Catholicism*, 1080; *United States Catholic Catechism for Adults*, 223.

32   See Bob Moran, *A Closer Look At Catholicism* (Waco, Tex.: Word Books, 1986), 126.

Related to the teaching of transubstantiation, some Catholics believe that when the Mass is performed and the Eucharist is consecrated,[33] Jesus is sacrificed anew on behalf of the people. One Catholic priest penned this:

> Some Protestants, including many evangelicals, have recoiled from the popular, late medieval view that said the Mass was "another" sacrifice of Jesus for our sins. Since Jesus had died once and for all, no human ritual could repeat this. It was particularly unthinkable that some priest could do mumbo-jumbo and call down Jesus into those humble bits of bread and drops of wine. . . . While at Wheaton College in the autumn of 1983 . . . I heard Dr. Julius Scott . . . leading a Bible study. . . . Dr. Scott seemed to be teaching that Jesus continues to plead our cause before the Father. . . . I was delighted to hear Dr. Scott speak of this. . . . If Jesus was constantly interceding for us, . . . why couldn't we be one with him in this continual pleading and reminding through our ritual [the sacrifice of the mass]? . . . Somewhere in my Catholic training one or more teachers described the Mass as an "unbloody" sacrifice. . . . In the Mass . . . Jesus offers himself *sacramentally* to the Father. . . . It is not the same as Calvary, yet it is related at a very deep level. . . . We cannot rest content with a ritual enactment that is "mere memorial."[34]

Thus, a percentage of Catholics hold that when the Mass is performed, Jesus is sacrificed again.[35] While it is not identical to His sacrifice on Golgotha's cross, it is in substance the same.

---

33 The Catholic "eucharistic prayer" (or "sacrament prayer," as Mormons would call it) consists of the following words from the New Testament: "Take this, all of you, and eat it: This is my body which will be given up for you. Take this, all of you, and drink from it: this is the cup of my blood, the blood of the new and everlasting covenant. It will be shed for you and for all so that sins may be forgiven. Do this in memory of me." See Mark 14:22–25; Matthew 26:26–29; Luke 22:15–20; and 1 Corinthians 11:22–26.

34 Moran, *A Closer Look At Catholicism*, 121–24. Peter Kreeft noted, "The Eucharist does not repeat this sacrifice, but re-presents it to the Father." Kreeft, *Catholic Christianity*, 326. See also *United States Catholic Catechism for Adults*, 220–21.

35 There is no way to estimate the percentage of Catholics who interpret transubstantiation in this way. In my experience the numbers are low, however, at least one of the Catholics who read this text emphatically believes it in the aforementioned way. It is impossible to say more than this: some perceive the doctrine this way, and others do not.

LATTER-DAY SAINTS

Latter-day Saints, like Catholics, see this ordinance as originating with Jesus Himself. It was at the Last Supper, a Passover feast, that He first taught His disciples that the sacramental bread and wine represented His body and blood. However, hints of this doctrine are found elsewhere in Jesus' teachings. For example, in the sixth chapter of the Gospel of John we read, "Then Jesus said unto them, Verily, verily, I say unto you, Except ye eat the flesh of the Son of man, and drink his blood, ye have no life in you. Whoso eateth my flesh, and drinketh my blood, hath eternal life; and I will raise him up at the last day" (John 6:53–54). Whereas Catholicism sees something very literal in Jesus' words, Latter-day Saints do not take them literally. We believe the consecrated or blessed bread and water (used by Latter-day Saints instead of wine) remain bread and water in "substance" *and* "appearance." They only symbolize Christ's body and blood. Having said that, Latter-day Saints would acknowledge that something does happen to the bread and water through the blessing that is pronounced upon it. After it has been blessed, it has (in LDS belief) a power to bring God's Spirit to the partaker, and in so doing, it allows the person who worthily partakes to be sanctified and changed through consumption of the elements.

While both faiths accept this rite as a sacrament requisite for salvation, we differ not in the power of the blessed elements, but in their nature and in the way Jesus is "present" in them. Contrary to Catholic belief, Latter-day Saints do not accept the "real presence" of Jesus in the bread and water, but we do accept the real presence of His Spirit during the ordinance. Similarly, Mormons do not perceive Jesus as being re-sacrificed during the blessing on the bread and water/wine as some Catholics might, but in both faiths the sacrament of the Lord's Supper has the power to spiritually transport the participating Christian back to Christ's atoning sacrifice, which was made on his or her behalf. Thus, both faiths would agree that "Eucharist" or "Thanksgiving" is a perfect title for this rite. Ideally, as we partake, each of us is struck with the debt we owe to Him who knew no sin (2 Corinthians 5:21).

PENANCE OR RECONCILIATION

CATHOLICS

In Catholicism, penance consists of the prayers or works one performs at the direction of one's priesthood leader. It can also include acts of repentance independently performed as an expression of a desire to change or as evidence of sorrow for sin.[36] While some may "tongue-in-cheek" speak of "Hail Marys"[37] and "Our Fathers,"[38] these are nevertheless sincere acts of contrition performed by the faithful who wish to feel forgiveness for sins or inadequacies and who desire to draw closer to God.

Of contemporary Catholic approaches to repentance and confession, one Catholic text notes:

> For years, Catholics observed a weekly rite of . . . entering the confessional box to anonymously whisper [their sins] to the priest who sat on the other side of a tiny screen door. Today, most Catholics do not observe the weekly rite of confession, and the setting for the sacrament can include sitting face-to-face with a confessor in a room rather than the little black box.[39]

In the process of confession, the priest acts on behalf of Jesus.[40] He informs the person confessing what Jesus requires of the sinner in order to gain forgiveness. He also expresses Christ's forgiveness for sins committed that are now being confessed.[41]

---

36 See "Penance," in *Harper Collins Encyclopedia of Catholicism*, 982. One of my Catholic readers noted that a good Catholic should never let more than three months pass without participating in the sacrament of confession.

37 The Hail Mary or *Ave Maria* is a popular Catholic prayer that states, "Hail Mary, full of grace: The Lord is with thee. Blessed art thou among women, and blessed is the fruit of thy womb, Jesus. Holy Mary, Mother of God, pray for us sinners, now and at the hour of our death. Amen." The repeating of this prayer is sometimes performed as an effort toward repentance and increased spirituality.

38 The Our Father, Lord's Prayer, or *Pater Noster* comes from Luke 11:2–4 and Matthew 6:9–13, and, like the Hail Mary, is used not only as part of the Mass, but also as part of personal penance.

39 O'Gorman and Faulkner, *Complete Idiot's Guide to Understanding Catholicism*, 154.

40 *United States Catholic Catechism for Adults*, 238.

41 One Catholic author wrote, "The question is often asked by Protestants: Why must we confess to a priest and not just to God? . . . And the answer is that throughout scripture, God's forgiveness is always mediated. In the Old Testament God's forgive-

LATTER-DAY SAINTS

While Latter-day Saints don't think of the process of repentance in necessarily as structured of terms as Catholics might, the similarities between the Catholic and LDS approach should be quite obvious. As in Catholicism, in Mormonism serious sins should be confessed to a priesthood leader. In most cases the leader will assign certain things to be done. Prayer is always included, but often other acts are to be performed in an effort to facilitate repentance and change. Indeed, the LDS General Handbook of Instructions offers a very structured approach to serious transgressions. One might say that it offers an LDS version of Hail Marys and Our Fathers.[42] Latter-day Saint priesthood leaders, like Catholic priests, also act in the stead of Christ, both in their commission to lead one through the repentance process and in their belief that they have the right and authority to let one know when the Lord has forgiven them of serious sins that have been confessed and properly repented of. Major differences between Catholic and LDS approaches to repentance are more perceived than real. Official Catholic teaching is that priests themselves do not have the power to forgive sins. They are simply surrogates for Christ.[43]

---

ness was mediated by the high priest. . . . In the New Testament it was mediated by Christ on the Cross . . . and then it was mediated by his commission to his apostles. . . . The fact that Christ made forgiveness available to us so concretely through confession to a priest is a sacramental sign of his concrete presence. He—the one who alone can forgive sins—is just as really present [during confession] as his priest is." Kreeft, *Catholic Christianity*, 343.

42   See "Church Discipline," in *Church Handbook of Instructions, Book 1: Stake Presidencies and Bishoprics* [leadership handbook] (Salt Lake City: The Church of Jesus Christ of Latter-day Saints, 2006), 105–23.

43   Some lay Catholics would understand Jesus' words to His apostles in John 20:23—"Whose soever sins ye remit, they are remitted unto them; and whose soever sins ye retain, they are retained"—to be saying that parish priests do actually have the power to remit sins. However, Catholic commentators on the passage indicate that the context of the verse suggests that this forgiveness of sins has to do with their power to give the Holy Ghost to believers, which then remits sins. It is not a declaration (in mainstream U.S. Catholic thinking) of a priest's power to forgive sins. See, for example, Pheme Perkins, "The Gospel According to John," in *The New Jerome Biblical Commentary*, eds. Raymond E. Brown, Joseph A. Fitzmyer, and Roland E. Murphy (Englewood Cliffs, N.J.: Prentice Hall, 1990), 984; Raymond E. Brown, *The Anchor Bible—The Gospel According To John XIII–XXI* (New York: Doubleday, 1970), 1040–45; Peter F. Ellis, *The Genius of John* (Collegeville, Minn.: Liturgical Press,

The contemporary Catholic Church does not practice the "sale of indulgences," and thus Catholics do not believe that they can buy their way out of sin. Nor do Catholics hold that saying prayers, such as the Rosary or the Lord's Prayer, forgives sins. Rather, those are acts of repentance that are designed to change the heart, mind,

A COLLECTION OF THE ITEMS A CATHOLIC PRIEST WOULD USE TO PERFORM THE SACRAMENT OF "ANOINTING THE SICK" OR "LAST RITES"

and desires of the sinner. The prayers are no more designed as a way for the penitent to "earn" forgiveness than is an LDS priesthood leader's counsel to attend all three hours of Church on Sunday (something those working through the repentance process are often advised to do).

Finally, Catholics and Mormons are united in their belief that penance or reconciliation is requisite for salvation. As one Catholic source noted, "reconciliation is the point of" the sacrament of penance. If we do not repent—fully engaging in those things our priest or bishop instructs us to do—we have little hope of being reconciled with God at the judgment day.

1984), 294–95. Raymond Brown wrote that "in reaction to the Protestant reformers the Council of Trent [suggested] . . . that this verse should be understood [as referring to] the power exercised by the ordained priest in the Sacrament of Penance. . . . Many modern Roman Catholic scholars [however] do not think that this declaration of the Church necessarily concerns or defines the meaning that *the evangelist* [John] attached to the verse when he wrote it." Brown then added, "exegetically, one can call upon John xx 23 for assurance that the power of forgiveness has been granted; but one cannot call upon the text as proof that the way in which a particular community exercises this power is not true to scripture." In other words, Brown is noting that it is unclear exactly how John meant this to be understood, but many Catholic scholars reject the idea that John is saying parish priests hearing a confession are the fulfillment of John's words. Brown, *The Anchor Bible—The Gospel According To John XIII–XXI*, 1041, 1045.

ANOINTING OF THE SICK

CATHOLICS

Throughout its history, the Catholic Church has had a sacrament known as "anointing of the sick." It is based on the biblical practice of using oil, the laying on of hands, and prayer, for the healing of the sick (Mark 6:13; James 5:13–16). From about the ninth century onward, this sacrament was referred to as "last rights" or "holy unction," mainly because it was almost exclusively associated with those who were near death.[44] Since Vatican II (1962–65), however, the Catholic Church has sought to bring the rite back into alignment with the Bible, and thus today it is called "anointing of the sick" instead of "last rights." Contrary to popular belief, Catholics do not see this ordinance as necessary for one's salvation, nor do they believe in "deathbed repentance," which some have associated with "holy unction" or "last rights."[45] Rather, this sacrament is primarily "for the strengthening of those whose health is debilitated by physical illness or old age."[46]

As an additional element of this rite, one text notes:

> Until Vatican II, anointing was restricted to the ministry of the priest and was kept for "deathbed situations. . . ." It has become quite common on given Sundays throughout the year to make anointing ceremonies part of the Mass. At these ceremonies, people in need of special healing come forward for anointing. The membership of the Church witnesses, prays, and supports the persons's healing. In such a setting . . . a large group of people prays for those who are sick. The event opens the participants to shifts of conscious-

---

44   See Andrew D. Ciferni, "Anointing of the Sick," in *Harper Collins Encyclopedia of Catholicism*, 57, 58.

45   This sacrament or ordinance became associated with the "deathbed" specifically because, like baptism, it was viewed as being a "once in a lifetime rite." Once you had received it, you would never receive it again. Thus, most Catholics were hesitant to receive the ordinance until they thought they would die without it. Hence the name "last rights" and hence the tendency to receive it only upon one's death. Today, however, one may receive this sacrament more than once during life. See O'Gorman and Faulkner, *Complete Idiot's Guide to Understanding Catholicism*, 159.

46   Ciferni, "Anointing of the Sick," in *Harper Collins Encyclopedia of Catholicism*, 57.

ness, resulting in a deeper sense of community and aware-
ness of one's personal journey.[47]

Thus, there is a corporate side to this sacrament. Those who are
well are invited to exercise their faith on behalf of those who are sick
or afflicted. In this sacrament, there is a sense that both the sick and
those praying for the sick are blessed through their participation in this
sacrament.

LATTER-DAY SAINTS

Latter-day Saints also believe in the anointing of the sick. We too
use consecrated oil. We too perform the laying on of hands and utter
inspired prayer. And, like Catholics, this rite is performed on the young
and the old alike whenever their health is in jeopardy. Mormons also
hold that the anointing of the sick has the power to bless both the sick
person being administered to and the person performing the ordinance
on behalf of the individual who is ill. Also as in Catholicism, Latter-day
Saints have a strong belief in the power of united or "corporate prayer"
on behalf of those who are sick or afflicted. This principle is heavily
emphasized in LDS temple worship.

The major differences between Catholic and LDS approaches to
this sacrament or ordinance have to do with who performs it and
the way in which it is performed. For Catholics, a priest should perform this sacrament. Whereas in Mormonism, any worthy, ordained
Melchizedek Priesthood holder can perform the rite; he need not be a
presiding authority in a congregation. Additionally, the Catholic performance of this rite is often preceded by the sacrament of confession
(or reconciliation) and followed by the sacrament of the Eucharist (or
the Lord's Supper). Latter-day Saints, on the other hand, do not receive
a confession from those being anointed and blessed neither do they
traditionally offer the Holy Communion (i.e., the Lord's Supper) after
they have been blessed.

Finally, in Mormonism the person being anointed and blessed has
consecrated olive oil placed only upon the crown of their head. In Ca-

---

47   O'Gorman and Faulkner, *Complete Idiot's Guide to Understanding Catholicism*, 160.
      See also *United States Catholic Catechism for Adults*, 256

tholicism, the oil is placed upon the forehead and the hands of the person being anointed, usually being rubbed on in the shape of a cross.

In the end, Catholics and Latter-day Saints see the purpose of this sacrament or ordinance as being the same—a potential restoration of health and an offering of peace, comfort, strength, and direction to the person experiencing a trial. Both faiths accept James' declaration that the individual being blessed can, through this rite, receive a remission of his or her sins (James 5:14–15).

MARRIAGE

CATHOLICS

Since the thirteenth century, the Catholic Church has held marriage to be a sacrament. Off and on for several centuries, celibacy was seen as a higher way of living one's faith—a demonstration of greater spiritual piety.[48] However, in recent years there has been a shift in thinking regarding marriage and celibacy. While Catholics do not see marriage as a sacrament necessary for salvation, they also do not see celibacy as a practice that earns one a higher heavenly reward. One must simply choose a vocation in life. That vocation may include a marital partner, or it may be practied as a single individual.

Because the consent of both of those being married is required for a marriage to be valid, "The Catholic Church teaches that the spouses, *not the witnessing priest or deacon*, are the ministers of the sacrament" of marriage.[49] Certainly a Catholic priest is involved in the rite, but the individuals entering into the covenant effect the covenant. The priest is but a witness of what they accomplish between themselves.

In Catholic thought, the dual purpose of marriage is (1) to attend to the well-being of one's spouse and (2) to procreate and rear

---

48   The Council of Trent (AD 1545–1563), for example, held that celibacy was "superior" to marriage as a way of life. See James K. Voiss, "Celibacy, Clerical," in *Harper Collins Encyclopedia of Catholicism*, 291.

49   See Michael G. Lawler, "Marriage," in *Harper Collins Encyclopedia of Catholicism*, 821; emphasis added.

children.[50] While it is not heavily stressed in Catholicism today,[51] the Church officially holds that marriages are for the duration of the mortal life of both partners.[52] Thus, if one of the two spouses dies, the marriage would remain intact until the other also passes.[53]

Additionally, Catholics hold that there are two types of marriages, civil and sacramental. The *Encyclopedia of Catholicism* states, "A sacramental marriage is . . . more than the civil marriage of a man and woman; it is more than human covenant. It is also a religious marriage and covenant. God and God's Christ are present in it, theologically third partners in it, from its beginning."[54] Thus, for Catholics, while a civil marriage can be dissolved, a sacramental marriage that has been consummated is "absolutely indissoluble." Only sacramental marriages "are held to be for the whole of life."[55]

---

50   The Vatican II document known as "The Pastoral Constitution of the Church in the Modern World" indicates that, while creating human life is part of the "proper mission" of married couples, nonetheless, marriage is not "solely for procreation" or giving birth to children. See *Gaudium et Spes* [or "The Pastoral Constitution of the Church in the Modern World"], part 2, chapter 1, section 50, as found in Austin Flannery, ed., *Vatican Council II: The Conciliar and Post Conciliar Documents*, new rev. ed. (New York: Costello Publishing, 1992), 953–54.

51   By this I mean that while the Catholic Church still holds that a sacramental marriage (i.e., one performed by the Church) *cannot* be dissolved (see Matthew 19:6), the once common practice of excommunicating those who divorced and then remarried (without Church approval) has been abolished. In addition, annulments (instead of divorce) have become more common in Catholicism, and one Catholic scholar noted that "virtually all diocese in the United States expend considerable resources for this ministry" (i.e., performing annulments). Pope John Paul II emphasized the need for the Church to offer pastoral services and compassionate understanding to those who have experienced a divorce and the related suffering and trauma. See John Lahey and Edward Scharfenberger, "Divorce," in *Harper Collins Encyclopedia of Catholicism*, 423.

52   See Lawler, "Marriage," in *Harper Collins Encyclopedia of Catholicism*, 825.

53   Many Catholics today see marriage as being until "death do you part." Some "old school" Catholics hold that the death of a spouse leaves the marriage intact until the remaining spouse passes away, but many maintain that once a husband or wife dies, the surviving spouse is single again, as though he or she had never been married.

54   Lawler, "Marriage," in *Harper Collins Encyclopedia of Catholicism*, 825.

55   Lawler, "Marriage," in *Harper Collins Encyclopedia of Catholicism*, 826. See also Kreeft, *Catholic Christianity*, 355–56. One Catholic reader suggested that Roman Catholics who choose to have a civil marriage rather than a sacramental one are really living in sin because they are not married in the eyes of God. In many parishes, Catholics who have chosen to marry outside of the Church are not allowed to partake of the sacrament of the Lord's Supper, or Holy Communion. Again, this is not a universal belief in Catholicism, but it is a belief that is certainly held by some Catholics.

LATTER-DAY SAINTS

Like Catholics, Mormons also see marriage as a sacrament.[56] We too see it as having a dual purpose: the unifying of the husband and wife and the rearing of a righteous posterity. And, like Catholics, Latter-day Saints see a distinction between a civil marriage and one performed by God's authority.

Having said that, marriage is one of the subjects on which Catholics and Latter-day Saints greatly differ. While we would agree that celibacy is not a higher way to live God's laws, we would disagree that marriage is equivalent to celibacy in God's eyes. In other words, in the teachings of the restored gospel it is held that marriage is both the higher way to live and a requisite for salvation in the highest degree of the celestial kingdom (D&C 131:1–4).[57] Thus, from a Latter-day Saint perspective, a higher reward is available to those who seek to marry in God's holy temple.

The Latter-day Saints also differ with Catholics on who the "minister" of the sacrament of marriage is. Because, for Mormons, so much stress is placed on sealing keys and authority, the temple marriage, or "sealing," must be performed by one holding those same sealing keys given to Peter by Christ,[58] and later restored to Joseph Smith by Peter, James, and John.[59] In LDS thinking, the couple being sealed is not

---

56   Elder Jeffrey R. Holland noted that, for Latter-day Saints, "human intimacy is a sacrament." See *Morality* (Salt Lake City: Bookcraft, 1992), 162. This text is a compilation of the teachings of various General Authorities on the subject of morality.

57   Catholics rely upon Jesus' words in the gospels (see Mark 10:11–12; Matthew 5:32; and Luke 16:18) for their position that divorce is, in most cases, wrong. On this subject Latter-day Saints would agree. The Catholic understanding of the mortal or temporary nature of marriage could also be drawn from New Testament passages. See, for example, Matthew 22:30, which reads, "For in the resurrection they neither marry, nor are given in marriage, but are as the angels of God in heaven." See also Mark 12:25 and Luke 20:35. The Doctrine and Covenants clarifies the Latter-day Saint position on passages such as these. See, for example, D&C 132:15–17. See also Bruce R. McConkie, *Doctrinal New Testament Commentary*, 3 vols. (Salt Lake City: Bookcraft, 1987–88), 1:604–8; and D. Kelley Ogden and Andrew C. Skinner, *Verse by Verse: The Four Gospels* (Salt Lake City: Deseret Book, 2006), 486–88.

58   "And I will give unto thee [Peter] the keys of the kingdom of heaven: and whatsoever thou shalt bind on earth shall be bound in heaven: and whatsoever thou shalt loose on earth shall be loosed in heaven" (Matthew 16:19).

59   "And also with Peter, and James, and John, whom I have sent unto you, by whom I have ordained you and confirmed you to be apostles, and especial witnesses of my name, and bear the keys of your ministry and of the same things which I revealed unto

performing the sacrament of marriage. Rather, it is being performed on their behalf by one holding the restored sealing keys.

Both Catholics and Mormons see a dramatic difference between a civil and sacramental marriage—including the permanence of the latter—but unlike Catholics (who see marriage as "until death do us part"), Latter-day Saints believe that marriage is "for time and all eternity." Only transgression can break such a bond. Otherwise, once sealed, a companionship will last forever.

HOLY ORDERS

CATHOLICS

The sacrament of "holy orders" would be akin to the LDS principle of priesthood ordination. In Catholic thinking, this sacrament is not held to be requisite for salvation, although its role within the Church is, nonetheless, very important.

Catholics acknowledge many different New Testament priesthood offices, including apostle, prophet, teacher, bishop, etc. The absence of some New Testament offices and the presence of some non-biblical priesthood offices is explained in the following comment by one eminent Catholic ecclesiologist: "In practice and in understanding, Holy Orders has undergone profound changes from its origins in the [New Testament] period to the developments of the Second Vatican Council."[60] In other words, as the Church has developed and changed, so has the structure and understanding of the priesthood.

---

them" (D&C 27:12). "The voice of Peter, James, and John in the wilderness between Harmony, Susquehanna county, and Colesville, Broome county, on the Susquehanna river, declaring themselves as possessing the keys of the kingdom, and of the dispensation of the fulness of times!" (D&C 128:20). "The messenger who visited us on this occasion and conferred this Priesthood upon us, said that his name was John, the same that is called John the Baptist in the New Testament, and that he acted under the direction of Peter, James and John, who held the keys of the Priesthood of Melchizedek, which Priesthood, he said, would in due time be conferred on us, and that I should be called the first Elder of the Church, and he (Oliver Cowdery) the second. It was on the fifteenth day of May, 1829, that we were ordained under the hand of this messenger, and baptized" (JS—H 1:72).

60   Frederick J. Cwiekowski, "Holy Orders," in *Harper Collins Encyclopedia of Catholicism*, 620.

Just as the number, type, and nature of priesthood offices have developed since the close of the New Testament, so too have the qualifications for being ordained changed. In Catholicism those wishing to receive the priesthood must attend a seminary for four to six years. There they receive the equivalent of a graduate degree in theology or a related field.[61]

There have been other changes in the concept of priesthood over the nearly two millennia since the Catholic Church began. For example, since the 1960s, some responsibilities that were formerly reserved for priests and their superiors have been opened to performance by the laity. Today, Catholicism, like much of Protestantism, believes in a priesthood of all believers. From a Catholic perspective, all of the baptized faithful are called by God to be a "priestly people." While there is a difference between the laity's priesthood and that of those who have entered into "holy orders," that distinction has not been fully defined by the Catholic Church. The laity can now do things that prior to the 1960s only someone formally ordained could do, such as distribute the sacrament of the Eucharist. For Catholics, the sacrament of holy orders sets certain men apart as symbolic representations of Christ—who is the ultimate priesthood authority in the Church.[62]

LATTER-DAY SAINTS

While Latter-day Saints do not use the term "holy orders," the concept of priesthood ordination exists within Mormonism. As in Catholicism, we have a very structured priesthood with numerous offices and various responsibilities.

We too acknowledge that a number of post-biblical roles or offices have been developed to meet the needs of an expanding and changing Church. For example, the Bible does not mention regional representatives or area authorities—the latter of which we currently have, and the former of which we once had but no longer do. Similarly, the terms "general authority" or "area presidency" do not appear in the Bible, but

---

61   It was the Council of Trent (AD 1545–1563) that decreed the creation of the first seminaries, and it was the 1917 Code of Canon Law that first made seminary training a prerequisite for priesthood ordination. See Joseph M. White, "Seminary," in *Harper Collins Encyclopedia of Catholicism*, 1181–82.

62   Cwiekowski, "Holy Orders," in *Harper Collins Encyclopedia of Catholicism*, 625.

they are certainly a part of the modern LDS Church. Like Catholics, Mormons see priesthood holders as earthly representations of and representatives of the Lord Jesus Christ. It is His authority we profess to hold, and His power we seek to exercise.

There are some differences between LDS and Catholic views of priesthood ordination. While Latter-day Saints see the laity as heavily involved in many aspects of the kingdom, we reject the notion of a priesthood of all believers. For us, the priesthood holder is decidedly different from the non-priesthood holder, and from an LDS perspective, there are no ordinances that the unordained can perform.[63]

Additionally, Mormons hold that formal education and priesthood ordination are unrelated. Men certainly receive priesthood training in their various quorums, but the equivalent of a college education is not a prerequisite for ordination. An LDS Melchizedek Priesthood holder can be a high school dropout or a PhD. Personal righteousness and faith in Jesus Christ are the primary factors that determine who is ordained and who is not.[64]

SUMMARY OF THE SACRAMENTS

While we have slightly different notions about each of the sacraments we have been discussing, it should be clear to the reader that Mormons, like Catholics, would consider each of these seven rites as sacramental. As Elder Jeffery R. Holland stated, "A sacrament could be any one of a number of gestures or acts or ordinances that unite us with God and his limitless powers. . . . Those special moments of union with God are sacramental moments . . . when we formally take the

---

63   Latter-day Saint sisters do not hold priesthood or "share" in the priesthood with their husbands. However, those who have received their temple endowment can be "set apart" as temple workers, whereby they have "authority" given them to perform, within the walls of the temple, ordinance work. It should be stressed that those who do so have received, through the laying on of hands, the "authority" to act in such a capacity, and thus are to be distinguished from other sisters who, as lay members, attend the temple.

64   This is in no way to suggest that those who are ordained in the Catholic Church are somehow not personally righteous or believing. On the contrary, the commitment required to be ordained in Catholicism establishes that those who seek out this vocation are exactly that! However, in Mormonism there is no academic training required to qualify one for ordination. In Catholicism, academic training is paramount.

hand of God and feel his divine power."[65] In Mormonism, each of the aforementioned seven rites are designed to suppress the natural man within us and to bring out the divine within us. Like Catholics, we certainly feel the power of a God-given ordinance to spiritually unite us with our God.

---

65   Holland, "Of Souls, Symbols, and Sacraments," as cited in *On Earth As It Is in Heaven*, 193.

THE SALE OF INDULGENCES

So often, when Mormons and Protestants hear the word "indulgences," the thought that comes to mind is of one of corruption or the purchasing of the right to sin. In reality, this is a complete misunderstanding of the doctrine of the Catholic Church. The world "indulgence" comes from Latin and means "tenderness" or "kindness."[1] While that might seem strange to the average Latter-day Saint, specifically because of our standard interpretation of indulgences, when one understands the actual doctrine, "kindness" is exactly what comes to mind. Indeed, one commentary on the catechism of the Catholic Church states, "The scandalous *sale* of indulgences for money was the abuse that sparked the Protestant Reformation. But the theology behind the Church's practice of *granting* indulgences is beautiful and profound."[2]

CATHOLICS

An indulgence is *not* the absolution from sin or the forgiveness of sins.[3] Christ is the only being that can actually remit or forgive one's

---

1   David Kennedy, "Forgiveness," in *Encyclopedia of Christianity*, ed. John Bowden (New York: Oxford University Press, 2005), 476.

2   Peter J. Kreeft, *Catholic Christianity: A Complete Catechism of Catholic Beliefs based on the Catechism of the Catholic Church* (San Francisco, Calif.: Ignatius Press, 2001), 346.

3   Kennedy, "Forgiveness," in *Encyclopedia of Christianity*, 476; Kenan B. Osborne, "Indulgences," in *Harper Collins Encyclopedia of Catholicism,* ed. Richard P. McBrien (San Francisco, Calif.: HarperSanFrancisco, 1995),Calif.: HarperSanFrancisco 662; and Kreeft, *Catholic Christianity*, 346.

sins. Catholicism is quite firm on this point. Indulgences have to do with the consequences or penalties for our sins and not with the actual forgiveness of the sinful acts. The *United States Catholic Catechism for Adults* explains indulgences in this way:

> Every sin has consequences. . . . The necessity of heal-
> ing these consequences, once the sin itself has been forgiven,
> is called temporal punishment. Prayer, fasting, almsgiving,
> and other works of charity can take away entirely or dimin-
> ish this temporal punishment. . . . "Through indulgences the
> faithful can obtain the remission of temporal punishment
> resulting from sin, for themselves and also for the souls in
> Purgatory."[4]

In other words, if I have sinned, indulgences are acts or actions that have the power to remove punishment for the sins I've committed—but only after I have confessed those sins and obtained God's forgiveness (which, in some cases, may only come after talking to a priest).[5] So, according to Catholic thinking, if I commit a sin and then seek to repent of that sin through confession and repentance, I may still have an obligation to perform certain acts of penance traditionally assigned by my priest during my confession. For example, as part of the repentance process the priest will certainly require that I say a specified number of prayers, but then he may also instruct me to perform some kind of charitable service as a means of completing my repentance, as a form of restitution, so to speak.[6]

There are both partial indulgences and plenary indulgences, the latter of which remit *all* post-confession requirements for penance.[7] Pope Urban II granted the first plenary indulgences on the occasion of the first crusade (AD 1095).[8] He told those who were willing to assist in

---

4   *United States Catholic Catechism for Adults* (Washington, D.C.: United States Confer-
    ence of Catholic Bishops, 2006), 244–45.
5   Kennedy, "Forgiveness," in *Encyclopedia of Christianity*, 476. See also Diana Webb,
    "Pilgrimage," in *Encyclopedia of Christianity*, 942.
6   For the deceased, indulgences have the power to shorten the length of time they have
    to spend in purgatory after this life because of the sins they committed in mortality.
    See John Bowden, "Life After Death," in *Encyclopedia of Christianity*, 708; and Mickey
    L. Mattox, "Reformation," in *Encyclopedia of Christianity*, 1010.
7   Kennedy, "Forgiveness," in *Encyclopedia of Christianity*, 476.
8   Kennedy, "Forgiveness," in *Encyclopedia of Christianity*, 476.

**THE INTERIOR OF ST. PETER'S BASILICA,
SHOWING THE ALTAR AND DOMED CEILING.**

the crusade that they could do so "in lieu of all penance" they had been assigned for sins they had committed.[9]

Historically speaking, it is true that the sale of indulgences brought in significant revenue for the Church and that the money raised through indulgences financed the building of many of Europe's great cathedrals, including paying for the rebuilding of St. Peter's Basilica in Rome.[10] And while it is also true that during medieval times some senior clergy abused the principle, the Council of Trent (AD 1545–1563) put an end to such abuses.[11] The *Encyclopedia of Catholicism* notes the following as to how the sale of indulgences developed:

> When tariff penance began to establish itself in the Western Church from the ninth century onward, various penances that a person would find difficult to fulfill were commuted, e.g., into a specified number of prayers or a specified amount of alms. This gave rise to a mathematizing of Penance: e.g., a set number of fast days equaled a pilgrimage to Jerusalem. With the beginning of the Crusades . . . . indulgences became . . . monetary. Christians, unable to partake in the Crusades personally, could share in the merits of the Crusades by almsgiving."[12]

Like the Council of Trent, Vatican II also sought to reform both the theology behind indulgences and the practice, all in an attempt to avoid any "commercial overtones." Pope Paul VI made the use of indulgences—or the lack thereof—entirely voluntary.[13] Today traditional acts of penance rather than monetary contributions are the norm.

LATTER-DAY SAINTS

While all of this may seem rather strange to practicing Mormons, there are a number of parallels to indulgences in LDS thinking and practice.

---

9   Kennedy, "Forgiveness," in *Encyclopedia of Christianity*, 476.
10   Kennedy, "Forgiveness," in *Encyclopedia of Christianity*, 476.
11   Kennedy, "Forgiveness," in *Encyclopedia of Christianity*, 476.
12   Osborne, "Indulgences," in *Encyclopedia of Christianity*, 662–63. See also Paul Ballard, "Death," in *Encyclopedia of Christianity*, 329.
13   See Osborne, "Indulgences," in *Encyclopedia of Christianity*, 663.

First of all, no matter how popular the claim, at no point in history was it the *official* policy of the Catholic Church that one could purchase "free sins," per se, via an indulgence. This is an utter misrepresentation of the principle and its practice.

Second, the idea of a priesthood leader assigning penance as part of the repentance process after a sin has been confessed to one's bishop is commonplace in Mormonism. Like Catholics, Latter-day Saints hold that many serious sins have consequences that must be addressed after confession has taken place. An LDS bishop gives various requirements to a person working through the repentance process both in an effort to change the heart and life of the sinner and (occasionally) as an act of restitution. Thus, as in Catholicism, in Mormonism there can be post-confession works necessary in order to fully complete the repentance process or as a natural consequence of our sins.

Finally, the idea that the works of the living can somehow shorten the stay of the dead in purgatory should also sound familiar to Latter-day Saints. Our entire doctrine of work for the dead suggests that those in the spirit world who have accepted the fullness of the gospel anxiously await acts performed on earth by the living as a means of releasing them from spirit prison. Thus, like Catholics, Mormons hold that indulgences—or acts of "kindness" and "tenderness"—can be performed on behalf of the deceased in an effort to limit their stay in spirit prison.

SUMMARY

Mormons and Catholics both see the consequences of our sins as extending beyond the sins themselves. All sin has fallout. Often, even after we have confessed to our priesthood leader, there remains a need for further work in order to place ourselves fully within the good graces of our God. In Catholicism, those acts may consist of saying certain prayers or performing some alms. In Mormonism, on the other hand, it is more likely that we will be asked to do things, such as regularly attending our meetings or pay a full tithe, but the principle and the outcome are the same—namely, a sanctifying influence upon the one seeking forgiveness.

The two areas in which we differ (as it relates to this subject) are in how indulgences relate to the dead and in how they were purchased historically as a replacement for some other previously assigned form of penance.

From an LDS perspective, we do temple work on behalf of the deceased to enable them to leave spirit prison so that eventually they may inherit the celestial kingdom. Traditionally, there is no sense in Mormonism that our works in the temple on behalf of our deceased ancestors functions as a completion of the repentance process for them. In reality, however, it probably accomplishes exactly that. For just as the natural result of a Mormon accepting Christ is for that person to repent, enter into, and keep all of the covenants of the restored gospel—including the ordinances of the holy temple—so also are those in the spirit world being taught the gospel, in the process of repenting, and anxiously awaiting our performance of temple ordinances so that they may vicariously enter into those covenants requisite for their exaltation.

As it relates to the practice of indulgences as a replacement for other previously assigned forms of penance or personal spiritual realignment, Mormonism has no such concept. Unlike medieval Catholicism, Mormonism does not have a history of substituting one act of repentance (or penance) for another. This serves as the real distinction between Latter-day Saints and Roman Catholics on this matter.

POPES AND PROPHETS

One of the earmarks that sets Latter-day Saints and Catholics apart from the vast majority of other Christians is the fact that we both have a very structured hierarchy that includes a singular presiding figure. No other Christian denomination is quite as hierarchical as these two faiths. While the Church of England and the Eastern Orthodox Church each have a singular head (i.e., the Archbishop of Canterbury and the Ecumenical Patriarch), the universal power traditionally seen as resident in the pope or the LDS prophet sets them apart from the leaders of most other Christian denominations. How are these two leaders similar in their authority and responsibilities and how do they differ?

PRIMACY AND INFALLIBILITY

CATHOLICS

In Roman Catholicism, the pope (meaning "father" or "papa")[1] is perceived as the successor to the Apostle Peter, to whom Christ gave the "keys of the kingdom" (Matthew 16:18–19). He exercises "papal

---

1   Other titles for the pope include "Vicar of Jesus Christ," "Successor of the Chief of the Apostles," "Vicar of Peter," "Supreme Pontiff of the Universal Church," "Patriarch of the West," "Primate of Italy," "Archbishop and Metropolitan of the Roman Province," "Sovereign of the Vatican City State," "Servant of the Servants of God," etc. It should be noted that the title "pope" was not reserved for the bishop of Rome until AD 1073. Prior to that time all Roman Catholic bishops were referred to as "pope." See Richard P. McBrien, *Lives of the Popes* (San Francisco, Calif.: HarperSanFrancisco, 1997), 17.

primacy," which means that he is unique among all other bishops, but he is not "over" them.[2] He is the head of the college of bishops and is seen as "first among equals," in that he is seen as equal to the other bishops but not the same as them. Thus, when the bishop of Rome speaks, he always speaks as a representative of the college of bishops and never as a "private leader."[3] His position in relation to the other bishops in the college is comparable to an LDS high priest group leader; he has no additional authority or keys but is called to lead, preside, and ensure the orthodoxy of his group. Hence, his calling is "to be the guardian of the supreme confession of the apostolic faith."[4]

According to current Catholic teaching, the early Christian Church was not monoepiscopal, meaning it was not run by a solitary man or bishop.[5] Even though Rome had primacy early on, its initial role was one of advisor, counselor, or "court of last resort." Other bishops would appeal to Rome and its bishop for help with disputes or conflicts they could not settle themselves.[6] It wasn't until the eleventh century that the pope began to be seen as presiding over the "universal" or whole Church. One Catholic theologian wrote:

> Before the beginning of the second millennium . . . popes functioned largely in the role of mediator. . . . They did not appoint bishops. They did not govern the universal Church through the Roman Curia. They did not impose or enforce clerical celibacy. They did not write encyclicals or authorized catechisms for the whole Church. They did not retain for themselves alone the power of canonization. They did not even convene ecumenical councils. . . . The Second Vatican Council (1962–65) brought the Church's understanding of the papacy, and of papal primacy in particular, more in line once again with that of the first millennium, in contrast with that of the second millennium. The council viewed the papacy in increasingly communal and collegial terms. In other words, the pope is no longer to be conceived of as an

2   See Jean M. R. Tillard, "Primacy, Papal," in *Harper Collins Encyclopedia of Catholicism*, ed. Richard P. McBrien (San Francisco, Calif.: HarperSanFrancisco, 1995), 1052.
3   See Tillard, "Primacy, Papal," in *Harper Collins Encyclopedia of Catholicism*, 1052.
4   See Tillard, "Primacy, Papal," in *Harper Collins Encyclopedia of Catholicism*, 1052.
5   See McBrien, *Lives of the Popes*, 18.
6   See McBrien, *Lives of the Popes*, 18.

absolute monarch. . . . According to the Second Vatican Council, the pope exercises supreme authority over the whole Church, but the other bishops also share in that authority.[7]

Thus, the office or position of pope started as a small, mostly honorific position, which grew to hold almost incomprehensible power, but in recent years it has begun to return to the more honorific position it held for the first millennia of Christianity. Of course, related to the issue of papal primacy is the concept of papal infallibility.

Historically speaking, the concept of the infallibility of the pope arose in the fourteenth century, but it wasn't formally defined as dogmatic until 1870.[8] The basic principle is that a pope, when he speaks in his official capacity as pope,[9] cannot err on matters of doctrine or morality. This does not mean that he cannot sin. Nor does it mean that he is "omniscient" or "all knowing."[10] In addition, his "infallibility" only applies when (1) he is formally speaking as head of the Church, (2) he is speaking on a matter of faith or morality—not on policy or discipline—and (3) he must be intending to bind the whole Church by the things he is saying. Thus, the pope is *not* infallible, but, rather, he can speak infallibly on certain matters. Having said that, many Catholics hold that "infallibly" pronounced teachings can change, and that "individual popes [have] erred in matters of doctrine and even . . . deviate[d] from the faith."[11] Thus, one must not misunderstand the official Catholic position on the scope and nature of

---

7   See McBrien, *Lives of the Popes*, 19.

8   Even when it was declared as dogma, at least one-fifth of the bishops in attendance at the council questioned the move. Some worried about how it would strain relationships with other Christian denominations. Some felt that the theological implications of the pronouncement and the definition of what it meant to be "infallible" were not fully fleshed out. Some questioned the truthfulness of the very idea of papal infallibility. Some questioned how a pope could declare himself infallible. Should this not come from the college of bishops, and should they not be universally in agreement on the matter? The controversy continues to exist today—more than 130 years after the principle was pronounced dogmatically. See John T. Ford, "Infallibility," in *Harper Collins Encyclopedia of Catholicism*, 664.

9   Traditionally, Catholics refer to such "official" utterance as *ex cathedra* or "from the chair."

10   Ford, "Infallibility," in *Harper Collins Encyclopedia of Catholicism*, 664–65.

11   See McBrien, *Lives of the Popes*, 21–22.

papal power. Christ conferred "infallibility" upon His Church—not upon the pontiff. Thus, the pope is only exercising (or drawing upon) authority that does not belong to him.[12] Hence, he is traditionally *not* seen as incapable of having personal opinions, even opinions that might be in error. As one Catholic scholar wrote, "Only God is infallible, totally immune from error. If infallibility is to be predicated of anyone else, it can only be in a very restricted sense."[13]

LATTER-DAY SAINTS

Latter-day Saints do not attribute "infallibility" to the President of the Church, at least not in the sense that when he speaks he is incapable of expressing personal opinions. However, like Catholics, we do believe that the President of the Church has the ability to be guided by God beyond his natural ability and that God will "protect" the Church from being lead down false paths that would harm the salvation of its members, particularly doctrinal and moral paths. In the *Doctrine and Covenants* we read, "The Lord will never permit me [Wilford Woodruff] or any other man who stands as President of this Church to lead you astray. It is not in the programme [sic]. It is not in the mind of God. If I were to attempt that, the Lord would remove me out of my place, and so He will any other man who attempts to lead the children of men astray from the oracles of God and from their duty."[14] Thus, in a sense, we would have to say that on certain matters the Lord has assured His Church that He will keep them "infallibly" on the right path. Some Latter-day Saints argue that the President of the Church must (or will) say "thus saith the Lord" when he is speaking as a prophet rather than as a man—when he is speaking "infallibly." President Wilford Woodruff once noted:

---

12   On a related note, the pope is not alone in his ability to exercise the "infallibility" of the Church. The college of bishops, whether assembled in a council or scattered throughout the world, can also speak infallibly if they speak on a matter of doctrine or morality and with a corporate voice. See Ford, "Infallibility," in *Harper Collins Encyclopedia of Catholicism*, 664.

13   Ford, "Infallibility," in *Harper Collins Encyclopedia of Catholicism*, 664.

14   Wilford Woodruff, *61ˢᵗ Semi-Annual Conference of The Church of Jesus Christ of Latter-day Saints* (Salt Lake City: The Church of Jesus Christ of Latter-day Saints, 1890), also found in the Doctrine and Covenants, "Excerpts from Three Addresses by President Wilford Woodruff Regarding the Manifesto," 292.

Some had thought that revelation had ceased, but this is not the case. The Lord is with us and gives us revelation. But I will say for myself that I wish to avoid saying thus saith the Lord as far as I can when I give the will of the Lord to the people. In the days of Joseph Smith it was thus saith the Lord almost daily until the revelations now embodied in the Book of Doctrine and Covenants had been given. Since that day President Brigham Young, John Taylor, and myself have seldom used the words (thus saith the Lord) when giving the word of the Lord to the people.[15]

The LDS and Catholic positions on this matter are not sizably different. In both cases it is acknowledged that neither pope nor prophet claims to speak for God every time he talks. Both faiths would acknowledge that prophets and popes have opinions, and both churches would argue that, on matters germane to salvation, God keeps His mouthpiece "infallibly" accurate.

APOSTOLIC SUCCESSION

CATHOLICS

Catholics believe in the principle of apostolic succession, meaning they hold that there is an unbroken line of authority that can be traced from Peter to the current Church. It must be remembered, however, that contemporary Catholicism does *not* claim that there is an unbroken line of *popes*, from Peter to the current pontiff.[16] In official Catholic thought, it is the bishops that succeeded Peter not the popes.[17]

---

15   Wilford Woodruff, *Wilford Woodruff's Journal, 1833–1898, Typescript*, ed. Scott G. Kenney, 9 vols. (Midvale, Utah: Signature Books, 1983–84), 9:168.

16   One Catholic ecclesiologist wrote, "The leaders whose names are found in later lists of successors to Peter at Rome were probably the prominent presbyter-bishops of the city, some of whom may have exercised leadership concurrently. These lists come from a later period in which authors simply assumed that the structures of their day were also in place in the earlier hundred years of Roman Christianity." Frederick J. Cwiekowski, *The Beginnings of the Church* (New York: Paulist Press, 1988), 185.

17   Rome was not led by a single bishop until circa AD 140–150. Prior to that time it was led by a collective leadership of bishops. Thus, Peter's successor could not be a pope seated in Rome. No such person (or office) existed at that time, and Catholicism makes no claim that it did. See Cwiekowski, *Beginnings of the Church*, 185. See also Francis A. Sullivan, "Apostolic Succession," in *Harper Collins Encyclopedia of Catholicism*, 77–79.

Therefore, since there have been bishops since New Testament times, an unbroken line of authority exists in them, back to Peter. In this sense, Catholics proclaim they have apostolic authority.

Wild claims are *often* made to disprove apostolic succession in the Catholic Church. For example, one regularly finds reference to a supposed woman pope named "Pope Joan," who gave birth to a child during a procession. There is also occasional reference to the ordination of a donkey as pope. While entertaining, these myths have no factual basis. More to the point, the Catholic Church of today is very open about the gaps in the succession of popes and the presence of some forty-two "antipopes" who have claimed a right to preside over the Church.[18] However, the existence of these antipopes is not seen as problematic because, as noted above, the Catholic Church's official position is that it was the bishops, not the popes, that succeeded Peter. So, although some might be uncomfortable with the human side of Catholic history, it does not affect or change their basic claim as to how they have apostolic succession.

LATTER-DAY SAINTS

Latter-day Saints hold strongly to a doctrine of apostolic succession, but, like Catholics, we do not claim an unbroken line from Peter to the current President of the Church. Instead, we hold that Christ sent the Prophet Joseph angelic ministrants who held the priesthood keys that were lost when the last New Testament apostle died.

- Moroni brought the "keys of the record of the stick of Ephraim" (or Book of Mormon).
- John the Baptist restored the Aaronic Priesthood, including the "keys of the ministry of angels."
- Elijah conferred upon Joseph the "keys to turn hearts of fathers to children and children to their fathers."

---

18   An "antipope" is an individual whose claim of authority is rejected by the Church as invalid. Often antipopes would reign at the same time as a legitimate pope and thereby split allegiances within the membership of the Church. In modern Catholic sources one frequently finds reference to the fact that some 180 years of Catholic history have seen an antipope claiming rights to "Peter's throne." Indeed, the antipope Benedict XIII laid claim to the papacy for some twenty-three years.

- Adam brought the "keys" of temple ordinances, particularly the endowment.[19]
- Peter, James, and John restored the Melchizedek Priesthood and the apostolic office.

There were many other angels who appeared and restored keys, authority, rites, etc. to the Prophet Joseph. The point is that Latter-day Saints trace their apostolic succession back from the current President of the Church to Joseph Smith and from Joseph Smith to whichever angel restored any given key. For example, from the resurrected Peter, who ordained Joseph Smith an apostle, we trace his authority directly back to Christ. Thus, it is in this sense that we claim apostolic succession.

Thus, Latter-day Saints and Catholics both see the importance of priesthood authority, particularly that of presiding or "apostolic" authority, and while Mormons speak of "keys," and Catholics do not, both faiths acknowledge that the New Testament apostles held something— some power or authorization from Christ —which the average member of the Church did not. That unique authority that Peter and his colleagues in the Twelve held is what both Latter-day Saints and Catholics claim to have. Thus, the major way

PETER—BELIEVED BY LAY CATHOLICS TO HAVE BEEN THE FIRST POPE—HOLDS THE "KEY OF THE KINGDOM OF HEAVEN" (MATTHEW 16:19).

19   Joseph indicated that, whenever "the Keys" have been brought from heaven "they are revealed . . . by Adam's authority." Andrew F. Ehat and Lyndon W. Cook, *The Words of Joseph Smith: The Contemporary Accounts of the Nauvoo Discourses of the Prophet Joseph Smith*, Religious Studies Monograph Series, no. 6 (Provo, Utah: Religious Studies Center, Brigham Young University, 1980), 8. Indeed, one LDS scholar wrote, "According to Joseph Smith, if Adam did not personally reveal the ordinances, he would send messengers who would teach his posterity the endowment counsels that would lead them in the way of life and salvation." Andrew F. Ehat, "Joseph Smith's Introduction of Temple Ordinances and the 1844 Mormon Succession Question" (master's thesis, Brigham Young University, 1981), 256 n. 86.

in which we differ on this matter has to do with how that apostolic authority was passed down from Peter to the current head of our respective faiths.

REVELATION

CATHOLICS

In November of 1964, the Catholic Church declared that the pope, in concert with the college of bishops, seeks to define doctrine through a process of seriously and zealously examining scripture and the tradition of the Church, through which they then formulate what they find into a doctrinal pronouncement. However, the Church added, "they do not admit any new public revelation as pertaining to the divine deposit of the faith."[20]

While Catholicism certainly believes in "modern-day revelation," more often than not that revelation is defined by contemporary Catholics as "God's self-communication" or "divine self-disclosure" to man. In other words, revelation consists of God inviting human beings to have a relationship with Him. He does this, of course, primarily through His Holy Spirit. One Catholic theologian wrote, "The event of divine revelation is repeated every time God invites a human being into an interpersonal dialogue of friendship. This endlessly repeated event of divine self-disclosure remains dependent on the revelation completed through Christ (and his apostles) and adds nothing essential to its content."[21] Thus, while personal revelation is held to be almost commonplace among those who seek a relationship with God, Catholicism generally holds that the Bible consists of a "once-and-for-all" revelation that "completes" God's revealed word to the whole Church.[22]

---

20   *Lumen Gentium* [or "Dogmatic Constitution on the Church"], chapter 3, section 25, in Austin Flannery, ed., *Vatican Council II: The Conciliar and Post Conciliar Documents*, new rev. ed. (New York: Costello Publishing, 1992), 381.

21   Gerald O'Collins, "Revelation," in *Harper Collins Encyclopedia of Catholicism,* ed. Richard P. McBrien (San Francisco, Calif.: HarperSanFrancisco, 1995), 1113.

22   See O'Collins, "Revelation," in *Harper Collins Encyclopedia of Catholicism*, 1112.

LATTER-DAY SAINTS

Like Catholics, Latter-day Saints believe in "modern-day revelation." For us that is two-fold. We accept the idea that God seeks to "disclose" Himself to each of His children by sending them opportunities for spiritual experiences. Through these experiences the seeds of testimony are planted and begin to grow within the hearts and minds of the faithful.

Mormons also hold, however, that God speaks in post-biblical times to living apostles and prophets. These revelations constitute communications of biblical proportion and nature and are directed at the entire Church, rather than just to a singular person. From a Latter-day Saint perspective, the canon cannot be closed. God continues to speak, in the biblical sense of the word, to modern-day prophets and apostles and will do so until the end of time.

Catholics and Mormons are very similar in their approach to personal revelation. Both faiths believe in its existence and in God's earnest desire to speak to His children. We differ most on our understanding of the degree to which the Holy Bible constitutes God's final universal word to mankind. From a Catholic perspective, the Bible was the end of that type of revelation. From a Latter-day Saint perspective, it was but one example of that type of revelation.

HIERARCHY STRUCTURE

Over the two millennia that the Catholic Church has existed, its hierarchy (or leadership) has developed into a rather complex and ordered system of officers and offices. One might make a similar claim about the Latter-day Saint hierarchical priesthood structure, although ours had done all of its developing in two hundred years rather than two thousand. What Catholics often refer to as the "magisterium" of the Church, Mormons simply refer to as the "Church leadership." The following chart, although overly simplistic, shows basic comparisons between the various major leadership positions in the Catholic and LDS faiths.

ROMAN CATHOLIC	LATTER-DAY SAINT
Pope or Bishop of Rome	Prophet or First Presidency
College of Cardinals	Quorum of the Twelve Apostles
Archbishop	Quorums of the Seventy
Bishop	Stake President
Priest	Bishop
Laity	Laity

While our structure is similar, the day-to-day responsibilities of the various officers in the Catholic Church, when compared to their LDS counterparts, are significantly different.

As part of his responsibilities, the pope celebrates the Mass with some frequency; whereas the prophet traditionally does not bless the sacrament. The pope is the head of both the Church and also the Vatican City State, which is its own sovereign nation.[23] The prophet, on the other hand, presides over only the Church, not any political entity. In his capacity as the head of a nation, the pope regularly meets with dignitaries from the more than 100 nations that have diplomatic relations with the Holy See. The prophet, although occasionally entertaining dignitaries from various states and nations, has no diplomatic ties with any nation. The pope, who presides over more than a billion people, necessarily delegates the running of the Church to many committees, individuals, and entities. The Prophet, on the other hand, is significantly involved in the day-to-day decisions and operations of the much smaller Mormon church and, in most cases, is directly involved in the decisions that determine all general Church policies, all major financial expenditures, the content of general Church curriculum, etc. Suffice it to say, there is much that would be different in a typical day of a Catholic pope and an LDS prophet.

---

23   The Vatican City State is the smallest sovereign state in the world. It comprises just under 109 acres and houses approximately 1,000 residents—although some 4,000 people work in the state. It was established in 1929, and the pope is its head.

SCRIPTURE

While we've already alluded to this to some degree in the previous section, a more extensive treatment of the topic of holy scripture is appropriate, particularly in light of the fact that Latter-day Saints and Catholics each have a somewhat unique perception of scripture when compared to the protestant world.

CATHOLICS

The Catholic Church believes in the Holy Bible as the inspired word of God. Included in that would be the Old and New Testaments and the Apocrypha.[1] Catholics hold the Bible to be of both divine and

---

1   The Catholic Apocrypha consists of fifteen Old Testament books that are not found in the Hebrew Bible but were included in Jerome's Latin Vulgate Bible. They are 1st and 2nd Esdras, Tobit, Judith, Additions to the Book of Esther, Wisdom of Solomon, Sirach or Ecclesiasticus, Baruch, Letter of Jeremiah, Song of the Three Young Men and Prayer of Azariah, Susanna, Bel and the Dragon, Prayer of Manasseh, and 1st and 2nd Maccabees. In 1546 the Council of Trent declared these books canonical, with the exception of 1st and 2nd Esdras and the Prayer of Manasseh. This remains the position of the Catholic Church today. See John J. Collins, "Apocrypha," in *Harper Collins Encyclopedia of Catholicism,* ed. Richard P. McBrien (San Francisco, Calif.: HarperSanFrancisco, 1995), 71. When Joseph Smith was working on his inspired version of the Holy Bible, he inquired of the Lord as to whether he should also translate the Apocrypha. In response to the inquiry the Lord gave him the revelation we call section 91 of the Doctrine and Covenants. In it we learn the following about the Apocrypha: "There are many things contained therein that are true" (91:1), and "It is mostly translated correctly" (91:1). However, "There are many things contained therein that are not true" (91:2)—much of which are the "interpolations . . . of men" (91:2). Joseph learned that if the reader is directed by the Spirit when reading it, he or she would "obtain benefit"

human origins—God being the author but inspired humans being the recorders of that sacred text.[2] Traditionally they hold the Bible to be inerrant on matters pertinent to our salvation but not necessarily on matters of culture, archaeology, history, and the like.[3] Thus, in official Catholic teaching, the Bible likely contains some errors on non-essential things, but on salvific matters, it is without error.

Prior to Vatican II, Catholic theologians held that there were two sources for God's revelations—scripture and tradition.[4] Indeed, the sixteenth century Council of Trent declared that the gospel is "contained in written books and in unwritten traditions."[5] However, Vatican II's "Dogmatic Constitution on Divine Revelation" stepped away from Trent's "two source" approach to scripture.[6] Today Catholic theologians would be more inclined to say, "Scripture has been and remains our primary, although not exclusive, source for Catholic doctrines."[7] Nevertheless, tradition does have its place in Catholic approaches to scripture.[8] For example, the development of the New Testament came about through a process of tradition, and all scrip-

---

therefrom (91:5), but, in the end, the Lord told Joseph that "it [was] not needful that it should be translated" (91:6).

2   See Bob Moran, *A Closer Look At Catholicism* (Waco, Tex.: Word Books, 1986), 77; John R. Donahue, "Bible," in *Harper Collins Encyclopedia of Catholicism*, 166; Raymond Collins, "Bible, Church Teachings on the," in *Harper Collins Encyclopedia of Catholicism*, 167.

3   See Donahue, "Bible," in *Harper Collins Encyclopedia of Catholicism*, 165; Moran, *Closer Look At Catholicism*, 67; Collins, "Bible, Church Teachings on the," in *Harper Collins Encyclopedia of Catholicism*, 167; *Dei Verbum* [or "Dogmatic Constitution on Divine Revelation"], chapter 3, section 21, in Austin Flannery, ed., *Vatican Council II: The Conciliar and Post Conciliar Documents*, new rev. ed. (New York: Costello Publishing, 1992), 757.

4   See Moran, *Closer Look At Catholicism*, 64.

5   Moran, *Closer Look At Catholicism*, 65.

6   See Moran, *Closer Look At Catholicism*, 65; Donahue, "Bible," in *Harper Collins Encyclopedia of Catholicism*, 165; Susan K. Wood, "Tradition," in *Harper Collins Encyclopedia of Catholicism*, 1262.

7   Moran, *Closer Look At Catholicism*, 60. See also Donahue, in "Bible," in *Harper Collins Encyclopedia of Catholicism*, 165.

8   One Catholic source notes, "General usage distinguishes between Tradition (capital 'T') as the process of transmission, tradition (small 't,' singular) as the content of what is transmitted, and traditions (small 't,' plural) as the particular customs of separate Churches or movements." Wood, "Tradition," in *Harper Collins Encyclopedia of Catholicism*, 1261.

ture must be understood against a backdrop of tradition and context.[9]

9   It wasn't until the end of the second century that Christians began to take an interest in determining a uniquely Christian "canon." See Harry Y. Gamble, "Canon—New Testament,"
in *The Anchor Bible Dictionary*, ed. David Noel Freedman, 6 vols. (New York: Doubleday,
1992), 1:853. Christians initially saw themselves as Jews who had found the Messiah, so
the Jewish canon was their canon. It was also only after the prophets and apostles were
killed that Christians saw the need to write down (and preserve) what had been passed
down orally. It was specifically the influence of Marcion that forced the creation of the New
Testament canon. See Justo L. González, *The Story of Christianity*, 2 vols. (Peabody, Mass.:
Prince Press, 2001), 1:61. Marcion was "one of the most influential heretics of the second
century." Everett Ferguson, ed., *Encyclopedia of Early Christianity* (New York: Garland
Publishing, 1990), 568. He taught that the god of the Old Testament was not the "true
God," but rather a wicked god that was ignorant and contradictory. According to Marcion,
the "true God"—or Christian God—requires nothing of us. He doesn't even want us to
obey Him; He just wants our love. He held that there would be no judgment day because
God is so loving that He will forgive everyone of everything. Marcion also claimed that
Jesus was *not* born of Mary, but rather had simply appeared on the earth as a grown man,
and that the Old Testament was good for history but doctrinally corrupt. So, he created
the first New Testament canon. It contained the Gospel of Luke and ten of the epistles of
Paul—each of which had been edited to remove any quotes from the Old Testament. All of
the other gospels and New Testament books he believed were heavily corrupted by the Jewish Christians. Marcion's canon and teachings quickly gained popularity, so the Christians
felt a need to produce a canon that could combat his version of the New Testament and his
teachings that were found therein. Hence, the first authorized New Testament was born.
One New Testament canon scholar wrote,

> The canon which finally emerged contained only a fraction of the
> Christian literature that had been produced in the early period. Many
> other writings (gospels, acts, letters, and apocalypses) achieved wide
> currency and attained the status of scripture in some areas without in
> the end becoming canonical. So, for example, the *Apocalypse of Peter*
> and the *Shepherd of Hermas* were scarcely less popular than the Revela-
> tion to John in the 2nd century; the *Gospel of Thomas* and the *Gospel
> of Peter* were reckoned by some no less authoritative than any other
> gospel; the letters known as *I Clement* and *Barnabas* were esteemed
> and quoted as scripture by many; the *Acts of Paul* also was held in high
> regard in some areas. (Gamble, "Canon—New Testament," in *Anchor
> Bible Dictionary*, 1:855)

Although no ecumenical council was ever called for the sole purpose of determining
canon, several did deal with defining the scope of the Church's canon (i.e., Laodicea in
AD 363, Hippo in AD 393, and Carthage in AD 397). A couple of factors determined
which early Christian texts made it into the emerging fourth-century Christian canon.
First of all, they looked at how much support a book had from major figures within the
Church. For example, Athanasius convinced people that John's revelation should be kept.
Similarly, Hilary, Ambrose, and Jerome all fought to make the book of Hebrews canonical. Second, the popular use of a book in various congregations had significant influence
on which books received canonical status. For example, during the persecutions of the
early Christians, scriptures were often confiscated and destroyed. In order to pacify their
antagonists, Christians often had to surrender their scriptures. In so doing, some would
select what they deemed as less valuable texts and offered these up to their persecutors, all

Thus, tradition is not separate from scripture, but rather is part of the development of scripture.[10] As one Catholic theologian noted, "In the early Church an oral tradition preceded the written tradition collected in the Scriptures. In this sense tradition logically and chronologically precedes Scripture."[11] In the Vatican II "Dogmatic Constitution on Divine Revelation," we are told that the Church "has always regarded, and continues to regard the Scriptures, taken together with sacred tradition, as the supreme rule of her faith."[12] Tradition is the means by which the truths Christ has revealed to His apostles are passed on to succeeding generations.[13] That process of passing on scripture through tradition includes God's act of inspiring those who, after the close of the New Testament, have interpreted, applied, preserved, and passed on God's revealed words. From a Catholic perspective, then, one cannot ignore tradition and context and still gain an accurate understanding of what God intended for us to understand through His word.

Finally, while Catholics generally hold the Bible in its entirety to be scripture, Vatican II declared the preeminence of the four gospels, in that they are the principle witness to the life and teachings of Christ.[14]

LATTER-DAY SAINTS

"Canon" is a Greek word that literally means a "measuring stick." Thus, we call the officially recognized books of scripture "the canon" because they are the "standard" or "rule" by which we measure doctrine. The canon is what is used to distingush "sound" doctrine from heresy. Non-LDS scholars will sometimes make a distinction between "scripture" and "canon." Something can be "scriptural" and not be part

---

the while hiding the scriptural books they most loved or revered. See Gamble, "Canon—New Testament," in Anchor Bible Dictionary, 1:857. The popularity of a given book among the members of the various Christian congregations made a difference in whether it attained canonical status.

10   See Wood, "Tradition," in *Harper Collins Encyclopedia of Catholicism*, 1261; Moran, *Closer Look At Catholicism*, 78.

11   Wood, "Tradition," in *Harper Collins Encyclopedia of Catholicism*, 1261.

12   *Dei Verbum* [or "Dogmatic Constitution on Divine Revelation"], chapter 6, section 21, in *Vatican Council II: The Conciliar and Post Conciliar Documents*, 762.

13   See Wood, "Tradition," in *Harper Collins Encyclopedia of Catholicism*, 1261.

14   Collins, "Bible, Church Teachings on the," in *Harper Collins Encyclopedia of Catholicism*, 167.

of one's "canon." "Scripture" might be defined as that which is "religiously authoritative"—something outside of the "canon" that may still be used to "measure" the orthodoxy of a teaching or belief. "Canon," on the other hand, is usually used by Latter-day Saints to mean the definitive list of "scripture" that seems fairly set—the "standard works" of the Church.

- The Old Testament
- The New Testament
- The Book of Mormon
- The Doctrine and Covenants
- The Pearl of Great Price

While we acknowledge these aforementioned texts as both "scripture" and "canon," there are other "authoritative" teachings that fall outside of our canon and yet are held as important "measuring sticks" in determining sound doctrine. We have the teachings of the living prophets—the monthly First Presidency message in the *Ensign*, for example—that seem to have "scriptural," but not necessarily canonical, status within the Church. There are the general conference talks given by members of the First Presidency and Quorum of the Twelve that also fall under this umbrella. Of course, there are also these words from the Doctrine and Covenants, which imply "scripture," but not necessarily "canonicity" for any words spoken under the influence of the Holy Spirit: "And whatsoever they shall speak when moved upon by the Holy Ghost shall be scripture, shall be the will of the Lord, shall be the mind of the Lord, shall be the word of the Lord, shall be the voice of the Lord, and the power of God unto salvation" (D&C 68:4).[15] So, the question of what constitutes "canon" and "scripture" for Latter-day Saints is not as cut-and-dried as some might wish to suggest.

In general terms, Mormons traditionally hold that the four standard works of the Church are the inspired and binding word of God. We make no claims of inerrancy for *any* book of scripture. Of the Holy Bible, our position is that it is the "word of God as far as it is translated

---

15   A discussion about scripture and canonicity potentially provokes questions such as these: What about the comments of past General Authorities vs. present General Authorities? Or how about texts that once were held to be "canonical"—like the *Lectures on Faith*—but no longer enjoy that status?

correctly" (Article of Faith 8). As to the Book of Mormon, Moroni put it best when he said, "if there are faults [within the text] they are the mistakes of men"—not the fault of God.[16] Similar statements could be made regarding any of our standard works. While we do not claim inerrancy for them, we do insist on their inspired nature. Through the standard works, the Lord has spoken to His Church.

And what of "tradition"? Like Catholics, Latter-day Saints would acknowledge that it is a significant part of our means of understanding God's word and will. The teachings of each of the presidents of the Church and the discourse of modern prophets and apostles greatly influence what Mormons perceive as doctrinal. Elder Jeffery R. Holland spoke of "the formula" by which the gospel is taught in the restored church: "personal testimony, the teachings of the living prophets, and the written record of the scriptures."[17] Those three together constitute the scripture, tradition, and canon of Mormonism.

Personal testimony falls under the category of D&C 68:4 (i.e., "whatsoever they shall speak when moved upon by the Holy Ghost shall be scripture").

The teachings of living prophets and apostles constitute the "tradition" of Mormonism (i.e., "the means by which the truths Christ has revealed to His apostles are passed on to succeeding generations").

Our "canon" consists of the standard works of the Church (i.e., the Holy Bible, the Book of Mormon, the Doctrine and Covenants, and the Pearl of Great Price).

SUMMARY

In what ways are Catholics and Mormons similar in their view of scripture? We each accept the Holy Bible as the word of God. We each acknowledge the authoritative place of written, canonized scripture in the formulation and preservation of doctrine. Both faiths hold that God can and does reveal to chosen leaders what He intended the scriptures to mean and how He intended them to apply to the Church and its membership. Neither of us hold the scriptures to be inerrant, and

---

16   See the title page of the Book of Mormon.
17   See Jeffrey R. Holland, *Christ and the New Covenant: The Messianic Message of the Book of Mormon* (Salt Lake City: Deseret Book, 1997), 65–66.

both traditions hold that God, through His Holy Spirit, is the author of scripture, but that man is the one commissioned to pen what God is revealing to and through him.

In the end, the real difference between LDS and Catholic approaches to scripture has to do with the "open" or "closed" nature of the canonical books. Catholics speak of the "complete and once-and-for-all" nature of the New Testament.[18] It is the last and definitive word of God through apostles or prophets. Outside of tradition, no more is needed; no more will come. Latter-day Saints, on the other hand, feel that God continues to speak through modern prophets and apostles and that the additional revelation they receive for the Church today is crucial to the salvation of mankind. Thus, while we do not regularly add to the content of our bound standard words, we do believe that God regularly reveals His will for the Church—in biblical fashion—through living oracles, namely, the First Presidency of the Church and the Quorum of the Twelve Apostles.

---

18   See Gerald O'Collins, "Revelation," in *Harper Collins Encyclopedia of Catholicism*, 1112.

THE GREAT APOSTASY

While the word "apostasy" literally means a renunciation of one's religious faith or an abandonment of a previously held loyalty, when Mormons speak of the "Great Apostasy" they are referring to the LDS belief that first century Christianity was lost after the death of Jesus and the apostles. Roman Catholics, on the other hand, are more inclined to speak less in terms of a general, Church-wide apostasy, and more of individual apostasy and its influence over the Church. Nevertheless, both faiths acknowledge the reality that Christianity, over its approximately two millennia of existence, has experienced dramatic changes and frequent challenges from those who have proposed alternate systems of belief and salvation. Were these developments, challenges, and changes bad? Did they harm the Church or advance it? Was God behind such acts of doctrinal evolution?

CATHOLICS

Roman Catholic scholars are quite open about developments in and evolution of Christianity's doctrines, theology, and liturgical rites over the two millennia since Christianity was officially begun.[1] Such

---

1   As a singular example, one Catholic scholar wrote, "In practice and in understanding, Holy Orders has undergone profound changes from its origins in the NT period to the developments of the Second Vatican Council (1962–65)." Frederick J. Cwiekowski, "Holy Orders," in *Harper Collins Encyclopedia of Catholicism,* ed. Richard P. McBrien (San Francisco, Calif.: HarperSanFrancisco, 1995), 620. See also Anthony Sherman, "Baptism," in *Harper Collins Encyclopedia of Catholicism,* 133–38; Mary Piil, "Con-

changes are not seen in Catholicism as signs of a "great apostasy." Rather, in many cases they are seen as evidence that God was indeed with the Church, moving it forward as times changed, and as the needs of the Church and its people evolved.

It is commonplace for non-Catholics to cite papal corruption—particularly during the middle ages—as evidence that God is no longer with the Church.[2] However, Catholics traditionally ignore such arguments, noting Christ's declaration, which says, "They that be whole need not a physician, but they that are sick" (Matthew 9:12). Catholics would argue that if the sinful behavior on the part of a Church leader qualifies the Church as apostate, then there isn't a denomination existent that hasn't succumbed. All humans sin, and, unfortunately many leaders do also—as Judas's example proves.

Thus, Catholics openly acknowledge the need for reform in periods like the fourteenth and fifteenth centuries,[3] but they do not concede that God would ever allow the Church to fall into general apostasy.[4]

firmation," in *Harper Collins Encyclopedia of Catholicism*, 346–50; Regis A. Duffy, "Eucharist," in *Harper Collins Encyclopedia of Catholicism*, 481–87; Kenan Osborne, "Reconciliation," in *Harper Collins Encyclopedia of Catholicism*, 1083–87; Andrew D. Ciferni, "Anointing of the Sick," in *Harper Collins Encyclopedia of Catholicism*, 57–61; and Richard P. McBrien, *Lives of the Popes* (San Francisco, Calif.: HarperSanFrancisco, 1997), 17–23.

2   Much has been written about the "bad popes" of the Catholic Church. See, for example, E. Russell Chamberlin, *The Bad Popes* (Gloucestershire: Sutton Publishing, 2003); E. Russell Chamberlin, "Rating the Popes," in McBrien, *Lives of the Popes*, 434–38; Brandon Toropov, *The Complete Idiot's Guide to The Popes and the Papacy* (Indianapolis, Ind.: Alpha Books, 2002), 47–55, 91–92, 95, 108–12, and 152–53; and Karl Keating, *Catholicism and Fundamentalism: The Attack on 'Romanism' by 'Bible Christians'* (Fort Collins, Colo.: Ignatius Press, 1988).

3   For example, one Catholic scholar wrote, "The fourteenth and fifteenth centuries were among the darkest in the history of the Church in the West. The papal monarchy that developed in the twelfth and thirteenth centuries had become a bloated bureaucracy with an insatiable appetite for money and power. . . . During these years the clergy became increasingly corrupt. . . . Clerical immorality, greed, and arrogance were blamed for what was perceived as religious decline. The need for reform was universally acknowledged but was thwarted by the self-interest of the hierarchy and of secular rulers who profited by the abuses." R. Emmett McLaughlin, "Reformation, the," in *Harper Collins Encyclopedia of Catholicism*, 1091.

4   Many Catholics see passages like Matthew 16:18 as proof of this belief.

LATTER-DAY SAINTS

Latter-day Saints would likely agree that the sinfulness of individuals—even leaders—does not constitute a general apostasy of the Church. A number of LDS General Authorities, particularly in the early days of the Church, were excommunicated for sinful practices or apostate teaching.[5] However, the Church did not fall into apostasy because of the sinful choices of these wayward men. Thus, while personal apostasy or sinfulness is never good, particularly in a Church leader, it is insufficient to constitute a general apostasy of the Church akin to what Latter-day Saints hold the early Christian Church went through.

From an LDS perspective, the cause of the Great Apostasy of early Christianity was the loss of priesthood keys.[6] Elder Bruce R. McConkie

WHILE SOME DOCTRINES AND RITES BECAME CORRUPTED OVER TIME, THE MOST IMPORTANT LOSS DURING THE GREAT APOSTASY WAS PRIESTHOOD KEYS.

---

5   As examples, Oliver Cowdery (Assistant President of the Church), Sidney Rigdon (First Counselor in the First Presidency), Frederick G. Williams (Second Counselor in the First Presidency), William Law (Second Counselor in the First Presidency), John C. Bennett (Additional Counselor in the First Presidency), Amasa Lyman (Additional Counselor in the First Presidency), Albert Carrington (Assistant Counselor to the First Presidency), Thomas B. Marsh (President of the Quorum of the Twelve Apostles), William E. McLellin (Quorum of the Twelve Apostles), Luke S. Johnson (Quorum of the Twelve Apostles), William B. Smith (Quorum of the Twelve Apostles), Orson Pratt (Quorum of the Twelve Apostles), John F. Boynton (Quorum of the Twelve Apostles), Lyman E. Johnson (Quorum of the Twelve Apostles), John E. Page (Quorum of the Twelve Apostles), Lyman Wight (Quorum of the Twelve Apostles), John W. Taylor (Quorum of the Twelve Apostles), Richard R. Lyman (Quorum of the Twelve Apostles), Joshua Butterfield (First Council of the Seventy), John Gaylord (First Council of the Seventy), Benjamin Clapp (First Council of the Seventy), George P. Lee (First Council of the Seventy), and John Corrill (Second Counselor to Presiding Bishop) were all excommunicated. Some came back to the Church and were rebaptized. Others remained outside of the faith after their excommunication.

6   By priesthood keys we mean that which was restored to the Prophet Joseph Smith and gives a man a right to be president. Prophets, apostles, sealers, stake presidents,

wrote, "With the coming of the great apostasy, vacancies no longer were filled in the Quorum of the Twelve, and when the last apostle ceased to minister among mortals, the keys of the kingdom no longer were exercised, and the so-called Christian Church was no longer the Lord's Church."[7] Thus, although doctrines and ordinances have changed over the two thousand years that Christianity has existed, the Great Apostasy was not caused by those changes. Rather, those changes happened as a result of the loss of the apostolic keys, and the martyrdom of the general authorities that once held them.

SUMMARY

Latter-day Saints and Catholics are basically in agreement that the Church of the New Testament evolved in dramatic ways after the first century. We would also agree that sin among priesthood leaders, while always bad, is not sufficient to constitute a general apostasy of the Church.

The place where Catholics and Mormons would most disagree on this subject would be in how they view the evolution of the rites and doctrines of the early Church. Whereas Catholics see it as progress, and potentially a sign that God is moving the work forward, Latter-day Saints would argue that such evolution is a mark of apostasy, and a sign that the apostolic keys and governance of the New Testament Church have been lost.

---

bishops, elder's quorum presidents, teacher's and deacon's quorum presidents all hold keys. However, men who are simply ordained to the priesthood, but are not serving in any of the aforementioned capacities, do not hold priesthood keys. Thus, when the Great Apostasy was in full-swing at the end of the first century, once the keys were lost, the Melchizedek Priesthood continued to be upon the earth for some time. The loss of keys did not remove valid priesthood, but it did strip the Church of apostles and prophets, the ability to perform sealing ordinances, and the general Church governance which the First Presidency and Quorum of the Twelve provide today. Hence, from an LDS perspective, the Church quickly fell into disarray once it was no longer being run on a general level. Well-meaning local leaders sought to pick up the slack, but the lack of general leadership allowed the Church to go in many different directions.

7   Bruce R. McConkie, *Mormon Doctrine*, 2d ed. (Salt Lake City: Bookcraft, 1979), 50, s.v. "apostolic succession."

THE GREAT
AND ABOMINABLE CHURCH

Like the members of every other Christian denomination, Latter-day Saints are sometimes curious about the identity of the "great and abominable church" (1 Nephi 13:6), the "mother of harlots" (1 Nephi 14:16–17), the "whore of all the earth" (D&C 29:21)—she who caused what we refer to as the "Great Apostasy."

In the Book of Revelation, John associates the "mark of the beast"—the number 666—with the "great and abominable" church (Revelation 13:18). From the Protestant Reformation onward, various Christians have associated that mark, and that "church," with Roman Catholicism.[1] A number of clever connections have been made in an effort to "prove" that the pope is the anti-Christ and that the Catholic Church is the "great and abominable" church. Such connections include supposed symbolic meanings behind papal titles,[2]

---

1   See, for example, Charles F. Pfeiffer and Everett F. Harrison, eds., *The Wycliffe Bible Commentary* (Chicago, Ill.: Moody Press, 1975), 1517, which states, "The majority of commentators, since the time of the Reformation, identify her with the papacy, as Luther, Tyndale, Knox, Calvin . . . Alford, Elliott, Lange, and many others."

2   During the Protestant Reformation, it was common to see some reference to the Catholic Church in the number 666. Thus, the Greek word *lateinos*, which totals 666, was interpreted as a reference to the "Roman empire" or the "Roman Church." The phrase, "the Latin kingdom," if written in Greek, gave one a sum of 666 as did the title "Italian church." The Latin phrases, *Vicarius Generalis Dei In Terris* or *Vicarius Filii Dei* (supposedly inscribed on the papal coronation tiara), have also been said to total 666, as does the Greek word *papeiskos* (which has been used for "pope"). Having said that, it has been noted that the pope has no such "official title," and his papal tiara apparently bears no such inscription. Thus, as one LDS scholar notes, "His real title,

suspicious geography,[3] the wearing of certain colors by the clergy,[4] claims about the existence of some kind of secret society designed to hide the "real truth" about Catholicism,[5] etc. Of course, all of these

---

Vicarius Christi (Vicar of Christ), only adds up (with a disappointing thud) to 214." Barry Bickmore, "'Clearing Up Misconceptions', A review of Patrick Madrid, *Pope Fiction: Answers to 30 Myths and Misconceptions about the Papacy,*" in *FARMS Review of Books* 13, no. 2 (2001): 198–99. One source suggests that the Reformation's association of the number 666 with the pope and the Catholic Church was a direct result of Catholics claiming that Martin Luther was the anti-Christ. "At the time of the Wars of Religion, a Catholic mystic called Petrus Bungus, in a word published in 1584–1585 at Bergamon, claimed to have demonstrated that the German reformer [Martin] Luther was none other than the Anti-Christ since his name, in Roman numerals [LVTHERNVC], gives the number 666. But the disciples of Luther, who considered the Church of Rome as the direct heir of the Empire of the Caesars, lost no time in responding. They took the Roman numerals contained in the phrase *VICARIUS FILII DEI* ('Vicar of the Son of God') which is on the papal tiara, and drew the conclusion that one might expect. The title totals 666." Georges Ifrah, *The Universal History of Numbers* (New York: John Wiley & Sons, 2000), 260–61. See also John J. Davis, *Biblical Numerology* (Grand Rapids, Mich.: Baker Book House, 2000), 128, 132, 145; and William Barclay, "Great Themes of the New Testament," in *Expository Times* 70 (1959): 296. Curiously, but not significantly, not only does the name Luther (when written in Roman numerals) total 666, but also the word "Saxon" (also used by Catholics in reference to Luther), when written in Greek, totals 666. Barclay, "Great Themes of the New Testament," 296.

3   When John the Revelator states, "The seven heads are seven mountains, on which the woman [or the whore] sitteth" (Revelation 17:9), many commentators have seen this as a reference to Rome, the headquarters of the Catholic Church, and thus have drawn the conclusion that the great and abominable church is Roman Catholicism. See, for example, Uriah Smith, *Daniel and Revelation* (Mountain View, Calif.: Pacific Press, 1944), 644; and David Hocking, *The Coming World Leader* (Portland, Ore.: Multnomah Press, 1988), 246–47.

4   Some would see both John (Revelation 17:3–4, 18:16) and Nephi's (1 Nephi 13:7–8) symbolic description of the clothing of the great and abominable as a reference to the dress of the pope or the liturgical garb of a priest officiating during the Mass.

5   See Jack T. Chick, *Alberto: Parts 1–5* (Chino, Calif.: Chick Publications, 1979, 1981–83, 1985); and John Cornwell, *Hitler's Pope: The Secret History of Pius XII* (New York: Viking, 1999). See also Dan Brown's grossly misrepresentative portrayal of Opus Dei in his 2003 book, *The Da Vinci Code.* Opus Dei is a Catholic organization, officially recognized by the Roman Catholic Church, that simply seeks to bring faith into the day-to-day life—more particularly into the professional life—of Roman Catholics worldwide. While Brown's book, *The Da Vinci Code,* is a fictional novel, it portrays members of Opus Dei is ways that might be construed as reality rather than fiction. For example, members of the movement are portrayed as monks, but there are no monks in Opus Dei. Brown suggests that they are involved in criminal behavior. In reality, the organization exists to promote the exact opposite. Members of Opus Dei are depicted in *The Da Vinci Code* as practicing extreme forms of self-mortification. Yet again, no such behaviors are encouraged or practiced by members of Opus Dei. Brown's suggestion that that Opus Dei is a cult that practices brainwashing and coer-

supposed parallels between scriptural descriptions of the "great and abominable" church and Roman Catholicism are misunderstandings about what the scriptural authors intended.

While it is true that the "great and abominable church" caused the Great Apostasy of first century Christianity, Catholicism could not be "the whore of all the earth."[6] Latter-day Saints hold that Catholicism is

cion is ridiculous. Opus Dei is not a denomination of Catholicism. It is not a secret society. It is not some clandestine arm of the Vatican seeking to bring to pass evil and works of darkness. *The Da Vinci Code's* representation of Opus Dei was generally inaccurate, misleading, and offensive.

6   Some Latter-day Saints are wont to quote the first edition of *Mormon Doctrine* to establish that The Church of Jesus Christ of Latter-day Saints holds that Catholicism is the "church of the devil." In that work, Bruce R. McConkie—who was *not* a member of the Quorum of the Twelve at the time the text was written—penned these words: "*The Roman Catholic Church* [is] specifically—singled out, set apart, described, and designated as being 'most abominable above all other Churches.' (1 Ne. 13:5.) Such agencies have been and are founded by the devil who is an enemy to all righteousness. It is also to the Book of Mormon to which we turn for the plainest description of the Catholic Church as the great and abominable Church. . . . (1 Ne. 13:24–42.) . . . Nephi beheld further that this Church was the 'mother of abominations,' and . . . [that it ruled] from Rome, the city built on 'seven mountains.'" See Bruce R. McConkie, *Mormon Doctrine*, 1st ed. (Salt Lake City: Bookcraft, 1958), s.v. "church of the devil." It should be noted that Brother McConkie later removed those words from his book, and during his tenure as an apostle, he was decidedly cautious about expressing this same opinion in public settings. Like anyone else, Brother McConkie was entitled to his personal opinions. And, prior to his call to the Twelve, he had expressed what he, at that time, believed to be the case. In his introduction to his first edition, Brother Mc-Conkie noted that he was "solely" and "fully responsible" for the content of the book. It was published by neither the Church nor Deseret Book. It appears that his views on the identity of the great and abominable church softened and expanded somewhat after he first penned them in *Mormon Doctrine*. Years later, Elder McConkie—having been called to the Quorum of the Twelve Apostles—discussed what he believed the great and abominable church to be. As an apostle, he wrote:

> There was . . . a church of the devil in the pre-existence. Lucifer was its head. . . . There has always been a church of the devil on earth. . . . The Prophet Joseph Smith said: 'the devil always sets up his kingdom at the very same time in opposition to God.' (*Teachings*, p. 365). Thus when Adam and Eve taught the gospel to their children, 'Satan came among them, saying . . . believe it not; and they believed it not, and they loved Satan more than God. And men began from that time forth to be carnal, sensual and devilish.' . . . In 201 A.D. . . . the Nephite people 'began to . . . build up churches unto themselves to get gain, and began to deny the true church of Christ. And it came to pass that . . . there were many churches in the land . . . which professed to know Christ, and yet they did deny the more parts of his gospel, insomuch that they did . . . multiply exceedingly because of iniquity, and because of the power of Satan who did get hold upon

of fourth century origins, and yet the Great Apostasy takes place begin-ning in the middle of the first century. Thus, Catholicism could not have caused the Apostasy, and, therefore, could not be the "great and abominable church." From an LDS perspective, the Catholic Church simply didn't exist when the Apostasy took place.

Additionally, Nephi speaks of the "great and abominable church" removing many "plain and precious things" from the scriptures (1 Nephi 13:26). However, those "plain and precious" things Latter-day Saints see as taken from the Bible were already gone by AD 313. Thus, again, Catholicism could not be the "church of the devil."

Finally, Nephi speaks of the "church which is most abominable above all other churches, which slayeth the saints of God, yea, and

their hearts. And . . . they did persecute the true church of Christ . . . . Thus, apostasy . . . overran the Nephite people. . . .Satan . . . was setting up his church again among them." [Bruce R. McConkie, *Doctrinal New Testament Commentary*, 3 vols. (Salt Lake City: Bookcraft, 1987–88), 3:547–48]

Notice that Elder McConkie sees the great and abominable (or the church of the devil) as causing the apostasy among the Nephites. Certainly there was no Catholic Church in the Americas at this point. Elder McConkie wrote that "there were many churches comprising Lucifer's earthly kingdom." McConkie, *Doctrinal New Testament Commentary*, 3:549. While Elder McConkie believed that some of Satan's "churches" were worse than others, he was very cautious (as an apostle) with regard to what he publicly taught about the great and abominable church. Of the church of the devil in these last days, Elder McConkie wrote that it "is not one [church] among many [churches], but it is all the forces of evil linked together." McConkie, *Doctrinal New Testament Commentary*, 3:551; See also Bruce R. McConkie, *The Millennial Messiah* (Salt Lake City: Deseret Book, 1982), 51–55. I do not wish to imply that Bruce R. McConkie saw the great and abominable church as something entirely separate from Catholicism. In an effort to be fair, after he made his changes to the text of *Mormon Doctrine,* for the most part he ceased to refer to the Catholic Church as the great and abominable. Yet, it does seem clear that Elder McConkie (until the time of his death) held that the church of the devil was an evolving institution that, at different times, used different vehicles to further its work. One of those vehicles, in Elder McConkie's opinion, was some of the world's various Christian denominations. He made it quite clear that he did not believe that all were "highjacked" by Satan to the same degree. Some religions, he believed, were worse than others in that they taught things that simply were contrary to the divinely inspired teachings and will of God. Elder McConkie (as an apostle) was traditionally cautious to not specifically name any given church as more or less a part of the great and abominable church. For a review of early LDS claims that Roman Catholicism is the Great and

Abominable Church, and Catholic claims that the Mormonism is that same evil institution, see Matthew J. Grow, "The Whore of Babylon and the Abomination of Abominations: Nineteenth-Century Catholic and Mormon Mutual Perceptions and Religious Identity," in Church History, Volume 73 (March 2004): 139-167.

tortureth them and bindeth them down, and yoketh them with a yoke of iron, and bringeth them down into captivity" (1 Nephi 13:5). Latter-day Saints should remember that Catholics were persecuted—they were not the persecutors of early Christians. Thus, again, they do not qualify for the of "the whore of all the earth."

CATHOLICS

While Catholics do not traditionally use the terms "great and abominable church" or "church of the devil," they do see John's reference to that evil empire as important. As to who or what the "beast" and the anti-Christ are, the Catholic Church has taken no official position. The *Encyclopedia of Catholicism* states, "The imagery of the beast has been applied to various forces, secular and religious, that have been felt to be oppressive throughout the history of the Church. The immediate reference of the image in the historical context of [the Book of] Revelation was apparently the Roman Empire [of the first century]."[7] Of the anti-Christ, the same text states that it is:

> a personified opponent of Christians and of the good who appears in the last times in early Christian apocalyptic theology. While usually thought of in connection with the book of Revelation . . . the idea is common in . . . the [New Testament] under a variety of names, especially Belial or Beliar . . . perhaps Gog and Magog . . . or the beast. . . . It is not clear . . . whether the opponent is the devil or a human figure who represents the devil.[8]

LATTER-DAY SAINTS

Latter-day Saints sometimes vary on how they understand the "great and abominable church" and the anti-Christ. We know that its main damage to the early Christian Church was done very early in Christianity's history. The things that happened *after* the mid-second century were really offspring of the great and abominable "church." In an effort to define the movement that brought down the first century Christian Church, Stephen E. Robinson wrote:

---

7   "Beast of the Apocalypse," in *Harper Collins Encyclopedia of Catholicism,* 146.

8   Carolyn Osiek, "Antichrist," in *Harper Collins Encyclopedia of Catholicism*, 65.

Can we, then, identify the historical agency that acted as the great and abominable Church in earliest Christianity? Such an agent would have had its origins in the second half of the first century and would have done much of its work by the middle of the second century. This period might be called the blind spot in Christian history, for it is here that the fewest primary historical sources have been preserved. We have good sources for New Testament Christianity; then the lights go out, so to speak, and we hear the muffled sounds of a great struggle. When the lights come on again a hundred or so years later, we find that someone has rearranged all the furniture and Christianity has become something very different from what it was in the beginning. That different entity can accurately be described as hellenized Christianity.[9]

SUMMARY

Roman Catholicism is not, nor could be, the "great and abominable church" of the Bible and the Book of Mormon. From an LDS perspective, its arrival on the scene is too late, its influence too good,[10] and its design too lofty to qualify as one of Satan's ultimate instruments against the truth.

---

9   Stephen E. Robinson, "Warring Against the Saints of God," *Ensign* (January 1988): 38–39.

10   Latter-day Saints should realize that Catholicism had done a number of things that have benefited all of Christendom, Mormons included. In his article "Catholicism's Contribution to God's Plan," Latter-day Saint scholar Gerald Hansen Jr. offered a number of ways in which the Catholic Church blessed the Christian world during the Great Apostasy: (1) For centuries "Catholicism was the standard and disseminator of moral standards in Europe and other parts of the world." (2) It "kept alive for 2,000 years the idea of Jesus as the Savior of the world." (3) "The New Testament" likely would "not exist without the Catholic Church." (4) "Music as we know it in the West began its development in the Catholic mass." (5) "Art in the West was kept alive and developed . . . mostly through the Church." (6) "Universities were essentially a Catholic invention." (7) Catholicism engendered a mindset that made modern science possible." (8) "Monks . . . copied books, and kept learning alive during times of illiteracy." Gerald Hansen Jr., "Catholicism's Contribution to God's Plan," *Perspective* 6, no. 2 (Autumn 2006): 84–97. Whereas Mormonism tends to heavily emphasize the positive aspects of the Protestant Reformation in preparing the world for the Restoration, there are many things in Catholic history that have also served to prepare the world for the coming forth of the fullness of the gospel of Jesus Christ through the Prophet Joseph Smith.

THE VATICAN IS WORLD HEADQUARTERS FOR THE ROMAN CATHOLIC CHURCH, THE RESIDENCE OF THE POPE, AND THE SMALLEST SOVEREIGN STATE IN THE WORLD.

From a Catholic perspective, while the exact nature and identity of today's "great and abominable church" is not known, it is certainly seen as being, at the very least, secular and religious forces in the last days who seek to oppress Christianity and thwart good. Catholic scholars acknowledge the seat of the "church of the devil," described by John (Revelation 17:9), as likely a reference to Rome. However, it has no connection to Vatican City, the seat of today's Roman Catholic Church. Rather, it is a reference to ancient Rome, the goddess Roma, worldliness, sin, etc.[11]

While, from a Latter-day Saint perspective, the "great and abominable church" still exists today, like Catholics, we too would acknowledge that it has evolved and diversified from its first century version, which we might best label as Hellenism. Today, the "church of the devil" encompasses any movement—political, social, religious, monetary, etc.—that seeks to thwart good, advocate evil, and stop the furtherance of the work, words, and Church of God upon the earth.

---

11   See, for example, Adela Yarbro Collins, "The Apocalypse (Revelation)," in *The New Jerome Biblical Commentary,* eds. Raymond E. Brown, Joseph A. Fitzmyer, and Roland E. Murphy (Englewood Cliffs, N.J.: Prentice Hall, 1990), 1012.

Thus, LDS and Catholic understandings of what the "great and abominable church" was are slightly different (i.e., specifically Hellenism as opposed to ancient Rome and its goddess), nevertheless, our understandings of what it is today are very similar.

SAINTS

For Protestants and Latter-day Saints alike, there is sometimes a great deal of misunderstanding about the Roman Catholic position on saints and their role within the Church and salvation. Some of those misunderstandings have arisen because popular practice and the Church's official position have not always been the same. While some might assume that Catholics both pray to and worship deceased Christians (whom they refer to as saints), context is important for understanding what certain acts of piety mean, and what the Catholic Church officially teaches on this matter.

CATHOLICS

It is true that around the fifth century the Catholic Church encouraged the veneration of relics among new converts to help them "solidify their faith."[1] This probably did more harm than good, as it encouraged a practice the Church would later have to fight in order to end. For example, as early as the end of the eighth century, the Church found itself in a constant battle to keep its members from placing saints, angels, and the Virgin Mary above Christ in their acts of veneration, honor, and worship. The Second Council of Nicaea (AD 787) stressed that Jesus is the only one "worthy" of "worship and adoration."[2] By the

---

1   See Richard P. McBrien, *Lives of the Saints* (San Francisco, Calif.: HarperSanFrancisco, 2001), 6.

2   See McBrien, *Lives of the Saints*, 6.

late Middle Ages, petitioning saints for help became somewhat popular as the Church taught that they dwelt in heaven in close proximity to God, thus having direct access to him. Thus began the Catholic practice of appealing to saints in an effort to convince God to heed a specific request.[3] In an effort to correct potentially skewed understandings of the role of saints within the Church, during the Second Vatican Council the Church shifted the emphasis from "the saints as miracle workers to the saints as models."[4] Of course, old traditions die slowly. However, the Roman Catholic Church's position has been, and remains to this day, that saints' lives are simply examples to us that holiness is an achievable goal for any Christian who seeks it.[5] Thus, saints are not to be worshiped, but rather emulated in their examples, achievements, and particularly in their devotion to God. But what of prayer to saints? Certainly that happens within the Church. Of this practice, one Catholic author wrote:

> We ask fellow Christians on earth to pray for us, why shouldn't we ask those who are in heaven to pray for us, too? The "Hail Mary" is our way of asking Mary to pray with us as a senior prayer partner. You mustn't imagine that we are praying to Mary and the saints instead of God. We are asking them to pray for us, and with us as prayer partners. If you had a prayer partner named Richard and you sent him an email asking him to pray for your father who has had an operation, we wouldn't say you are praying to Richard instead of to God. . . . Asking saints in heaven to help was part of the ancient Hebrew tradition. The parable of Lazarus and the rich man indicates that Jesus accepted the idea that people in heaven could intercede for those on earth (Luke 16:22–28).[6]

The idea that Catholics are not really praying to saints, but rather asking that they pray with them, is a commonly held view in Roman

---

3   See McBrien, *Lives of the Saints*, 7–8.
4   McBrien, *Lives of the Saints*, 2.
5   See McBrien, *Lives of the Saints*, 8.
6   Dwight Longenecker and David Gustafson, *Mary: A Catholic–Evangelical Debate* (Grand Rapids, Mich.: Brazos Press, 2003), 175–76.

Catholic writings.[7] They are simply "invoking" or "calling upon" them for help. In support of this, notice the language of the popular Catholic prayer—the "Hail Mary"—which states, "Holy Mary . . . pray for us sinners." Clearly Mary is being asked to add her prayers to ours. However, she is not being "prayed to" in the sense that one would pray to God.

According to Catholic thought, one should not worship or give adoration to anyone or anything other than God. However, the saints and angels deserve our respect and veneration for who they are and how they lived their lives. But respect and veneration is decidedly different than worship.[8] So, while Catholics might speak of "patron

ROMAN CATHOLICISM TEACHES THAT THE VIRGIN MARY ADDS HER PRAYERS TO OURS, HENCE, THE FAMOUS LINE FROM THE POPULAR CATHOLIC PRAYER, "HOLY MARY... PRAY FOR US SINNERS, NOW AND AT THE HOUR OF OUR DEATH. AMEN."

---

7   For example, one Catholic scholar wrote, "Ecumenically . . . a main point of contention is the Catholic practice of invoking Mary as well as other saints and asking her to 'pray for us.' . . . Within a rightly ordered faith this is an expression of our solidarity in the communion of saints, analogous to asking other living persons to pray for us." Elizabeth A. Johnson, "Blessed Virgin Mary," in *Harper Collins Encyclopedia of Catholicism,* ed. Richard P. McBrien (San Francisco, Calif.: HarperSanFrancisco, 1995), 838. Elsewhere we read, "We do not pray to the saints as gods. We merely pray to the saints that they will intercede for us before God. . . . Why can't we ask them—just like we ask our family and friends—to do us a favor? Why can't they obtain a blessing for us? Why can't they plead our case and present our petitions before Almighty God?" Paul L. Williams, *The Complete Idiot's Guide to the Lives of the Saints* (Indianapolis, Ind.: Alpha Books, 2001), 81. Another penned this, "Prayer is the act by which one enters into conscious, loving communion with God. . . . When prayer is directed to the mother of Christ or a saintly intercessor, the one prayed to is viewed as connected with God" and is appealed to as a heavenly prayer partner of sorts. Margaret Dorgan, "Prayer," in *Harper Collins Encyclopedia of Catholicism,* 1037. See also *United States Catholic Catechism for Adults* (Washington, D.C.: United States Conference of Catholic Bishops, 2006), 146–47.

8   See Williams, *Complete Idiot's Guide to the Lives of the Saints,* 81–82; Peter J. Kreeft, *Catholic Christianity: A Complete Catechism of Catholic Beliefs based on the Catechism of the Catholic Church* (San Francisco, Calif.: Ignatius Press, 2001), 414–15.

saints" as guardian angels, of sorts, technically they are simply righteous individuals now dwelling in the presence of God who deserve our respect or veneration[9] because of the way they lived. They are seen as having the power to "bend God's ear" on our behalf because they have been exalted and now dwell in his presence. In that context, they may act as special protectors or intercessors.[10] But Catholics do not perceive themselves as "praying" to these saints—nor do they believe that answered prayers, miracles, or forgiveness of sins comes from saints. Rather, they come from God, although a saint may have interceded to help secure this blessing for the mortal requesting it.[11] As the Second Vatican Council (1962–65) taught, "it is fitting to love the saints who are our brothers and sisters in Christ," but any devotion directed to them "is ultimately directed toward God."[12]

LATTER-DAY SAINTS

While Latter-day Saints do not request intercession of deceased individuals, we certainly do look to certain figures from our past as exemplars whom we venerate. President Brigham Young once noted:

> Many . . . of the first Elders of the Church, were looked upon almost as angels. They were looked upon by the young members as being so filled with the Spirit and power of God that we were hardly worthy to converse with them. You hear the names of Bishop Partridge, of Brother W. W. Phelps, who is now sitting on this stand, of Parley P. Pratt, of David Whitmer, of Oliver Cowdery, and the names of many others of the first Elders who had been up to Zion, and I declare to you that brethren in other parts of the land, those who had not seen the persons named, felt that should they come into their presence they would have to pull off their shoes, as the ground would be so holy upon which they trod.[13]

---

9   To "venerate" is to show some sign of respect. See "Veneration of the Cross," in *Harper Collins Encyclopedia of Catholicism*, 1307.

10   See "Patron Saint," in *Harper Collins Encyclopedia of Catholicism*, 971.

11   See Regina Coll, "Saints," in *Harper Collins Encyclopedia of Catholicism*, 1156.

12   Coll, "Saints," in *Harper Collins Encyclopedia of Catholicism*, 1156.

13   John A. Widtsoe, comp., *Discourses of Brigham Young* (Salt Lake City: Bookcraft, 1998), 129.

President Young was correct in his assessment of how Latter-day Saints tend to view some of the early leaders of the Church and even the famed Mormon pioneers. Indeed, a primary example would be the Prophet Joseph Smith, who is, to a great extent, the LDS version of a "patron saint." Most practicing Mormons hold him in very high regard. Like Catholics with their saints, Mormons would certainly argue that we do not pray to Joseph Smith, nor do we expect miracles at his hands.[14] However, certain successors of Joseph Smith have taught that he does play an intercessory role akin to that of Catholic saints. For example, President Brigham Young stated, "No man or woman in this dispensation will ever enter into the celestial kingdom of God without the consent of Joseph Smith."[15] Why is that the case? According to President Young, it is because Joseph Smith holds the "keys" over this last dispensation. Thus, he must intercede on behalf of those living in the dispensation of the fullness of times. They must accept the work of the restoration he was sent by the Father to establish. As they do so, his keys are utilized on their behalf. He is not to be worshiped or prayed

---

14   Having said that, Joseph, like the Virgin Mary, has been seen by a number of Latter-day Saints since his passing. He appeared to his successor, Brigham Young, shortly after Brigham took over for the Prophet Joseph, and then apparently appeared to him again on Brigham's deathbed. See Hugh Nibley, "Teachings of Brigham Young," in *Encyclopedia of Mormonism,* ed. Daniel H. Ludlow, 4 vols. (New York: Macmillan, 1992), 4:1609; and Robert L. Millet, *Alive in Christ: The Miracle of Spiritual Rebirth* (Salt Lake City: Deseret Book, 1997), 200–201. The Prophet Joseph also appeared to his wife Emma shortly before she died—some thirty five years after his martyrdom. See Joseph Fielding Smith, *Origin of the Reorganized Church and the Question of Succession* (Salt Lake City: Deseret News, 1909), 113. Wilford Woodruff indicated that Joseph appeared to him numerous times after he had been martyred. See Wilford Woodruff, *Wilford Woodruff's Journal, 1833–1898, Typescript,* ed. Scott G. Kenney, 9 vols. (Midvale, Utah: Signature Books, 1983–84), 5:237. Many, many others made similar claims of post-martyrdom appearances of the Prophet Joseph Smith. In the sense that he has appeared to his devotees with some frequency after his death, Joseph seems to parallel the Virgin Mary or other Catholic saints. Regarding the appearances of Mary, one Catholic text notes, "Apparitions . . . of Mary have multiplied . . . especially in the later decades of the twentieth century. Some of these the Church had declared inauthentic . . . some of them, after long and careful investigation, she has declared 'worthy of belief' (such as those at Lourdes, France, in 1854, and at Fatima, Portugal, in 1917). Many of them are still under investigation.. . . . These are private revelations, not Church dogma, and Catholics are not bound to believe in them." Peter J. Kreeft, *Catholic Christianity: A Complete Catechism of Catholic Beliefs based on the Catechism of the Catholic Church* (San Francisco, Calif.: Ignatius Press, 2001), 420.

15   Brigham Young, in *Journal of Discourses,* 26 vols. (Liverpool: F. D. Richards, 1855–86), 7:289.

to. But, from an LDS position, veneration is owed him for all he has done. As President John Taylor noted about the LDS understanding of Joseph Smith's work as an intercessor: "Joseph Smith, the Prophet and Seer of the Lord, has done more, save Jesus only, for the salvation of men in this world, than any other man that ever lived in it" (D&C 135:3). Thus, Latter-day Saints *do* see the Prophet Joseph as having an intercessory role in helping you and I lay hold on God and salvation via the works Joseph performed and the things he restored.

In addition, a number of the Brethren have taught that there are angels who intercede, protect, or provide in the lives of the Saints, sometimes in response to prayers, and sometimes simply because intercession is desperately needed. These heaven-sent beings act as "guardian angels" or "patron saints" of sorts, and while the Holy Ghost is seen as the ultimate "guardian angel" or "patron saint," Latter-day Saints acknowledge that other deceased disciples are used by the Father to meet the needs of His children upon the earth.[16] For example, Moroni came in answer to Joseph's prayer (JS—H 1:29–30); Gabriel (or Noah) came in response to Zacharias's prayers (Luke 1:13); an angel who was not a member of the Godhead came to John the Revelator, speaking by "divine investiture of authority" on behalf of the Lord (Revelation 19:10). Many other examples could be given. Latter-day Saints, like Catholics, believe that the members of the Godhead are not the only ones to interact with mankind. Stories in Mormonism of the deceased petitioning the living, particularly as it relates to the performance of temple ordinances, are legion.[17] And in LDS belief many an angel has been sent from the Father to address the needs of mankind, to intercede, or to do the Father's will. President Joseph F. Smith taught:

16   See, for example, David O. Mckay, *Conference Report*, October 1968, 86; Hyrum G. Smith, *Conference Report*, October 1928, 81–82; George Q. Cannon, *The Life of Joseph Smith, the Prophet* (Salt Lake City: Deseret Book, 1986), 494–95; Joseph Fielding Smith, *Doctrines of Salvation*, 3 vols. (Salt Lake City: Bookcraft, 1998), 1:54; Orson Pratt, in *Journal of Discourses,* 2:344; John A. Widtsoe, *Gospel Interpretations* (Salt Lake City: Bookcraft, 1947), 28–29; and Daniel H. Ludlow, *A Companion to Your Study of the Doctrine and Covenants,* 2 vols. (Salt Lake City: Deseret Book, 1978), 1:558. Many other examples could be given.

17   See, for example, Jacob Heinerman, *Temple Manifestations* (Salt Lake City: Hawkes Publishing Company, 1975); Margie Calhoun, *When Faith Writes the Story*, 2d ed. (Salt Lake City: Bountiful Press, 1993); and Margie Calhoun, *Stories of Insight and Inspiration*, 2d ed. (Salt Lake City: Bountiful Press, 1993).

Joseph, the prophet, and . . . the martyrs of this dispensation . . . are carefully guarding the interests of the kingdom
of God in which they labored and for which they strove
during their mortal lives. . . . We are closely related to our
kindred, to our ancestors, to our friends and associates and
co-laborers who have preceded us into the spirit world. . . .
Those who have been faithful, who have gone beyond, are
still engaged in the work for the salvation of the souls of
men, in the opening of the prison doors to them that are
bound and proclaiming liberty to the captives. . . . They see
us, they are solicitous for our welfare, they love us now more
than ever.[18]

An additional parallel between Catholic Saints and LDS belief is to
be found in the fact that Mormons see the various angels of the restoration as having specific, divinely assigned roles or parameters to their authority and intercession. For example, John the Baptist held and restored
the keys of the ministry of angels. Elijah restored the keys requisite for
family history work, thereby turning the hearts of fathers to children
and the children to their fathers. Adam held and restored keys associated with temple ordinances, particularly the endowment.[19] Many other
examples could be given.[20] The basic point is that Latter-day Saints see
angels as having specific "job descriptions." They have areas over which
they hold responsibility, and for which they have a right to intervene and

18   Joseph F. Smith, *Gospel Doctrine* (Salt Lake City: Bookcraft, 1998), 430–31.
19   Joseph indicated that whenever "the Keys" have been brought from heaven "they are
      revealed . . . by Adam's authority." Andrew F. Ehat and Lyndon W. Cook, *The Words of
      Joseph Smith: The Contemporary Accounts of the Nauvoo Discourses of the Prophet Joseph
      Smith*, Religious Studies Monograph Series, no. 6 (Provo, Utah: Religious Studies
      Center, Brigham Young University, 1980), 8.] Indeed, one LDS scholar wrote, "Ac-
      cording to Joseph Smith, if Adam did not personally reveal the ordinances, he would
      send messengers who would teach his posterity the endowment counsels that would
      lead them in the way of life and salvation." Andrew F. Ehat, "Joseph Smith's Introduc-
      tion of Temple Ordinances and the 1844 Mormon Succession Question" (master's
      thesis, Brigham Young University, 1981), 256 n. 86.
20   For example, Moroni is said to have held the keys of the record of the stick of Ephraim
      (or Book of Mormon). Elias held the keys to preside over the Restoration (under
      Adam). See Joseph Fielding Smith, *Teachings of the Prophet Joseph Smith* (Salt Lake
      City: Deseret Book, 1976), 157. Joseph of Egypt apparently held the keys of the Abra-
      hamic covenant and its promises. Abraham, Isaac, and Jacob (or Israel) each held keys
      associated with the Abrahamic covenant and its promises, and Peter, James, and John
      held the Melchizedek Priesthood and keys associated with the apostolic office.

interact with mankind. This is very similar to Catholic Saints, who function as patrons or intercessors for specific groups of people or for specific needs.[21]

When it comes to "saints," Catholics and Mormons are very similar. The direction of the petition may not always be the same (i.e., Mormons hold that sometimes mortals intercede on behalf of the dead, and sometimes they intercede on our behalf—D&C 128:15, 18). Nevertheless, the idea of intercessors outside of the Trinity or Godhead helping save those who cannot help themselves is commonly held by both faiths.

SUMMARY

Latter-day Saints and Catholics alike are instructed by their respective faiths to pray *only* to God. For Mormons that means directing one's prayers to the Father. For Catholics that means praying to the Trinity.[22] Certainly, in both traditions, some may choose to do otherwise,[23] but such an act would be contrary to the official teachings and counsel of the two faiths.

Both religions also acknowledge that God may sometimes work through deceased holy persons, now angels, in order to answer prayers or intervene on behalf of God's children. These persons or angels are traditionally individuals who are worthy of veneration but not worship. According to both faiths, whatever that intervening being brings

---

21   For example, the patron saint of priests is Jean-Baptiste Vianney, the patron saint of clerics is Gabriel, the patron saint of mothers is Monica, the patron of military chaplains is John Capistrano, the patron saint of theologians is Augustine, and the patron saint of the Church is Joseph.

22   Roman Catholics will sometimes direct prayers to the Father, other times to the Son, and sometimes to the Holy Spirit.

23   On one occasion, while attending a meeting on the campus of the University of Notre Dame, I witnessed a female Catholic scholar offer the Lord's prayer to "Mother in Heaven," by saying "Our Mother, which art in heaven, hallowed be thy name." Similarly, at the conclusion of an LDS religion class, I heard a female student offer the closing prayer to "Heavenly Mother." In both cases these women acted against their respective faith's teachings on the matter of prayer. One might take either experience as proof that both Catholics and Mormons pray to individuals other than God the Father. However, clearly one must make a distinction between what individual Catholics or Latter-day Saints choose to do, and what the official teaching of their respective faiths is on this matter. The membership of these two faiths are instructed to pray only to God—not to saints, Mary, Mother in Heaven, deceased ancestors, etc.

or does, it is only a manifestation of the Father's power and will. It is *never* to be connected with the power or will of God's angelic representative.

Additionally, both faiths' positions on "saints" and angels tend to be grossly exaggerated and terribly misunderstood by those outside of the faith.

Of course, there are differences in how each faith approaches the issue of saints or intercessors. For example, where Catholics would feel comfortable directly petitioning a deceased saint, Mormons would not. Catholics have a process whereby one is publicly and officially declared a saint (or "canonized"), but Mormons do not.[24] Catholic saints are assigned feast days on which they are celebrated, but Latter-day Saints have no such practice to commemorate the lives of those whom they see as now exalted or functioning as ministering angels. Likewise, in Catholicism the saints have assignments as "patrons" over countries, needs, or occupations. So, for example, Matthew is the patron saint over accountants, Francis de Sales is the saint of the deaf, and Patrick is the saint assigned over the nation of Ireland. True, in Mormonism certain angels hold specific keys and responsibilities. For example, Elijah holds the keys to turn hearts of fathers to children and children to their fathers; Adam possesses and reveals the keys of temple ordinances, particularly the endowment;[25] Peter, James, and John hold the keys over the Melchizedek Priesthood and the apostolic office. Nevertheless, Latter-day Saints do not see the specific ministry of an angel as being solely confined to a nation, occupation, or need.

---

24   The exception to this (in LDS thinking) might be that there is a specified way in which we make our "calling and election sure," namely by faithfully entering into and keeping covenants. In a sense, one might argue that the temple rite associated with this doctrine officially declares one a "saint."

25   See footnote 19 of this chapter.

MARY

With regard to all of the post-mortal press the Virgin Mary has received in the last two thousand years, one Calvinist-Anglican scholar posed the following question: "If in heaven with Jesus we are privileged to meet Mary and ask her what she thinks of all of this, what will she say?"[1] Catholics and Mormons would probably have different responses to this query. Nevertheless, Mary is a significant figure in both faiths because of her central role in the nativity story and in the life of our mutual Savior, the Lord Jesus Christ. With all that circulates and is sensationalized in the media, Latter-day Saints may be surprised to learn the Roman Catholic Church's official position on Mary.

CATHOLICS

Mary is a polarizing figure in Catholicism, and while she plays a very important role in their theology, not all Catholics are in agreement as to what that role is.

Certainly Mary is preeminent among saints.[2] Devotion to her in Catholicism is traditionally stronger than devotion to any other being, save the Trinity. However, some Catholics struggle to keep their devotion to her in proper perspective. One Catholic author wrote, "Catholics themselves agree that devotion to Mary can sometimes be distorted

---

1   J. I. Packer, "Foreword," in Dwight Longenecker and David Gustafson, *Mary: A Catholic–Evangelical Debate* (Grand Rapids, Mich.: Brazos Press, 2003), 14.

2   *United States Catholic Catechism for Adults* (Washington, D.C.: United States Conference of Catholic Bishops, 2006), 143.

and excessive."[3] Another wrote, "Honoring Mary should occur within the bounds of a rightly ordered faith and thus not overshadow the one triune God."[4] While sometimes lay Catholics do place too much focus on Mary, it seems fair to say that the Roman Catholic Church does not encourage its members to worship the Virgin Mary, pray to her, or place her above the Trinity. Rather, Mary is seen as an example of what Christians are destined to become and how they should empty themselves of personal desires in deference to the will of the Father.[5] Mary's words to the angel Gabriel establish why she is the ultimate example of Christian submission: "Behold the handmaid of the Lord; be it unto me according to thy word" (Luke 1:38).

Catholics are sometimes criticized for their perception of Mary as functioning in a mediating role between men and God. It is not uncommon to hear Protestants cite 1 Timothy 2:5—"For there is one God, and one mediator between God and men, the man Christ Jesus"—as evidence that Catholics are wrong in their understanding of Mary's role of mediation. Some Catholics see this as potentially problematic, and suggest that the fact that Jesus is both "judge" and "advocate" explains why the seeming contradiction between scripture and theology exists. One Catholic author noted that perhaps the Church's emphasis on Christ's role as judge has caused the apparent need for "another advocate."[6] Those who see no contradiction highlight the Church's official position, which is that "Christ alone is the merciful Savior and one Mediator between God and human beings."[7] It seems fair to say that Catholic perceptions of Mary as occupying a role of mediation are harmonious with the general idea of saints within Roman Catholic tradition. Mary may be the highest and most revered of saints,[8] but her mediating role is in keeping with what all saints do. She does, however,

---

3   Longenecker and Gustafson, *Mary: A Catholic–Evangelical Debate*, 43.
4   Elizabeth A. Johnson, "Blessed Virgin Mary," in *Harper Collins Encyclopedia of Catholicism,* ed. Richard P. McBrien (San Francisco, Calif.: HarperSanFrancisco, 1995), 837.
5   See Johnson, "Blessed Virgin Mary," in *Harper Collins Encyclopedia of Catholicism*, 836; Peter J. Kreeft, *Catholic Christianity: A Complete Catechism of Catholic Beliefs based on the Catechism of the Catholic Church* (San Francisco, Calif.: Ignatius Press, 2001), 404.
6   See Longenecker and Gustafson, *Mary: A Catholic–Evangelical Debate*, 204.
7   Johnson, "Blessed Virgin Mary," in *Harper Collins Encyclopedia of Catholicism*, 837.
8   *United States Catholic Catechism for Adults*, 143.

seem to exercise a bit more clout with the heavenly hierarchy in light of her role as the mother of Jesus.

Perhaps the most controversial aspect of "Mariology" has to do with discussions of her role as "co-redemptrix." Over the years, literally millions of requests have been sent to Rome by faithful Catholics pleading with the Pope to declare Mary to be "co-redemptrix" with Christ.[9] Pope John Paul II publicly used the title "co-redemptrix" in reference to Mary no less than six times during his pontificate.[10] There is some question among Catholics as to what exactly it would mean for Mary to be "co-redemptrix" with Jesus. Some say it does *not* mean she is equal with Christ, *only* that she cooperates with Him in our redemption.[11] Others see the title as implying just the opposite.[12] In what ways is Mary seen as co-redemptrix? First and foremost, it is because of her role in the incarnation. She cooperated with God, and thereby gave birth to Jesus. Had she not done so, Jesus would not have been born, and thus you and I would not be saved.[13] As one source states, "Inasmuch as Jesus came into the world through Mary we have to admit that the grace of Jesus

STATUES OF THE VIRGIN MARY, SUCH AS THIS ONE ATOP A CATHEDRAL IN CROATIA, ARE COMMONPLACE IN AND ON CATHOLIC CHURCHES, CATHEDRALS, AND SCHOOLS.

---

9   See Andrew Murr, Christopher Dickey, Eric Larson, Sarah Van Boven, and Hersch Doby, "Hail, Mary," in *Newsweek*, August 25, 1997, 49; and Sean Horrigan, "Mary, Co-Redemptrix?" in *Dallas Morning News*, August 16, 1997, G1, G4.

10   Horrigan, "Mary, Co-Redemptrix?" G4; See also Murr, Dickey, Larson, Van Boven, and Doby, "Hail, Mary," 54.

11   See Longenecker and Gustafson, *Mary: A Catholic–Evangelical Debate*, 194; Horrigan, "Mary, Co-Redemptrix?" G4; and *United States Catholic Catechism for Adults*, 143–47.

12   See, for example, comments in Longenecker and Gustafson, *Mary: A Catholic–Evangelical Debate*, 199200.

13   Longenecker and Gustafson, *Mary: A Catholic–Evangelical Debate*, 195; and Horrigan, "Mary, Co-Redemptrix?" G4.

Christ came through Mary. . . . She is not the source of that grace. She is merely a vehicle for it."[14] Additionally, Luke 2:35 speaks of Mary sharing in Jesus' suffering; specifically that she, with Him, would suffer during His passion.[15] Thus, this adds to her qualifications as "coredemptrix." In the end, Catholics see Mary as functioning as a sort of "Savior on Mount Zion" (see Obadiah 1:21), as do all of us. And in that sense, she can be seen as the "co-redemptrix" with Christ, just as you and I can.[16] However, as controversial as this has been—inside and outside of the Catholic Church—one author made this important clarification:

> Mary's role as Co-Redeemer and Mediatrix of grace is not formally defined dogma of the Catholic Church. It remains a pious opinion. . . . It is controversial even among Catholics. There are some ardent devotees of Mary who want the Church to define this role for Mary as a "final Marian dogma." . . . There are other Catholics who see the difficulties this would cause ecumenically. They think Mary has been honored enough.[17]

From an ecumenical position, the dogma of co-redemptrix is a public affairs nightmare. It has a great deal of potential to give non-Catholics the wrong impression with regard to Christ's unique role in mankind's salvation.[18] Perhaps this explains why the Vatican-appointed commission assigned to study the question as to whether Mary should officially be declared "co-redemptrix" strongly (twenty-three votes to zero) advised that the Church *not* pronounce this as official dogma.[19] Regardless of how Catholics feel about the subject, the Church would likely experience quite a backlash if they accepted the teaching as official.

---

14   Longenecker and Gustafson, *Mary: A Catholic–Evangelical Debate*, 200–201.

15   Longenecker and Gustafson, *Mary: A Catholic–Evangelical Debate*, 144.

16   See Horrigan, "Mary, Co-Redemptrix?" G4.

17   Longenecker and Gustafson, *Mary: A Catholic–Evangelical Debate*, 190–91. See also Murr, Dickey, Larson, Van Boven, and Doby, "Hail, Mary," 52; Horrigan, "Mary, Co-Redemptrix?" G1.

18   Johnson, "Blessed Virgin Mary," in *Harper Collins Encyclopedia of Catholicism*, 837.

19   Murr, Dickey, Larson, Van Boven, and Doby, "Hail, Mary," 49. See also Horrigan, "Mary, Co-Redemptrix?" G4.

Setting the issue of "co-redemptrix" aside, the Catholic Church has declared four other ideas about Mary as official doctrine.[20] It is official teaching that she (1) was a perpetual virgin, before, during, and after the birth of Jesus; (2) she is the "mother of God" or Theotokos; (3) she was born through what is known as the "immaculate conception"—meaning that Mary was conceived without original sin; and (4) her body and spirit were assumed (or taken up) into heaven at the end of her life.[21]

LATTER-DAY SAINTS

While in Latter-day Saint circles Mary is not looked upon with quite the awe and devotion as she is in Catholicism, her preeminence is acknowledged. Elder Bruce R. McConkie taught, "The greatest of all female spirits was the one . . . chosen and foreordained to be 'the mother of the Son of God, after the manner of the flesh.'"[22] On another occasion Elder McConkie noted the following:

> Can we speak too highly of her whom the Lord has blessed above all women? There was only one Christ, and there is only one Mary. Each was noble and great in the pre-existence, and each was foreordained to the ministry he or she performed. We cannot but think that the Father would choose the greatest female spirit to be the mother of his Son, even as he chose the male spirit like unto him to be the Savior.[23]

---

20   See *United States Catholic Catechism for Adults*, 143–46; Johnson, "Blessed Virgin Mary," in *Harper Collins Encyclopedia of Catholicism*, 836; Horrigan, "Mary, Co-Redemptrix?" G1; and Peter J. Kreeft, *Catholic Christianity: A Complete Catechism of Catholic Beliefs based on the Catechism of the Catholic Church* (San Francisco, Calif.: Ignatius Press, 2001), 404–21.

21   Catholics do not all agree as to whether Mary actually died and then was instantly taken up, or was taken up in a state akin to a translated being (in LDS theology). The *United States Catholic Catechism for Adults* suggests that she was instantly resurrected upon her death. However, not all Catholics would see it this way. *United States Catholic Catechism for Adults*, 144. See Elizabeth A. Johnson, "Assumption of the Blessed Virgin Mary," in *Harper Collins Encyclopedia of Catholicism*, 104.

22   Bruce R. McConkie, "Eve and the Fall," in *Woman* (Salt Lake City: Deseret Book, 1979), 59. Elsewhere he wrote, "Mary and Eve were two of the greatest of all the spirit daughters of the Father." Bruce R. McConkie, *The Mortal Messiah*, 4 vols. (Salt Lake City: Deseret Book, 1980–81), 1:23.

23   McConkie, *Mortal Messiah*, 1:326–27 n. 4. See also Robert L. Millet, "The Birth and Childhood of the Messiah," in Kent P. Jackson and Robert L. Millet, eds., *Studies in*

Another LDS author penned this about LDS constructs of the Virgin Mary:

> In the councils of heaven . . . Mary stood prominent among all female spirits. . . . Her place in history was foreordained. She was the one the Father had chosen to nurture his only child to be born in the flesh. There was no greater honor that the Father of us all could bestow upon any woman. . . . Of those born in the flesh there is no woman whom the Saints hold in greater esteem than Mary.[24]

Clearly, like Catholics, Mormons hold Mary, the mother of Jesus, in the highest regard and believe her to have been the greatest of all female spirits; one called, sustained, and foreordained to give birth to the Son of God, the Messiah, the Savior of "worlds without end" (Moses 1:33–35).

SUMMARY

Latter-day Saints and Catholics agree on Mary's greatness and chosen status. Both faiths would agree with Alma's description of her as "a virgin, a precious and chosen vessel, who shall be overshadowed and conceive by the power of the Holy Ghost, and bring forth a son, yea, even the Son of God" (Alma 7:10). Both would likely agree that, as a "savior on mount Zion" (see Obadiah 1:21), she assisted others in coming unto Christ and laying hold upon salvation—as each of us are commanded to do.

However, of the four officially declared Catholic dogmas about Mary, Latter-day Saints would only agree with one. We reject the "perpetual virginity of Mary" after Jesus' birth. We are inclined to be uncomfortable calling her the "mother of God" or Theotokos (meaning "God-bearer"), since, for Catholics, this title implies that she is the mother of the divine and mortal part of Jesus.[25] Latter-day Saints

---

Scripture, 5 vols. (Salt Lake City: Deseret Book, 1986), 5:142.

24   Joseph Fielding McConkie, *Witness of the Birth of Christ* (Salt Lake City: Bookcraft, 1998), 61–62.

25   The Council of Ephesus (AD 431) taught that Jesus was one divine person with one nature, rather than one human nature and one divine nature. Thus, Mary was the "Mother of God" in that she was not only the mother of his human side, but also of His divine side. See "Theotokos," in *Harper Collins Encyclopedia of Catholicism*, 1251; and "Mother of God," in *Harper Collins Encyclopedia of Catholicism*, 895.

see God the Father as the origin of Jesus' divine nature, and Mary as the origin of Jesus' human or mortal nature.[26] We see no evidence to support the belief that Mary was "assumed into heaven" at the end of her life. In other words, in LDS thinking, Mary was not (so far as we know) translated. Thus, beyond the virgin birth, our one point of agreement on doctrines surrounding Mary would have to do with her birth. While we do not use the term "immaculate conception" in reference to her birth, we would agree that she was born without the taint of original sin, meaning she did not inherit an accountability for Adam's sinful acts or a yearning for self-gratification that turned her away from God.[27] Of course, Mormons would argue that *everyone* is born without original sin (see Article of Faith 2) not just Mary. Thus, even in this aspect of "Mariology," we have different reasons than Catholics for our beliefs.

---

26   This is a rather complex Christological issue. We are intentionally speaking here in very simple and broad terms, primarily for the sake of brevity.

27   See Thomas A. Smith, "Original Sin," in *Harper Collins Encyclopedia of Catholicism*, 943. Note that even significant figures in Catholic thought have struggled with the implications of the dogma of the immaculate conception. Origin (AD 185–254) had issues with the teaching because it would imply that Mary did not need Jesus to die for her sins (as she was sinless), which contradicts Romans 3:23, which reads, "For all have sinned, and come short of the glory of God." Likewise, Thomas Aquinas indicated that, had Mary been sinless, she would not have needed redemption from He who "is the Saviour of *all* men" (1 Timothy 4:10; emphasis added). See Longenecker and Gustafson, *Mary: A Catholic–Evangelical Debate*, 108, 130.

ORIGINAL SIN

Franz Lebowits, the American humorist and author, is purported to have quipped, "Original thought is like original sin: both happened before you were born to people you could not have possibly met." I suppose this well encapsulates the paradox of original sin—a paradox acknowledged by Catholics and Mormons alike. We each acknowledge we're fallen. Both faiths attest to the fact that that fall came through the choice of Adam, yet the nature of the influence of that fall on human-kind is not universally understood.

CATHOLICS

A standard, universally accepted definition of "original sin" is im-possible to arrive at. Not all Catholics interpret the meaning of the term the same way, in part because there has been an evolution in thinking on this subject during the last two millennia.

First of all, in Catholicism the term is used both in reference to Adam's initial transgression and in the more general sense of the uni-versal human condition of sinfulness.[1] Augustine argued that Adam's sin is passed on to every human being through the lust involved in acts of procreation. He believed that, at birth, each of us inherits both the guilt and also the penalties for Adam's Edenic sin and that this mani-

---

[1] See Thomas A. Smith, "Original Sin," in *Harper Collins Encyclopedia of Catholicism*, ed. Richard P. McBrien (San Francisco, Calif.: HarperSanFrancisco, 1995), 943; and Bob O'Gorman and Mary Faulkner, *The Complete Idiot's Guide to Understanding Catholi-cism*, 2d ed. (Indianapolis, Ind.: Alpha Books, 2003), 260.

WHILE NOT ALL CATHOLICS DEFINE "ORIGINAL SIN" THE SAME, MOST ASSOCIATE IT WITH ADAM AND EVE'S CHOICE TO PARTAKE OF THE "FORBIDDEN FRUIT" BECAUSE OF THE ENTICEMENTS OF THE "SERPENT" OR SATAN.

fests itself as a yearning for self-gratification.[2] During the Middle Ages, however, views of original sin emphasized humanity's lack of sanctifying grace rather than mankind's yearning for self-gratification.[3] In other words, theologians of that era believed less that we inherited a corrupt nature from Adam and more that we acquired a strained relationship with God from him.[4] Thomas Aquinas, on the other hand, held that original sin made us weak and disordered as humans but that baptism would take away that sinful or weakened state. However, both the yearning for self-gratification and the reality of eventual death remained as consequences of Adam's choice in Eden. Thus, according to Aquinas, while the sin is removed at baptism, the consequences remain.[5]

Today many Catholic theologians define original sin less in Augustinian terms and more along the lines of the universal situation—all of us are born into a world filled with sin, temptations and evil desires. Thus, the original sin of Adam and Eve has created for us an earthly inheritance that is tragically flawed.[6] As one Catholic text states, "The ultimate human dilemma is to exist in the midst of a sinful world, yet strive for goodness. Part of the struggle is to overcome a lower nature that sometimes wants to pull us off

---

2   See Smith, "Original Sin," in *Harper Collins Encyclopedia of Catholicism*, 943.

3   See Smith, "Original Sin," in *Harper Collins Encyclopedia of Catholicism*, 943.

4   See O'Gorman and Faulkner, *Complete Idiot's Guide to Understanding Catholicism*, 260.

5   See Smith, "Original Sin," in *Harper Collins Encyclopedia of Catholicism*, 943; O'Gorman and Faulkner, *Complete Idiot's Guide to Understanding Catholicism*, 260.

6   See Smith, "Original Sin," in *Harper Collins Encyclopedia of Catholicism*, 943–44.

course."[7] This "ultimate human dilemma" is a popular contemporary approach to the doctrine of original sin.

LATTER-DAY SAINTS

Latter-day Saints tend to recoil at the phrase "original sin," in part because our perceptions of what the term means for contemporary Catholics is not always accurate[8] and in part because the Book of Mormon seems to condemn the dogma.

> For, if I have learned the truth, there have been disputations among you concerning the baptism of your little children. . . . Listen to the words of Christ, your Redeemer, your Lord and your God. Behold, I came into the world not to call the righteous but sinners to repentance; the whole need no physician, but they that are sick; wherefore, little children are whole, for they are not capable of committing sin; wherefore the curse of Adam is taken from them in me, that it hath no power over them. . . . And after this manner did the Holy Ghost manifest the word of God unto me; wherefore, my beloved son, I know that it is solemn mockery before God, that ye should baptize little children. Behold . . . teach . . . repentance and baptism unto those who are accountable and capable of committing sin; yea, teach parents that they must repent and be baptized, and humble themselves as their little children, and they shall all be saved with their little children. And their little children need no repentance, neither baptism. Behold, baptism is unto repentance to the fulfilling the commandments unto the remission of sins. But little children are alive in Christ, even from the foundation of the world; if not so, God is a partial God, and . . . a respecter to persons; for how many little children have died without baptism! Wherefore, if little children could not be saved without baptism, these must have gone to an endless hell. Behold . . . he that supposeth that little children need baptism . . . hath neither faith, hope, nor charity; wherefore, should he be cut off while in the thought, he must go down to hell (Moroni 8:5 and 8–14).

---

7   O'Gorman and Faulkner, *Complete Idiot's Guide to Understanding Catholicism*, 261.

8   See, for example, Joseph Fielding Smith, *Doctrines of Salvation*, 3 vols. (Salt Lake City: Bookcraft, 1998), 2:49–51 and 3:284; and Larry E. Dahl and Donald Q.Cannon, eds., *Encyclopedia of Joseph Smith's Teachings* (Salt Lake City: Bookcraft, 1997), 114.

While there is no question that this passage condemns the rite of infant baptism, and, by implication, an Augustinian view of original sin, few Catholics today assume that (1) children are sinful, (2) children who die unbaptized go to hell, and (3) infants are held accountable prior to their ability to make informed choices.[9] Thus, this passage clearly condemns an Augustinian view of original sin in children, but it is less germane to current Catholic views of original sin.

As implied above, Latter-day Saints generally avoid the use of the term "original sin," except in a pejorative sense. However, the term has been used many times by presidents of the Church in reference to the Fall and Adam's original transgression. Jesus came to rescue us from "original sin," meaning the conditions caused by Adam's Fall.[10] Mormons see the consequences of Adam's choice (sickness, disease, a veil of forgetting, temptation, physical death, temporary separation from God, etc.) as affecting everyone—they do not go away simply by repenting[11]—however, we are not held accountable for the "sin" or transgression of Adam (see Article of Faith 2). With that being said, we do commit personal sins, perhaps, in part, because of the fallen world we have "inherited" from Adam and Eve. These we must repent of. But these are *our* fault. They represent *our* choices. Adam is no more responsible for these personal choices than you and I are for his. Mormons would likely see their view of original sin as being tied to this declaration:

> For the natural man is an enemy to God, and has been from the fall of Adam, and will be, forever and ever, unless he yields to the enticings of the Holy Spirit, and putteth off the natural man and becometh a saint through the atonement of Christ the Lord, and becometh as a child, submissive, meek, humble, patient, full of love, willing to submit to all things which the Lord seeth fit to inflict upon him, even as a child doth submit to his father (Mosiah 3:19).

---

9   See our discussion of limbo and the salvation of little children in chapter eight above.
10   See, for example, John A. Widtsoe, comp., *Discourses of Brigham Young* (Salt Lake City: Bookcraft, 1998), 21, 27, and 153; Smith, *Doctrines of Salvation*, 1:105, 126; and G. Homer Durham, ed., *Discourses of Wilford Woodruff,* (Salt Lake City: Bookcraft, 1998), 3.
11   See Widtsoe, *Discourses of Brigham Young*, 153.

Summary

Contemporary Catholic and LDS beliefs on the subject of "original sin" are basically the same. Both faiths hold that we have inherited a fallen world filled with temptations and sin from Adam and Eve. Both traditions see mankind as estranged from God by virtue of the Fall. While a small percentage of Catholics still hold that at birth children inherit some part of Adam's sin—an idea Latter-day Saints would reject—the frank reality is that most Catholics do not believe this. Like Mormons, the average Roman Catholic sees "original sin" as being not about the sinfulness of babies, but rather about the common lot of humankind—we dwell in a fallen world and are fallen human beings who all too frequently make sinful choices. This condition has come to us all through the Fall of Adam and Eve.

THE CROSS

One text on symbolism rightly notes that "in religion and art, the cross is the richest and most enduring of geometric symbols."[1] Regardless of one's denomination, it seems each and every Christian would be inclined to acknowledge the factual nature of this statement. Even those of non-Christian traditions recognize the cross and its inherent meaning. In Mormonism, as in Catholicism, the cross is an enduring symbol of the atoning sacrifice of the Lord Jesus Christ. No true Christian can look upon that symbol without being reminded of that greatest of all events—Jesus' act of redemption on behalf of all humankind.

CATHOLICS

Upon entering any Catholic Church one will see prominently displayed—usually over or on the altar but potentially in other parts of the Church—a crucifix, which is a cross with a sculpted figure of Christ on it.[2] Crosses also commonly adorn the steeples of the Church and the vestments of the priest who presides at the Mass. For Catholics, these serve as a poignant reminder of both "the act of redemption" performed by Christ on our behalf and of "the imitation of Christ," the daily taking up "their own crosses" (see Matthew 10:38; Mark 8:34;

---

1 Jack Tresidder, *Symbols and their Meanings* (London: Duncan Baird Publishers, 2000), 146.

2 The displaying of a crucifix on the altar or above the altar during the mass is said to be requisite.

and Luke 9:23 and 24:27), which all Catholics believe they are called to perform as committed Christians.[3] One Catholic author penned this:

> The crucifix . . . connects [Catholics] to the story of Jesus. . . . Catholics prefer the crucifix to the plain cross because of the emotions it evokes—it helps them feel more connected to Jesus as human. For many non-Catholics, the image of Jesus' crucified body seems harsh. But for Catholics, the image of Jesus on the cross makes the story of his life, death, and resurrection come alive.[4]

Beyond the practice of displaying crosses and crucifixes, it is common for Catholics, as an act of public or private devotion, to "cross" themselves, meaning to take the three middle fingers on the right hand and draw them up to touch the forehead, then down to touch the chest, and then over to touch the right and then left shoulders, thereby forming a cross on one's person. This is done as a reminder of the need of every Catholic to sanctify his or her daily life.

LATTER-DAY SAINTS

Latter-day Saints sometimes act as though they have an aversion to the cross. We certainly don't use it in our worship or architecture. We do not make the sign of the cross with our hands, and we do not display crucifixes in our buildings or homes.

It should not be misunderstood, however. The cross does have its place in Mormonism. It is heavily present in Latter-day Saint scripture. The Holy Bible, which we believe to be the word of God, time and again speaks of the "cross of Christ" and its saving influence upon repentant sinners (Romans 6:3–6; Galatians 2:20 and 6:14; Ephesians 2:14–16; Philippians 3:17–18; and Colossians 1:18–20 and 2:10–14). The LDS scriptural canon commands the followers of Christ to take up their personal crosses in the image and pattern of Christ's life (Matthew 10:38; Mark 8:34; and Luke 9:23 and 24:27). Even the Book of Mormon (1 Nephi 11:33; Jacob 1:8; Alma 21:9; Helaman 14:15; and 3

---

3   See "Cross," in *Harper Collins Encyclopedia of Catholicism*, ed. Richard P. McBrien (San Francisco, Calif.: HarperSanFrancisco, 1995), 381; and "Crucifix," in *Harper Collins Encyclopedia of Catholicism*, 382–83.

4   Bob O'Gorman and Mary Faulkner, *The Complete Idiot's Guide to Understanding Catholicism*, 2d ed. (Indianapolis, Ind.: Alpha Books, 2003), 117.

**"THE CRUCIFIXION," HARRY ANDERSON, GOSPEL ART PICTURE
KIT #230, © 2002 BY INTELLECTUAL RESERVE, INC.**

Nephi 27:13–14) and the Doctrine and Covenants (D&C 21:9; 35:2;
46:13–14; 53:2; and 138:35) use the image or symbol of the cross as a
reminder of what Jesus has done on our behalf.

The cross is also present in art utilized by The Church of Jesus
Christ of Latter-day Saints. While the crucifixion of Jesus is by no
means the most commonly depicted religious scene in LDS chapels,
the Church does utilize images of the crucified Savior in its curriculum
and teaching aids. For example, in the Church produced *Gospel Principles* manual, which is part of standard ward Sunday School curriculum.
the "visual aids" section of the book has a picture of the crucified Lord.[5]
In the 2003 *Teachings of the Presidents of the Church: David O. McKay*
manual there is a painting of Jesus showing His disciples the wounds in
His hands caused by His crucifixion.[6] In the "Gospel Art Picture Kit,"
which appears on the Church's website and in Church meetinghouse
libraries, picture #230 is "The Crucifixion" by Seventh-day Adventist
Harry Anderson.

5   See "Visual Aids—Support Materials" in *Gospel Principles* [Sunday School teacher's
     manual] (Salt Lake City: The Church of Jesus Christ of Latter-day Saints, 1992), 8.
6   See *Teachings of the Presidents of the Church: David O. McKay* [Melchizedek Priesthood
     and Relief Society course of study] (Salt Lake City: The Church of Jesus Christ of
     Latter-day Saints, 2003), 60.

Significantly, the one ordinance Mormons call their "sacrament" is a commemoration of the crucifixion of Christ. Likewise, the Apostle Paul informs us, "Know ye not, that so many of us as were baptized into Jesus Christ were baptized into his death?" (Romans 6:3; see also D&C 76:51). Latter-day Saints do acknowledge and symbolically represent the crucifixion. We simply do it in a different way than some of our brothers and sisters from other Christian traditions.

There may be a number of reasons why this seeming discomfort with images of the crucifixion and the cross exist. One LDS scholar noted of early Mormonism:

> Crosses were seldom if ever placed on our meetinghouses. Inasmuch as many of our early converts came from a Puritan background, they, like the Puritans, were essentially anti-ceremonial, including the non-use of crosses. For that matter, early Baptists did not have crosses on their Churches for a long time, at least until they began to move into mainstream Protestantism.[7]

Thus, just as our worship services reflect the largely protestant milieu in which Mormonism "grew up," so also our disuse of the cross may be explained as stemming from this same cultural trend.

An additional reason, more commonly cited by Latter-day Saints, is the fact that we tend to stress Jesus' triumph over sin and death. One LDS scholar wrote:

> Latter-day Saints . . . like the earliest Christians, are reluctant to display the cross because they view the "good news" of the gospel as Christ's resurrection more than his crucifixion. . . . The LDS conception of the Plan of Salvation is comprehensive. It encompasses a Council in Heaven; Jehovah's (Jesus') acceptance of his role as Savior; the virgin birth; Jesus' life and ministry; his saving suffering, beginning in Gethsemane and ending with his death at Golgotha; his burial; his preaching to the spirits of the righteous dead; his physical resurrection; and his exaltation to the right hand of the Father. No one symbol is sufficient to convey all this.

---

7   Robert L. Millet, "Where Did the Cross Go?" (presentation to the BYU religious education faculty, Brigham Young University, Provo, Utah, September 16, 2005), 13. Copy in the author's possession.

Moreover, the cross, with its focus on the death of Christ, does not symbolize the message of a living, risen, exalted Lord who changes the lives of his followers.[8]

Thus, for Latter-day Saints the cross is a Christian symbol, but a symbol of only one aspect of Christ's glorious life and ministry. For Mormons, the cross tends to remind them of that brief window of time when Jesus subjected Himself to the awful consequences of Satan's power over humankind. Latter-day Saints prefer to think of Jesus in terms of having overcome that, rather than suffering because of it.[9]

---

8   Roger R. Keller, "Cross," in *Encyclopedia of Mormonism,* ed. Daniel H. Ludlow, 4 vols. (New York: Macmillan, 1992), 1:344–45.

9   President Gordon B. Hinckley stated:

> Following the renovation of the Mesa Arizona Temple some years ago, clergy of other religions were invited to tour it on the first day of the open house period. Hundreds responded. In speaking to them, I said we would be pleased to answer any queries they might have. Among these was one from a Protestant minister. Said he: "I've been all through this building, this temple which carries on its face the name of Jesus Christ, but nowhere have I seen any representation of the cross, the symbol of Christianity. I have noted your buildings elsewhere and likewise find an absence of the cross. Why is this when you say you believe in Jesus Christ?" I responded: "I do not wish to give offense to any of my Christian colleagues who use the cross on the steeples of their cathedrals and at the altars of their chapels, who wear it on their vestments, and imprint it on their books and other literature. But for us, the cross is the symbol of the dying Christ, while our message is a declaration of the Living Christ." He then asked: "If you do not use the cross, what is the symbol of your religion?" I replied that the lives of our people must become the most meaningful expression of our faith and, in fact, therefore, the symbol of our worship. I hope he did not feel that I was smug or self-righteous in my response. . . . Well might many ask, as my minister friend in Arizona asked, if you profess a belief in Jesus Christ, why do you not use the symbol of His death, the cross of Calvary? . . . This was the cross, the instrument of His torture, the terrible device designed to destroy the Man of Peace, the evil recompense for His miraculous work of healing the sick, of causing the blind to see, of raising the dead. . . . Because our Savior lives, we do not use the symbol of His death as the symbol of our faith. But what shall we use? No sign, no work of art, no representation of form is adequate to express the glory and the wonder of the Living Christ. He told us what that symbol should be when He said, "If ye love me, keep my commandments" (John 14:15). As His followers, we cannot do a mean or shoddy or ungracious thing without tarnishing His image. Nor can we do a good and gracious and generous act without burnishing more brightly

Finally, one text argues that the cross as a religious symbol was adopted by Christianity from Paganism, and thus it should not be used by Latter-day Saints simply because of its non-Christian origins.[10] True, the use of physical crosses or crucifixes as symbols of Jesus was not a practice of the New Testament Christians. Even the portrayal of Jesus on the cross in religious art was avoided in the first centuries of Christianity.[11] Indeed, the first known use of an image of the crucified Christ was in Rome around the fifth century.[12] The custom of using crosses and crucifixes developed much later. It wasn't until the fourth century that crosses became venerated symbols in the Church,[13] it wasn't until the sixth century that crosses began to appear on Church steeples,[14] and it wasn't until the Middle Ages that crucifixes became common within the Catholic Church.[15] Thus, as Latter-day Saints so often argue, if a practice is a post-New Testament development that has not found support in modern scripture, we tend to avoid it.

SUMMARY

While Catholics use crosses and crucifixes and make the sign of the cross, Mormons do not, but we are, nevertheless, united in what the cross means to both of our faiths. Like Catholics, when Latter-day Saints see a religiously employed cross, we think of Jesus Christ and His infinite and eternal sacrifice on behalf of all of humankind. To the parishioners of both faiths, it is a symbol of the central figure of Chris-

---

the symbol of Him whose name we have taken upon ourselves. And so our lives must become a meaningful expression, the symbol of our declaration of our testimony of the Living Christ, the Eternal Son of the Living God. (Gordon B. Hinckley, "The Symbol of Our Faith," *Ensign* [April 2005]: 3,4, 6)

10   See Darrick T. Evenson, *The Gainsayers* (Bountiful, Utah: Horizon Publishers, 1989), 163–66.

11   See "Crucifix," in *Harper Collins Encyclopedia of Catholicism*, 383.

12   See Diane Apostolos-Cappadona, "Symbols," in *Encyclopedia of Christianity*, ed. John Bowden (New York: Oxford University Press, 2005), 1167.

13   See Joanne M. Pierce, "Vestments and Objects," in Geoffrey Wainwright and Karen B. Westerfield Tucker, eds., *The Oxford History of Christian Worship* (Oxford: Oxford University Press, 2006), 854.

14   See Millet, "Where Did the Cross Go?" 10.

15   See Apostolos-Cappanona, "Symbols," in *Encyclopedia of Christianity*, 1167; Pierce, "Vestments and Objects," in *Oxford History of Christian Worship*, 854.

tianity, Jesus of Nazareth. On this we are united. From an LDS author we find this:

> The word *cross* in reference to the crucifixion of Jesus comes to mean more than simply the mode of torture and execution invented by the Persians and perfected by the Romans. It was a sign, a token of the Atonement. To say that one believed in and taught the cross was to say that one accepted the reality of the lowly Nazarene's suffering and death as having divine redemptive power.[16]

It seems important to note that even though Latter-day Saints may not use crosses, we do have our own religious symbols. Robert L. Millet noted:

> We have no quarrel with those who speak reverently of the cross, for so did those whose writings compose a significant portion of the New Testament and those who spoke or wrote what is contained in our own scriptural records. The cross is a symbol. We are not opposed to symbols, for our people erect statues of the angel Moroni atop our most sacred edifices and wear CTR rings on their hand. . . . The key is not to become obsessed with the symbol, but to allow the symbol to point beyond itself toward that which is of deepest significance. Thus we do not worship Moroni; we look upon those statues and are reminded that through the instrumentality of Moroni and a whole host of divine messengers the everlasting gospel of Jesus Christ has been restored to the earth (Revelation 14:6–7). When we see a CTR ring, we are reminded that the followers of the Good Shepherd must do more than talk the talk; they must walk the walk, must conform their lives to the pattern He has shown and live a life befitting a true disciple.[17]

Thus, like Catholics, we use symbols in our daily expressions of faith that would have been foreign to New Testament Christians.

As to making the sign of the cross, again, Mormons do not. However, we do make physical gestures in our temples that are Christocen-

---

16   Millet, "Where Did the Cross Go?" 6.

17   Millet, "Where Did the Cross Go?" 13. "CTR" stands for "choose the right," and jewelry adorned with those letters is commonly worn by Latter-day Saints.

tric in nature and that carry basically the same meaning as the cross in that, among other things, they are designed to remind those who make them of the atoning sacrifice of the Lord Jesus Christ on their behalf.[18]

Mormons and Catholics really don't disagree on the issue of the cross. As noted above, we all see it as symbolizing the same thing. Catholics employ it; Latter-day Saints employ other symbols. Neither hold that Jesus or the early Christians would have used this symbol, but in the end, we all think of the same thing when we see it.

---

18   Todd Compton, "Symbolism," in *Encyclopedia of Mormonism,* 3:1430; Heber C. Kimball, in *Journal of Discourses,* 26 vols. (Liverpool: F. D. Richards, 1855–86), 10:44; David B. Haight, *A Light unto the World* (Salt Lake City: Deseret Book, 1997), 56–57; and David E. Sorensen, "Small Temples—Large Blessings," *Ensign* (November 1998): 65.

CREEDS

Our English word "creed" comes from the Latin *credo*, which means literally "I believe." Thus, creeds are formal statements defining what a given group or individual believes. Perhaps the most widely used summarization of Christian doctrine in the world is the fourth century Nicene Creed. It states:

> We believe in one God the Father Almighty, Maker of heaven and earth, and of all things visible and invisible. And in one Lord Jesus Christ, the only-begotten Son of God, begotten of the Father before all worlds, God of God, Light of Light, Very God of Very God, begotten, not made, being of one substance with the Father by whom all things were made; who for us men, and for our salvation, came down from heaven, and was incarnate by the Holy Spirit of the Virgin Mary, and was made man, and was crucified also for us under Pontius Pilate. He suffered and was buried, and the third day he rose again according to the Scriptures, and ascended into heaven, and sitteth on the right hand of the Father. And he shall come again with glory to judge both the quick and the dead, whose kingdom shall have no end. And we believe in the Holy Spirit, the Lord and Giver of Life, who proceedeth from the Father and the Son, who with the Father and the Son together is worshipped and glorified, who spoke by the prophets. And we believe one holy catholic and apostolic Church. We acknowledge one baptism for

the remission of sins. And we look for the resurrection of the dead, and the life of the world to come. Amen.

Catholics, Eastern Orthodox, and many Protestants use this creed, or a variation of it,[1] in their worship services or as part of their basic theology.

CATHOLICS

In Catholicism, the Nicene Creed is recited as part of every Mass. After the priest delivers his homily, and the congregation has been given a few moments to reflect on it, all rise to recite the Creed in unison.

From a Catholic perspective, the creed simply clarifies what Catholics unitedly and officially believe. The *Encyclopedia of Catholicism* notes that most religions of the world have creeds, or formal statements of faith, that they recite: Jews, Muslims, Hindus, Buddhists, and others declare their faith through the use of creeds.[2]

LATTER-DAY SAINTS

Most Latter-day Saints will be familiar with Joseph Smith's declaration that, during the First Vision, the Father told him that "all [the] creeds [of Joseph's contemporaries] were an abomination" in His sight (JS—H 1:19). Joseph also once noted, "I cannot believe in any of the creeds of the different denominations, because they all have some things in them I cannot subscribe to, though all of them have some truth. I want to come up into the presence of God, and learn all things; but the creeds set up stakes, and say, 'Hitherto shalt thou come, and no further'; which I cannot subscribe to."[3]

---

1   Variations of the "Nicene Creed" (AD 325) include the "Apostles Creed" (AD 390), the "Nicene-Constantinopolitan Creed" (a modified version of the Nicene Creed affirmed in AD 381), the "Athanasian Creed" (formulated between AD 381 and AD 451), and the "Creed of the Third Council of Constantinople" (AD 680–681). The "Old Roman Creed" (circa. AD 150), a short statement about belief in the Godhead, predates the Nicene Creed, and is sizably less developed than the Nicene or post-Nicene creeds.

2   See Robert A. Krieg, "Creeds," in *Harper Collins Encyclopedia of Catholicism,* ed. Richard P. McBrien (San Francisco, Calif.: HarperSanFrancisco, 1995), 378.

3   Joseph Fielding Smith, comp., *Teachings of the Prophet Joseph Smith,* (Salt Lake City: Deseret Book, 1976), 327.

There is a general feel among Latter-day Saints, perhaps because of these statements by the Prophet Joseph, that we do not believe in or use creeds. Indeed, one LDS author wrote, "The Church of Jesus Christ of Latter-day Saints has no creed, as that term is understood in traditional theology."[4] If the "traditional" understanding of a creed is, as the *Encyclopedia of Catholicism* states, a "concise, authorized [statement] of the essential tenets of religious belief that a believing community employs primarily in its worship and initiation rites,"[5] then we most certainly do have and use LDS creeds. We have our thirteen articles of faith, which we regularly recite, not only in answers to questions about our beliefs (as in the Wentworth letter),[6] but also as a sort of "rite of passage" from Primary into the Young Men and Young Women organizations of the Church. Each week the young women of the Church stand and recite the following statement:

> We are daughters of our Heavenly Father, who loves us, and we love Him. We will "stand as witnesses of God at all times and in all things, and in all places" as we strive to live the Young Women values, which are: Faith, Divine Nature, Individual Worth, Knowledge, Choice and Accountability, Good Works, and Integrity. We believe as we come to accept and act upon these values, we will be prepared to strengthen home and family, make and keep sacred covenants, receive the ordinances of the temple, and enjoy the blessings of exaltation.

This is as creedal as one could hope for, and it is even recited while standing at each Sunday gathering of the young women of the Church. Those who have served missions for the Church within the last few decades will likely remember standing and quoting Doctrine and Covenants section 4 as a sort of "creed of missionaries." Such a practice is common in the missions of the world.

---

4   Gary P. Gillum, "Creeds," in *Encyclopedia of Mormonism*, ed. Daniel H. Ludlow, 4 vols. (New York: Macmillan, 1992), 1:343.

5   Krieg, "Creeds," in *Harper Collins Encyclopedia of Catholicism*, 378.

6   Joseph penned the Articles of Faith in a March 1842 letter addressed to John Wentworth, the editor and proprietor of the *Chicago Democrat*. Written at Wenworth's request, the "Wentworth Letter" was Joseph's effort to explain in a systematic way what the Church believed on a variety of significant theological topics. Thus, this was a creedal statement.

SUMMARY

Contrary to popular belief, like Catholics, Latter-day Saints do have creedal statements that we use in our worship, in some rites of passage, and as clarifying declarations as to what we believe. In both Catholic and LDS practice, these can clarify to those outside of our faith what we believe, but they are more often used to remind those within our respective faiths what we profess and believe.

Other than in their doctrinal content and in the fact that Mormons prefer to not use the word "creed," are there any differences between Catholic and LDS creeds? Not particularly. Some LDS authors have tried to argue that creeds are limiting, but LDS declarations of belief are not.[7] In support of their argument, they cite Joseph's statement that "creeds set up stakes, and say, 'Hitherto shalt thou come, and no further'; which I cannot subscribe to."[8] While Joseph is correct that any creed *can* "set up stakes" or boundaries if one is not susceptible to change and revelation, to be fair, one must acknowledge that the Catholic Church has changed its creed numerous times as their understanding of certain doctrinal points have changed.[9] The Nicene Creed, penned in AD 325, was modified in AD 381, again in AD 390, again sometime around AD 451, and again in AD 680–681. The Catholic Church has not been limited by its creeds anymore than Mormons have been limited by their articles of faith, which, incidentally, not only focus on a select number of doctrines, but have also been changed a number of times in our history.[10]

---

7   See Gillum, "Creeds," in *Encyclopedia of Mormonism*, 1:343.

8   Smith, *Teachings of the Prophet Joseph Smith*, 327.

9   It seems fair to say that Joseph's concern was less about creeds, and more about creeds filled with falsehoods. Creeds that teach false doctrine harm adherents. However, having a creed is not innately problematic. It is the content of the creed that Joseph worried about. See Hoyt W. Brewster, Jr., "What was in the creeds of men that the Lord found abominable, as he stated in the First Vision?" in *A Sure Foundation: Answers to Difficult Gospel Questions* (Salt Lake City: Deseret Book, 1988), 210–14.

10   A few years after the publication of the "Wentworth Letter's" thirteen Articles of Faith, other similar lists or "articles" were issued and used by the Church. An 1834 version had only eight articles. An 1836 version had only five articles. An 1840 version had eighteen articles, while another 1840 version had nineteen. An 1842 version had sixteen articles. A version published in about 1845 had fifteen articles. An 1849 version had fourteen articles. Thus, clearly our "creeds" have themselves evolved over time. See David J. Whittaker, "Articles of Faith," in *Encyclopedia of Mormonism*, 1:67–69.

The doctrinal content in our creeds or articles is usually different, although not on all points, but on the general concept of what a creed is and how it is to be used, Catholics and Mormons are very close in their views.

LITURGY AND RITUAL

One thing almost always present in the various religious traditions of the world is ritual. The singing of a hymn; kneeling at a certain time, or at a certain place deemed holy; praying in a certain way; or wearing special clothing are but a few examples of the many rituals that comprise the forms of worship in the various faiths of the world.

By definition, rites or rituals are any ceremonial activities that are performed with regularity in a faith and that have proscribed rules for their valid performance. Liturgy is the united or corporate worship of a body of people who often use ritual or rites as part of the means of worship.

CATHOLICS
Catholic worship services can have a very high liturgy (meaning a highly ritualistic and formal ceremony) or a low liturgy (a ceremony with minimal ritual) based on the makeup of the congregation and the orientation of the parish priest or bishop. However, in comparison with an LDS sacrament meeting, Catholic worship services will almost always seem to be more ritualistic.

LATTER-DAY SAINTS
Mormons have a very low liturgy in their standard Sunday services. The most liturgical part of LDS corporate worship is the blessing and

passing of the sacrament. Beyond this, formal ritual is not part of how Latter-day Saints worship on the Sabbath.[1]

Yet, those who have participated in the rites and ordinances of an LDS temple know that the liturgy there is very high indeed. Symbolism abounds in LDS temples, in what we do, what we wear, what we say, and even in the architecture of the rooms in which we meet. Thus, while Mormons seem quite different from Catholics in their Sunday services, there are distinct parallels between how a High Mass would be celebrated and what a Latter-day Saint would experience in a holy temple.

HOW THE ENDOWMENT BECAME THE MASS[2]

Like modern Latter-day Saints, the early Christian Church had two different types of meetings. First of all there was the weekly synagogue service, which was in a number of ways like our sacrament services today. During the Sabbath worship services, the early Christians had scriptural readings and exhortations. They sang hymns. They held corporate (or group) prayers. But beyond their weekly Sabbath services, the early Christians also had what today we might call their "temple services" or meetings. Certainly, even after Jesus' death, the early Christians continued to attend Herod's temple.[3] But during His "forty-day ministry" Jesus revealed things to the first century Christians causing them to add additional rites that were not part of their synagogue or Sabbath meetings. They began to perform these temple-oriented rites in homes dedicated for that purpose. So the infant Christian Church had two kinds of meetings to serve members' spiritual needs, much as we do in Mormonism today.

As we've noted above, the early Christian Sabbath morning service resembled the synagogue or a combined Sunday School/sacrament service. In the "morning services," the newly baptized and those inves-

---

1   Certainly we have structure to our meetings, which itself is consistent. However, the format of our meetings is not ritual or rite so much as it is methodology or approach.

2   For a detailed discussion of the ideas contained in this section of the book, see Marcus Von Wellnitz, "The Catholic Liturgy and the Mormon Temple," *BYU Studies* 21, no. 1 (1981): 3–35.

3   See also Acts 2:46; Luke 4:16; John 18:30; Acts 3:1; 13:13–14; 17:1–2; 16:13; 18:4; and 19:9.

tigating the Church were invited to attend and learn more about the faith. This meeting was sometimes referred to as the "service of the catechumen." Since many of the early converts came from Judaism, this likely would have felt like a very familiar service to them.

On the evening of the Sabbath, they would hold a more formal ritualistic meeting that was temple oriented. In other words, they separated the two meetings much like Latter-day Saints used to separate the meetings of their current "three-hour block." Or, perhaps better explained, they separated their worship services from their temple services as we do today in Mormonism. The evening service of the early Christians—patterned after the things Jesus restored during His "forty-day ministry"—was more formal and ritualistic. This service was only open to worthy, initiated members. During this service the sacrament was blessed and passed.[4]

Soon the two meetings were combined into one, much like the LDS Church's meeting schedule consolidation in 1980. This may have been for convenience, as it was in modern times. The non-members and newly baptized converts were allowed to attend the first portion of the meeting. This short, initial meeting contained doctrinal teachings or sermons. After this the newly baptized and the investigators were dismissed and the more sacred things were discussed and performed. In effect, they now had two back-to-back meetings or "masses": the

---

4   As part of early Mormon temple worship, the sacrament was occasionally blessed and passed. See James E. Talmage, *The House of the Lord* (Salt Lake City: Deseret Book, 1971), 99; and David John Buerger, *The Mysteries of Godliness: A History of Mormon Temple Worship* (San Francisco, Calif.: Smith Research Associates, 1994), 74. This is generally not the case today, although there are certain exceptions. President N. Eldon Tanner of the First Presidency noted:

    On the first Thursday of every month the First Presidency meets with all the General Authorities—the members of the Twelve, the Seventy, and the Presiding Bishopric [in the Temple]. In this meeting all are advised of any changes in programs or procedures and instructed in their duties or responsibilities. The President calls on members to bear their testimonies, after which we all dress in our temple clothes, partake of the sacrament, and have a prayer circle with all members present participating. At the conclusion of the prayer all, other than the First Presidency and Quorum of the Twelve, are dismissed, and those remaining change to their street clothes and carry on with the regular business of the Thursday meetings. (N. Eldon Tanner, "The Administration of the Church," *Ensign* [November 1979]: 47–48)

missa catechumenorum or "mass of the catechumen," and the *missa sacramentorum* or "mass of the sacraments." Eventually the part of the service where the investigators were dismissed was dropped. One scholar noted, "When most of the people in Europe had converted to Catholic Christianity the combination service was no longer considered necessary and it was almost completely dispensed with."[1]

While this is a very general explanation, it shows how temple things were absorbed into the weekly worship service. Over time these things became the Catholic Mass. Hugh Nibley wrote, "Rome has not abolished the rites of the Temple . . . but simply taken them over, every particle of the ancient ordinances and imagery having been absorbed by the Christian sacraments."[2]

1   Von Wellnitz, "The Catholic Liturgy and the Mormon Temple," 6.

2   Hugh Nibley, "Christian Envy of the Temple," in *Mormonism and Early Christianity* (Provo, Utah: Foundation for Ancient Research and Mormon Studies, 1987), 403, in Von Wellnitz, "The Catholic Liturgy and the Mormon Temple," 35.

VESTMENTS, CLERICAL CLOTHING, AND TEMPLE GARMENTS

"The transforming effect of clothes," one source informs us, "has always given them considerable emblematic power."[1] In Mormonism, as in Catholicism, there are certain items of sacred or symbolic clothing one receives as a sign of one's commitment to or covenants with God and as a requisite for functioning in priestly matters. Anciently priestly clothing served as a symbol for the clothing and glory of God and His holy angels. In antiquity when mortals dressed themselves in sacred or symbolic clothing, it served as a representation of a change in role or status. In so doing they highlighted their transition from mortal to immortal, or from fallen man to authorized priest or priestess.[2] Today, in Mormonism and Catholicism, sacred clothing has strong symbolic representation of covenants, commitments, and authority.

CATHOLICS

In Roman Catholicism you see two classes of symbolic clerical clothing: those emblematic items traditionally worn as "street clothes" by priests once final vows have been taken,[3] and the symbolic cloth-

---

1   Jack Tresidder, *Symbols and Their Meanings* (London: Duncan Baird Publishers, 2000), 134.

2   See John Tvedtnes, "Priestly Clothing in Bible Times" in Donald W. Parry, ed., *Temples of the Ancient World* (Provo, Utah: Foundation for Ancient Research and Mormon Studies, 1994), 665, 666.

3   Roman Catholic nuns also have their habit, although in most cases neither nuns nor priests today are nearly as strict as they once were when it comes to wearing clerical clothing when they are "off duty."

ing worn during liturgical functions such as the Mass. While each item of clerical clothing, particularly liturgical clothing, has a specific symbolic meaning,[4] in general they all represent the set apart aspect of the priest. He stands in for God and officiates on His behalf. Thus, he dons specific articles of clothing that will remind him of the various aspects of his calling as a priest and earthly representative of Christ.

LATTER-DAY SAINTS

As in Catholicism, in Mormonism you see two classes of symbolic clothing worn by endowed Latter-day Saints: the underclothing received in the temple by all who enter into covenants therein, and the symbolic outer clothing worn during the temple endowment, or other temple ordinances, known as the "robes of the holy priesthood."[5] While each item of temple clothing—the undergarments and temple robes—has a specific symbolic meaning,[6] in general they each represent the set apart aspect of the endowed person. While all Latter-day Saints are called to be a peculiar people (1 Peter 2:9; D&C 95:8), those who have made covenants in the holy temple are called to live a higher standard. As they wear the symbolic clothing they are reminded of their role as a priest or priestess unto the Most High God.[7]

SUMMARY

Catholic priests and nuns are in many ways like temple endowed Latter-day Saint men and women. Each has made higher covenants or additional vows when compared to their baptized brothers and sisters in the Church, and each was given certain items of symbolic clothing to wear as an earmark of their status as one set apart for a special purpose in the Church and upon the earth. Of the parallel that exists between the sacred vestments of the various Christian denominations

---

4   See Hugh T. Henry, *Catholic Customs and Symbols* (New York: Benziger Brothers, 1925), 69–78.

5   N. Eldon Tanner, "The Administration of the Church," *Ensign* (November 1979): 43.

6   See Alonzo L. Gaskill, *The Lost Language of Symbolism: An Essential Guide for Recognizing and Interpreting Symbols of the Gospel* (Salt Lake City: Deseret Book, 2003), 61–82 and 316–318.

7   See Joseph Fielding Smith, comp., *Teachings of the Prophet Joseph Smith* (Salt Lake City: Deseret Book, 1976), 362.

and the temple garments of Latter-day Saints, Elder Boyd K. Packer wrote:

> Members [of our Church] who have received their temple ordinances thereafter wear [a] special garment or underclothing. . . . The garment represents sacred covenants. . . There may be occasions when endowed members of the Church face questions [about] the garment. . . . On one occasion I was invited to speak to the faculty and staff of the Navy Chaplains Training School. . . . In the question-and-answer period one of the chaplains asked, "Can you tell us something about the special underwear that some Mormon servicemen wear?" . . . I responded with a question: "Which church do you represent?" In response he named one of the Protestant churches. I said, "In civilian life and also when conducting the meetings in the military service you wear clerical clothing, do you not?" He said that he did. I continued: "I would suppose that that has some importance to you, that in a sense it sets you apart from the rest of your congregation. It is your uniform, as it were, of the ministry. Also . . . it reminds you of who you are and what your obligations and covenants are. It is a continual reminder that you are a member of the clergy, that you regard yourself as a servant of the Lord, and that you are responsible to live in such a way as to be worthy of your ordination." The chaplains all seemed to consent to this appraisal of the value of their own clerical clothing. I then told them: "A major difference between your churches and ours is that we do not have a professional clergy, as you do. . . . The man who heads our congregation on Sunday as the bishop may go to work on Monday as a postal clerk, as an office worker, a farmer, a doctor; or he may be an air force pilot or a naval officer. By our standard he is as much an ordained minister as you are by your standard. . . . We draw something of the same benefits from this special clothing as you would draw from your clerical vestments. The difference is that we wear ours under our clothing instead of outside, for we are employed in various occupations in addition to our service in

the Church. These sacred things we do not wish to parade before the world."[8]

In light of Elder Packer's comments, and because of our own experience, once we have received our endowment in the temple, Latter-day Saints should have no difficulty seeing the strong similarities that exist between the clerical vestments of Roman Catholics and that which we wear in our temples and under our "street clothes."

---

8   Boyd K. Packer, *The Holy Temple* (Salt Lake City: Bookcraft, 1999), 75, 76, and 77–78.

CHALLENGES FOR
THE CATHOLIC CHURCH

It is perhaps unwise for a Latter-day Saint to comment on challenges the Catholic Church is currently facing or will likely face in the future. As an outsider, I certainly do not see all of the dynamics at play within the Catholic Church and among its members. Having received part of my graduate theological training at a Catholic university, I know firsthand that there are some very strong feelings among Catholics regarding where the Church has gone in the last four decades. Still, as a non-Catholic I may never fully understand, in a spiritual sense, what is being felt by conservative or liberal Catholics, or by the laity and the magisterium. My sense is that a polarity exists within the Church: conservatives and hierarchy vs. liberals and progressive laity. The "two sides," if you will, seem to have been at war—morally and theologically—since Vatican II (AD 1962–1965). As the distinguished Catholic theologian Hans Küng has noted, "parties in the Church are a real problem. Indeed . . . we are facing new polarizations in the Church."[1]

Rather than give my own insights into where the Church is going and what challenges it faces, I will confine my remarks in this section to concerns expressed by Catholic scholars and the Catholic laity. I will let them speak for themselves. Each sees a seeming crisis on the horizon, yet their reasons for concern are almost exactly the opposite.

---

1   Hans Küng, *Reforming the Church Today* (New York: Crossroad, 1990), 32. O'Gorman and Faulkner noted, "The Church seems split down the middle between conservatives and progressives." Bob O'Gorman and Mary Faulkner, *The Complete Idiot's Guide to Understanding Catholicism*, 2d ed. (Indianapolis, Ind.: Alpha Books, 2003), xv.

One of the major crises within the Church, expressed by liberals[2] and conservatives[3] alike, has to do with activity rates within the Church since Vatican II. Numbers have plummeted in important categories, and a turnaround seems unlikely. Note the U.S. statistics since Vatican II:

- **Number of Priests:**
  - 1965 = 58,000
  - 2002 = 45,000

- **Priests Ordained in a Given Year:**
  - 1965 = 1,575
  - 2002 = 450

- **Parishes without Priests:**
  - 1965 = 549
  - 2002 = 2,929

- **Seminarians Preparing for the Priesthood:**
  - 1965 = 49,000
  - 2002 = 4,700

There are more Catholics today, but fewer priests to serve them. How will practicing Catholics gain access to the sacraments of the Church if there are insufficient priests to provide them? Liberal and conservative Catholics see this as a major problem the Church is facing.

Like priests, the numbers of those choosing to make a lifelong commitment to the Church by becoming nuns has also dramatically dropped.

- **Nuns:**
  - 1965 = 180,000
  - 2002 = 75,000

---

2   See Küng, *Reforming the Church Today*, particularly 7–12.
3   See Kenneth C. Jones, *Index of Leading Catholic Indicators: The Church Since Vatican II* (Fort Collins, Colo.: Roman Catholic Books, 2003), 8–9. See also O'Gorman and Faulkner, *Complete Idiot's Guide to Understanding Catholicism*, 57–74.

This statistic has been a particularly strong blow to Catholic schools and charities, which have traditionally drawn much of their staff from the populous of nuns within the Church.

While the implications of the next set of statistics are not entirely clear, the fact that there has been a sharp decline in enrollments at Catholic high schools and grade schools suggests something is afoot. For some it implies that there has been a change in attitude among lay Catholics regarding the value of a strong, religiously centered, Catholic education.

- **Enrolled Catholic High School Students:**
  - 1965 = 700,000
  - 2002 = 386,000

- **Enrolled Grade School Students:**
  - 1965 = 4.5 million
  - 2002 = 1.9 million

The next two statistics are as ominous as the shortage of priests within the Church. The steep decline in infant baptisms and weekly Church attendance implies that, for some reason, many Catholics are feeling less commitment to the Church, or they feel less need for the Church in their daily lives.

- **Infant Baptisms Performed:**
  - 1965 = 1.3 million
  - 2002 = 1 million

- **Attendance at Church:**
  - 1965 = 74 percent attending weekly
  - 2002 = 25 percent attending weekly

In relation to the number of infant baptisms, the reader should be aware that there were 20 million more Catholics living in the U.S. in 2002 than there were in 1965. While it seems that the decline in infant baptisms is small, it is statistically much larger than it appears. Of course, part of that diminution is the result of a steep decline in birth-rates among Catholics since the 1960s. However, even that decline is a significant message about how lay Catholics feel about Church teachings on subjects like birth control.

Conservative Catholics argue that these statistical downturns show that the Church's change in direction during Vatican II harmed Catholicism. As one Catholic source noted, "Many of the faithful felt a deep loss as traditional and beloved beliefs and practices were altered or dropped altogether in an effort to update the Church. In addition, the Church lost some of its uniqueness. . . . Many Catholics were left with a vague sense of the Church being 'less Catholic' than it used to be."[4] Many conservative Catholics feel that changes in traditional practices and rites within the Church are nothing more than man-made efforts to appease liberals and non-Catholics, suggesting that the Church made a conscious decision to step away from its ancient roots. Conservatives express concerns not only about the plummeting statistics, but also about changes that may be encouraging the decline in activity. Things such as:

- The downplay of the doctrine of transubstantiation and the removal of the term from the liturgy, which has caused some Catholics to feel less reverence for the consecrated Eucharist.[5]
- The ban on kneeling when receiving communion has caused a loss of reverence for that which was considered holy.
- The active participation of the laity in the Mass has reduced the role, and in the minds of some, the importance of the priest.
- Bringing the Mass down to the level of the laity by permitting it to be celebrated in any language, and permitting "folk masses" for those who desire it, has caused a lack of reverence for what once provoked a sense of the sacred. These changes and allowances

---

4   O'Gorman and Faulkner, *Complete Idiot's Guide to Understanding Catholicism*, 68.
5   This list has been drawn from Michael Davies, *Liturgical Time Bombs in Vatican II: The Destruction of Catholic Faith Through Changes in Catholic Worship* (Rockford, Ill.: Tan Books and Publishers, 2003).

also imply that the Mass is not the creation of God, but rather the creation of men.

These are but a few of the many concerns that conservative Catholics have expressed and that they see as the cause of the decline in Catholic observance.

Liberal Catholics, on the other hand, often suggest that the statistics only go to show that the Church dragged its feet so long in refusing to make much needed changes that many formerly faithful Catholics have simply given up and left the Church. Hans Küng has referred to it as "the present impasse in the Catholic Church."[6] While conservatives have offered their list of changes the Church needs to make in order to avoid future collapse,[7] liberals have their own register too. One text offers the following list of concerns:

- The "Church is crippled by its failure to address fundamental justice issues within its own institutional structures."[8]
- Women continue to be oppressed and violently and unequally treated, yet in the 1960s the Church implied that it would do something about this.
- Many Catholics are "deprived of the Church's sacramental life because of the declining number of priests."
- Very seldom are the lay members of the Catholic Church "allowed by Church authorities to participate in decisions that affect their lives."
- The Pope and the Roman Curia continue to select bishops throughout the world without soliciting input from the congregations over which these bishops will preside.
- Various groups are "marginalized" in the Church "because of race and ethnic identity."

---

6   See Hans Küng, *Signposts For The Future* (New York: Doubleday, 1978), xi.
7   See, for example Davies, *Liturgical Time Bombs in Vatican II*; and Jones, *Index of Leading Catholic Indicators*.
8   This list has been drawn from Küng, *Reforming the Church Today*, 193–95.

- Theologians are silenced, and constructive opposition is condemned by Rome. "Blind obedience" and "loyalty oaths" are often demanded of scholars.
- The Church conducts "financial dealings in secret without accountability to her people."
- The Vatican downgrades the "importance of national bishops conferences."
- Countless Catholic parishes and schools are being closed throughout the United States, and yet the Church is doing nothing to help those who now find themselves without a parish or a school to attend.
- Too many of the youth have begun to see the Church as "authoritarian" and "hypocritical," and therefore "many young adults and children of Catholic families . . . are reluctant to affiliate with [the] Church."

These are only a few examples, but they do show the chief concerns of some of the most vocal, progressive Catholics. More could be given from both the conservatives and the liberals, but in the end, more would not necessarily help make the point.

What is curious is that on points that conservatives and progressives agree to be problematic, their reasoning is exactly the opposite. For example, progressives say that fewer and fewer men are joining the priesthood because of the antiquated but mandatory ban on celibacy for lay members. Conservatives, on the other hand, say that the decrease in priesthood ordinations is being caused by the fact that the Church (after Vatican II) allowed its lay members to do things formerly reserved for priests. Hence, if one can do priestly things without having to make the sacrifice of being a priest (including the sacrifice of celibacy), then why join the priesthood? Similar differences of interpretation as to the cause of the problems exist on nearly every major issue. Thus, Catholics seem united on the fact that major problems exist, but divided on what the causes are. Which side is right? I suspect both are, contingent upon whom you ask. In other words, it appears that Catholics cease practicing for a variety of reasons. No one explanation addresses all of the issues.

What can the Church do to reunite the progressives and conservatives? Perhaps that question is best left to Catholics to answer. From my vantage point there is little that can be done to heal the divide. For some time there have been essentially two Catholic churches—the old school of the conservatives and the new school of the progressives. The divide between the "two sides" appears to be getting wider, and no evident solution is on the horizon. If the two sides are not able to live side by side, tolerating each other—since accepting each other as equally valid is unlikely—then the Church is headed for rough times, indeed.[9]

---

9   None of this is to suggest that Latter-day Saints don't have their own struggles. Although The Church of Jesus Christ of Latter-day Saints continues to grow, we too struggle with many of the same issues Roman Catholics are confronted with. While not to the same degree as in Catholicism, there are occasional rifts between "liberal" and "conservative" Mormons. We constantly have the voice of dissenters to deal with. The media remains focused on sensationalist stories that paint the Church in a bad light, but it seldom wishes to report to good the LDS Church is accomplishing in the world. Our Church is growing at such a rate in certain parts of the world that we can hardly provide the leadership necessary from the new converts to address the needs on a local level. This brief list is but a sampling of our challenges for the future.

CONCLUSION

Like perceptions about Mormons, views of practicing Catholics are sometimes terribly skewed or stereotypical. One source notes, "A pop image of Catholics exists in the world of movies, television, and books: the Irish cop, the spunky nun, and a priest who refuses to break the seal of confession. Nostalgic remembrances, stereotypes, prejudice, and just plain curiosity surround this somewhat mysterious religion. Candles, incense, processions, statues, and visions of Mary . . ."[1] Many, if not all, of these come to mind when non-Catholics hear the word Catholicism.

So what really is a Catholic? Well, to some extent that depends upon where the Catholic lives and how he or she views the Church's role in his or her personal life. Catholics in Mexico often live their religion differently than Catholics in Germany, but those differences are cultural, not theological or sacramental.

In general terms, a practicing Catholic is not what stereotypes make them out to be. For example, *most* modern Catholics *don't* have a dozen kids, play bingo regularly, have visitations from the Virgin Mary, or go to confession every week. On the other hand, practicing contemporary Catholics do pray to God daily, read their Bible regularly, attend Church weekly, and contribute money and time to their

---

1   Bob O'Gorman and Mary Faulkner, *The Complete Idiot's Guide to Understanding Catholicism*, 2d ed. (Indianapolis, Ind.: Alpha Books, 2003), 1. One of my Catholic readers noted that Latter-day Saints should understand that a parish priest who breaks the seal of confession is traditionally excommunicated from the Church.

parish frequently. Devout Catholics believe repentance is to be found in a sincere change of heart and not simply in a quick "Hail Mary." Committed Catholics believe in the importance of being "honest, true, chaste, benevolent, virtuous, and in doing good to all men." Indeed, they "believe all things . . . hope all things . . . have endured many things, and hope to be able to endure all things. If there is anything virtuous, lovely, or of good report or praiseworthy," practicing Catholics "seek after" it (Article of Faith 13). In a nutshell, a practicing contemporary Catholic has standards much like an active modern Latter-day Saint, and, as shown, the official doctrine of the Catholic Church suggests that modern Catholics also have some beliefs very similar to Latter-day Saints.

Are we different? Yes. But it seems fair to say that our similarities are more than our differences. Catholics and Mormons alike are followers of the Lord Jesus Christ.[2] Each faith is a Bible believing, sac-

---

2   Unfortunately for us, some Catholics may not perceive Latter-day Saints as Christians. As silly as the claim sounds to Latter-day Saints, there are a couple of possible reasons why one might mistakenly assume Mormons are not Christians. First of all, some are simply ignorant of the Church's teachings and beliefs about Jesus. By definition, a Christian is someone who (1) professes belief in the teachings of Jesus Christ, (2) is a disciple or follower of Jesus Christ and His teachings, (3) conforms to the ethics or lifestyle of Christianity, and (4) professes or affirms Christianity. See *Merriam-Webster's Collegiate Dictionary*, 11th ed. (Springfield, Mass.: Merriam-Webster Inc., 2005), 220, s.v., "Christian"; *The American Heritage Dictionary*, 2d collegiate ed. (Boston, Mass.: Houghton Mifflin, 1985), 271, s.v., "Christian." On all accounts, Mormons quality (by a dictionary definition) as Christians. Second, some might assume that Mormons aren't Christian because our understanding of the nature of the Trinity or Godhead is slightly different from that of some of our Christian brothers and sisters. Some who believe in the post-biblical doctrine of the Trinity will sometimes claim that anyone who rejects this teaching is not a Christian. However, it is important to recognize that many of the various Christian denominations have slightly different understandings of the nature of the Godhead or Trinity. For example, the Eastern Orthodox faith holds that Jesus is subordinate to the Father, whereas Catholics hold Jesus to be co-equal with the Father. The Orthodox also claims that the Father is the sole source of the Holy Spirit, whereas Catholics and Protestants tend to say that the Spirit comes from both the Father and the Son. While the Orthodox differ on this aspect of believe, they are still considered Christian by others followers of Christ. Hence, minor differences in belief should not disqualify Latter-day Saints. Of course, there is also the official name of the Church—The Church of *Jesus Christ* of Latter-day Saints—that also clearly indicates that Mormons are Christians. There are also the testimonies or witnesses of Mormons themselves. Time and again we are asked, "Are you Christian?" or "Do you believe Jesus is your personal Savior?" or "Do you believe Jesus is the divine Son of God?" In every case we answer with a resounding "Yes!" Members of The Church of

rament participating, vestment wearing, heaven hoping people. Each teaches its people to love God, follow the advice of their Church leaders, and pray daily for the Lord's help and forgiveness. Both traditions see themselves as being called by God to teach and sanctify society through the things they teach, the way they live, and the moral wars they wage.

PRESIDENT GORDON B. HINCKLEY AND PRESIDENT THOMAS S. MONSON MEET WITH A ROMAN CATHOLIC PRIEST.
©INTELLECTUAL RESERVE, INC.

If speaking analogously, we would not compare Catholics and Mormons to a set of identical twins. We could, nonetheless, see them as siblings. They look somewhat alike but are not identical. They claim that same family (Christianity) and same Father (God). Because of their background and roots, they seek very similar things and have very similar standards, and, as members of a family do, they pull together when things get tough (something Mormons and Catholics have done on numerous occasions). President Thomas S. Monson noted:

> As a Church we try to . . . promote humanitarian initiatives. . . . Examples include: . . . [sending] food, clothing, furnishings, and capital contributions to Catholic Community Services and Catholic Relief Services. I'd like to say that we have sent millions of dollars of supplies through Catholic Charities. It has been a wonderful association, and we keep that current as of today.[3]

Just because we have some doctrinal differences doesn't mean that we can't—our shouldn't—work to change the world and better the

---

Jesus Christ of Latter-day Saints absolutely are Christians. Anyone who claims otherwise is simply misinformed.

3   Thomas S. Monson, "Our Brother's Keepers," *Ensign* (June 1998): 37–38. See also "Catholics Honor Church," *Ensign* (February 1988): 73–74; Nicole Seymour, "Atmit to the Rescue," *Ensign* (January 2006): 74–75; and Lisa Ann Jackson, "Church Sends Aid to Ethiopia," *Ensign* (June 2003), 76–77.

lives of those who live in it. Additionally, just because we do not see eye to eye on all issues does not mean that we should avoid testifying side by side that Jesus is the Christ. President Gordon B. Hinckley noted:

> We acknowledge without hesitation that there are differences between us. Were this not so there would have been no need for a restoration of the gospel. . . . I hope we do not argue over this matter. There is no reason to debate it. We simply, quietly, and without apology testify that God has revealed Himself and His Beloved Son in opening this full and final dispensation of His work. We must not become disagreeable as we talk of doctrinal differences. There is no place for acrimony. . . . We can respect other religions, and must do so. We must recognize the great good they accomplish. We must teach our children to be tolerant and friendly toward those not of our faith. We can and do work with those of other religions in the defense of those values which have made our civilization great and our society distinctive. . . . We can and do work with those of other religions in various undertakings in the everlasting fight against social evils which threaten the treasured values which are so important to all of us. These people are not of our faith, but they are our friends, neighbors, and co-workers in a variety of causes. We are pleased to lend our strength to their efforts.[4]

As noted earlier, Elder Orson F. Whitney of the Quorum of the Twelve reminded Latter-day Saints that God "is using not only his covenant people, but other peoples as well, to consummate a work, stupendous, magnificent, and altogether too arduous for this little handful of Saints to accomplish by and of themselves."[5] Thus, while we testify to the realities of the Restoration of the fullness of the gospel of Jesus Christ, we willingly accept all of the help we can get in sanctifying this fallen world.

It has been my goal in this small work to correct some of the standard misunderstandings, stereotypes, and misnomers Latter-day Saints might have about their Roman Catholic brothers and sisters. I have

---

4   Gordon B. Hinckley, "We Bear Witness of Him," *Ensign* (May 1998): 4–5.
5   Orson F. Whitney, *Conference Report*, April 1921, 32–33.

earnestly sought to accurately represent Catholicism, and to do so in a spirit of respect and Christian civility. It is my hope that this small work might encourage Latter-day Saints and Catholics alike to build upon their commonalities, and to treat each other with a greater degree of understanding, respect, and even appreciation for what we each contribute toward the common good. While the goal of this book has not been to convert Catholics to Mormonism, or Latter-day Saints to Catholicism, it is my sincere hope that it will convert both to a more Christlike treatment of each other and a greater appreciation for how God works through all who are willing to be instruments in His hands.

Appendix:
Current Demographics

When contrasting the demographics of Roman Catholicism with Mormonism, the sheer difference in numbers is almost incomprehensible. For example, for every one Mormon there are approximately eighty-five Catholics. Thus, even though The Church of Jesus Christ of Latter-day Saints is one of the fastest growing faiths in the world,[1] in total numbers it lags far behind Roman Catholicism.

While demographic comparisons between the two faiths can be made, there are few areas of overlap, namely because of the significant differences these two faiths have in ecclesiastical structure. For example, Latter-day Saint statistics often include the following:

- LDS missions (344)
- Missionary Training Centers (17)
- Temples in operation (124)
- Church owned and operated universities and schools (4)
- Seminary students enrolled (362,756)
- Institute students enrolled (358,516)
- Family History Centers (4,500)
- Countries with Family History Centers (70)
- Countries receiving humanitarian aid from the Church (163)

---

1   See Hugh Hewitt, *Searching for God in America* (Dallas, Tex.: Word Publishing, 1996), 121.

- Welfare service and humanitarian missionaries (3,552)
- Languages in which Church curriculum is available (178)
- Etc.

Many of these statistical breakdowns are simply not applicable to the Roman Catholic Church. Having said that, a number of areas relevant to Catholicism would have no parallel in Mormonism either. For example, the following statistics typically appear in lists of Catholic demographics:

- Cardinals (192)
- Patriarchs (10)
- Archbishops (962)
- Bishops (3,628)
- Priests (405, 891)
- Brothers (55,030)
- Nuns (767,459)
- Enrollees at major seminaries (113,044)
- Enrollees at Catholic kindergartens (63,073)
- Enrollees at Catholic elementary schools (91,090)
- Enrollees at Catholic secondary schools (38,277)
- Hospitals (5,246)
- Children in Catholic orphanages (10,163)
- Etc.

It is evident from these published statistics that Roman Catholics and Latter-day Saints have a different ecclesiastical structure, and, to some degree, a different emphasis. Nevertheless, as noted above, there are a few areas in which our statistics do converge. The following chart shows some of the more significant demographic parallels between Catholics and Mormons.

	CATHOLICS[2]	LATTER-DAY SAINTS[3]
Approximate Total Church Membership Worldwide	1.1 billion	13 million
Approximate Annual Baptisms of Children of Record	14 million	100,000
Approximate Annual Convert Baptisms	2.5 million	275,000
Approximate Total Number of Parishes or Wards Worldwide	217,000	27,500
Approximate Total Number of Dioceses or Stakes Worldwide[4]	2,000	3,000
Approximate Number of Lay Missionaries Currently Serving	186,000	53,000

2   Demographics taken from Matthew Brunson, ed., *Our Sunday Visitor's Catholic Almanac—2007 Edition* (Huntington, N.J.: Our Sunday Visitor Inc, 2006), 333.

3   Demographics taken from www.lds.org.

4   While I have drawn a comparison here between stakes and dioceses, the reader should be aware that a stake is a rather small organization in the LDS Church in comparison to a Catholic diocese. An LDS stake traditionally has somewhere between six and fifteen congregations. However, a Catholic diocese can have dozens of parishes under its jurisdiction. Thus, for some the comparison will seem a stretch. Having said that, in both Mormonism and Catholicism the stake or diocese is in charge of the congregations under its jurisdiction, and in both cases the head of the stake or diocese selects the leaders of the individual congregations within its jurisdiction (although, admittedly, in Mormonism the stake president may select or recommend a man to be ordained a bishop, but in the end the President of the Church calls him to that position and priesthood office).

BIBLIOGRAPHY

A Sure Foundation: Answers to Difficult Gospel Questions. Various authors. Salt Lake City: Deseret Book, 1988.

"Age of Reason." In *The Harper Collins Encyclopedia of Catholicism*, edited by Richard P. McBrien. San Francisco, Calif.: HarperSanFrancisco, 1995.

Andrews, Dean Timothy. *What is the Orthodox Church?* New York: Greek Orthodox Archdiocese of North and South America, 1964.

Apostolos-Cappadona, Diane. "Symbols." In *Encyclopedia of Christianity*, edited by John Bowden. New York: Oxford University Press, 2005.

Ballard, Paul. "Death." In *Encyclopedia of Christianity*, edited by John Bowden. New York: Oxford University Press, 2005.

Barclay, William. "Great Themes of the New Testament." *Expository Times* 70 (1959): 292–96.

"Beast of the Apocalypse." In *The Harper Collins Encyclopedia of Catholicism*, edited by Richard P. McBrien. San Francisco, Calif.: HarperSanFrancisco, 1995.

Bickmore, Barry. "'Clearing Up Misconceptions,' A review of Patrick Madrid, *Pope Fiction: Answers to 30 Myths and Misconceptions about the Papacy*." *FARMS Review of Books* 13, no. 2 (2001): 197–99.

Blair, Robert W. "Vocabulary, Latter-day Saint." In *Encyclopedia of Mormonism*, edited by Daniel H. Ludlow. 4 vols. New York: Macmillian, 1992.

Boff, Leonardo. *Trinity and Society*. London: Burns and Oates, 1988.

Boutin, Mourice. "Anonymous Christianity: A Paradigm for Interreligious Encounter?" *Journal of Ecumenical Studies* 20 (Fall 1983): 602–29.

Bowden, John, ed. *Encyclopedia of Christianity*. New York: Oxford University Press, 2005.

———. "Life After Death." In *Encyclopedia of Christianity*, edited by John Bowden. New York: Oxford University Press, 2005.

Brewster, Hoyt W. Jr. "What was in the creeds of men that the Lord found abominable, as he stated in the First Vision?" In *A Sure Foundation: Answers to Difficult Gospel Questions*. Salt Lake City: Deseret Book, 1988.

Brown, Raymond E. *The Anchor Bible—The Gospel According To John XIII–XXI*. New York: Doubleday, 1970.

———. Joseph A. Fitzmyer, and Roland E. Murphy, eds. *The New Jerome Biblical Commentary*. Englewood Cliffs, N.J.: Prentice Hall, 1990.

Brunson, Matthew, ed. *Our Sunday Visitor's Catholic Almanac—2007 Edition*. Huntington, N.J.: Our Sunday Visitor Inc., 2006.

Calhoun, Margie. *Stories of Insight and Inspiration*. 2d ed. Salt Lake City: Bountiful Press, 1993.

———. *When Faith Writes the Story*. 2d ed. Salt Lake City: Bountiful Press, 1993.

Cannon, George Q. *The Life of Joseph Smith, the Prophet*. Salt Lake City: Deseret Book, 1986.

"Catholics Honor Church." *Ensign* (February 1988): 73–74.

Cavadini, John C. "Hellenism." In *The Harper Collins Encyclopedia of Catholicism*, edited by Richard P. McBrien. San Francisco, Calif.: HarperSanFrancisco, 1995.

———. "Iconoclasm." In *The Harper Collins Encyclopedia of Catholicism*, edited by Richard P. McBrien. San Francisco, Calif.: HarperSanFrancisco, 1995.

Chamberlin, E. Russell. *The Bad Popes*. Rev. ed. (Gloucestershire: Sutton Publishing, 2003).

Chick, Jack T. *Alberto: Parts 1-5*. Chino, Calif.: Chick Publications, 1979.

Church Handbook of Instructions, Book 1, Stake Presidencies and Bishoprics [leadership manual]. Salt Lake City: The Church of Jesus Christ of Latter-day Saints, 2006.

Ciferni, Andrew D. "Anointing of the Sick." In *The Harper Collins Encyclopedia of Catholicism*, edited by Richard P. McBrien. San Francisco, Calif.: HarperSanFrancisco, 1995.

Clooney, Francis X. "Salvation Outside the Church." In *The Harper Collins Encyclopedia of Catholicism*, edited by Richard P. McBrien. San Francisco, Calif.: HarperSanFrancisco, 1995.

Coll, Regina. "Saints." In *The Harper Collins Encyclopedia of Catholicism*, edited by Richard P. McBrien. San Francisco, Calif.: HarperSanFrancisco, 1995.

Collins, John J. "Apocrypha." In *The Harper Collins Encyclopedia of Catholicism*, edited by Richard P. McBrien. San Francisco, Calif.: HarperSanFrancisco, 1995.

Compton, Todd. "Symbolism." In *Encyclopedia of Mormonism*, edited by Daniel H. Ludlow. 4 vols. New York: Macmillian, 1992.

Cornwell, John. *Hitler's Pope: The Secret History of Pius XII*. New York: Viking, 1999.

Cowan, Richard O. *Answers to Your Questions About the Doctrine and Covenants.* Salt Lake City: Deseret Book, 1996.

"Cross." In *The Harper Collins Encyclopedia of Catholicism*, edited by Richard P. McBrien. San Francisco, Calif.: HarperSanFrancisco, 1995.

Crowley, Paul. "Beatific Vision." In *The Harper Collins Encyclopedia of Catholicism*, edited by Richard P. McBrien. San Francisco, Calif: HarperSanFrancisco, 1995.

———. "Heaven." In *The Harper Collins Encyclopedia of Catholicism*, edited by Richard P. McBrien. San Francisco, Calif.: HarperSanFrancisco, 1995.

"Crucifix." In *The Harper Collins Encyclopedia of Catholicism*, edited by Richard P. McBrien. San Francisco, Calif.: HarperSanFrancisco, 1995.

Cunningham, David. *These Three are One.* Oxford: Blackwell Publishing, 1998.

Cyprian of Carthage. "The Epistles of Cyprian." In *Ante-Nicene Fathers*, edited by Alexander Roberts and James Donaldson. 10 vols. Peabody, Mass.: Hendrickson Publishers. 1994.

Cwiekowski, Frederick J. *The Beginnings of The Church*. New York: Paulist Press, 1988.

———. "Holy Orders." In *The Harper Collins Encyclopedia of Catholicism*, edited by Richard P. McBrien. San Francisco, Calif.: HarperSanFrancisco, 1995.

Dahl, Larry E. "Lectures on Faith." In *Encyclopedia of Latter-day Saint History*, edited by Arnold K. Garr, Donald Q. Cannon, and Richard O. Cowan. Salt Lake City: Deseret Book, 2000.

Dahl, Larry E., and Charles D. Tate, Jr., eds. *The Lectures on Faith in their Historical Perspective*. Provo, Utah: Religious Studies Center, 1990.

Dahl, Larry E. and Donald Q.Cannon, eds. *Encyclopedia of Joseph Smith's Teachings*. Salt Lake City: Bookcraft, 1998.

Dallavalle, Nancy. "Mystery." In *The Harper Collins Encyclopedia of Catholicism*, edited by Richard P. McBrien. San Francisco, Calif.: HarperSan Francisco, 1995.

Davies, Michael. *Liturgical Time Bombs in Vatican II: The Destruction of Catholic Faith Through Changes in Catholic Worship*. Rockford, Ill.: Tan Books and Publishers, 2003.

Davis, John J. *Biblical Numerology*. Grand Rapids, Mich.: Baker Book House, 2000.

"Deification." In *The Harper Collins Encyclopedia of Catholicism*, Richard P. McBrien. San Francisco, Calif.: HarperSanFrancisco, 1995.

Di Noia, Joseph A. "Purgatory." In *The Harper Collins Encyclopedia of Catholicism*, edited by Richard P. McBrien. San Francisco, Calif.: HarperSanFrancisco, 1995.

Donahue, John R. "Bible." In *The Harper Collins Encyclopedia of Catholicism*, edited by Richard P. McBrien. San Francisco, Calif.: HarperSanFrancisco, 1995.

Dorgan, Margaret. "Prayer." In *The Harper Collins Encyclopedia of Catholicism*, edited by Richard P. McBrien. San Francisco, Calif.: HarperSanFrancisco, 1995.

Doxey, Roy W. *The Doctrine and Covenants and the Future*. Salt Lake City: Deseret Book, 1954.

Duffy, Regis A. "Eucharist." In *The Harper Collins Encyclopedia of Catholicism*, edited by Richard P. McBrien. San Francisco, Calif.: HarperSanFrancisco, 1995.

Ehat, Andrew F. *Joseph Smith's Introduction of Temple Ordinances and the 1844 Mormon Succession Question*. Provo, Utah. Master's thesis, Brigham Young University, 1981.

Ehat, Andrew F., and Lyndon W. Cook, eds. *The Words of Joseph Smith: The Contemporary Accounts of the Nauvoo Discourses of the Prophet Joseph Smith*. Provo, Utah: Religious Studies Center, Brigham Young University, 1980.

Evenson, Darrick T. *The Gainsayers*. Bountiful, Utah: Horizon Publishers, 1989.

Faust, James E. "The Great Imitator." *Ensign* (November 1987): 33–36.

Ferguson, Everett, ed. *Encyclopedia of Early Christianity*. New York: Garland Publishing, 1990.

Finan, Barbara. "Holy Spirit." In Richard P. McBrien. *The Harper Collins Encyclopedia of Catholicism*. San Francisco, Calif.: HarperSanFrancisco, 1995.

Flannery, Austin, ed. *Vatican Council II: The Conciliar and Post Conciliar Documents*. New rev. ed. New York: Costello Publishing, 1992.

Ford, John T. "Infallibility." In *The Harper Collins Encyclopedia of Catholicism*, edited by Richard P. McBrien. San Francisco, Calif.: HarperSanFrancisco, 1995.

Francis, Mark R. "Sacrament." In *The Harper Collins Encyclopedia of Catholicism*, edited by Richard P. McBrien. San Francisco, Calif.: HarperSanFrancisco, 1995.

Gaillardetz, Richard R. "Syllabus of Errors." In *The Harper Collins Encyclopedia of Catholicism*, edited by Richard P. McBrien. San Francisco, Calif.: HarperSanFrancisco, 1995.

Gamble, Harry Y. "Canon—New Testament." In *The Anchor Bible Dictionary*, edited by David Noel Freedman. 6 vols. New York: Doubleday, 1992.

Gaskill, Alonzo L. "Maximus Nothus Decretum: A Look at the Recent Catholic Declaration Regarding Latter-day Saint Baptisms." In *FARMS Review of Books* 13, no. 2 (2001): 175–196.

————. *The Lost Language of Symbolism: An Essential Guide for Recognizing and Interpreting Symbols of the Gospel*. Salt Lake City: Deseret Book, 2003.

Gee, John. "'La Trahison des Clercs: On the Language and Translation of the Book of Mormon,' A Review of Brent Lee Metcalfe's *New Approaches To the Book of Mormon: Explorations in Critical Methodology*." *FARMS Review of Books* 6, no. 1 (1994): 51–120.

Gillum, Gary P. "Creeds." In *Encyclopedia of Mormonism*, edited by Daniel H. Ludlow. 4 vols. New York: Macmillian, 1992.

"Glossary." In *Encyclopedia of Mormonism*, edited by Daniel H. Ludlow. 4 vols. New York: Macmillian, 1992.

González, Justo L. *The Story of Christianity*. 2 vols. Peabody, Mass.: Prince Press, 2001.

Gospel Principles [Sunday School teacher's manual]. Salt Lake City: The Church of Jesus Christ of Latter-day Saints, 1992.

Grow, Matthew J. "The Whore of Babylon and the Abomination of Abominations: Nineteenth-Century Catholic and Mormon Mutual Perceptions and Religious Identity," in Church History, Volume 73 (March 2004): 139-167.

Haight, David B. *A Light unto the World*. Salt Lake City: Deseret Book, 1997.

Harner, Philip. *The "I AM" of the Fourth Gospel: A Study in Johannine Usage and Thought*. Philadelphia, Pa.: Fortress Press.

Hawkins, Carl S. "Baptism." In *Encyclopedia of Mormonism*, edited by Daniel H. Ludlow. 4 vols. New York: Macmillian, 1992.

Heinerman, Jacob. *Temple Manifestations*. Salt Lake City: Hawkes Publishing Company, 1975.

Henry, Hugh T. *Catholic Customs and Symbols*. New York: Benziger Brothers, 1925.

Hilkert, Mary Katherine. "Grace." In *The Harper Collins Encyclopedia of Catholicism*, edited by Richard P. McBrien. San Francisco, Calif.: HarperSanFrancisco, 1995.

Hinckley, Gordon B. "We Bear Witness of Him." *Ensign* (May 1998): 4–6.

————. "The Symbol of Our Faith." *Ensign* (April 2005): 3–7.

Hocking, David. *The Coming World Leader*. Portland, Ore.: Multnomah Press, 1988.

Holland, Jeffrey R. "Of Souls, Symbols, and Sacraments." Devotional at Brigham Young University, January 12, 1988.

————. *Christ and the New Covenant*. Salt Lake City: Deseret Book, 1997.

Holland, Jeffrey R., and Patricia T. Holland. *On Earth As It Is In Heaven*. Salt Lake City: Deseret Book, 1989.

Horrigan, Sean. "Mary, Co-Redemptrix?" *The Dallas Morning News,* August 16, 1997.

Hewitt, Hugh. *Searching for God in America.* Dallas, Tex.: Word Publishing, 1996.

Ifrah, Georges. *The Universal History of Numbers.* New York: John Wiley & Sons, 2000.

Jackson, Lisa Ann. "Church Sends Aid to Ethiopia." *Ensign* (June 2003): 76–77.

Jaques, John. *Catechism for Children, Exhibiting the Prominent Doctrines of the Church of Jesus Christ of Latter-day Saints.* Liverpool: F. D. Richards, 1854.

John Paul II. *Crossing the Threshold of Hope.* New York: Alfred A. Knopf, 1994.

Johnson, Elizabeth A. "Assumption of the Blessed Virgin Mary." In *The Harper Collins Encyclopedia of Catholicism,* edited by Richard P. McBrien. San Francisco, Calif.: HarperSanFrancisco, 1995.

———. "Blessed Virgin Mary." In *The Harper Collins Encyclopedia of Catholicism,* edited by Richard P. McBrien. San Francisco, Calif.: HarperSanFrancisco, 1995.

Joynt, R. J. "Are Two Heads Better Than One?" As cited in "Is Consciousness Important?" *British Journal of the Philosophy of Science* 35 (1984): 223.

"Judgement, Particular." In *The Harper Collins Encyclopedia of Catholicism,* edited by Richard P. McBrien. San Francisco, Calif.: HarperSanFrancisco, 1995.

Keating, Karl. *Catholicism and Fundamentalism: The Attack on 'Romanism' by 'Bible Christians.'* Fort Collins, Colo.: Ignatius Press, 1988.

Keller, Roger R. "Cross." In *Encyclopedia of Mormonism,* edited by Daniel H. Ludlow. 4 vols. New York: Macmillian, 1992.

Kelly, Geffery B. "'Unconscious Christianity' and the 'Anonymous Christian' in the Theology of Dietrich Bonhoeffer and Karl Rahner." *Philosophy and Theology* 9 (Autumn/Winter 1995): 117–49.

Kelly, J. N. D. *Early Christian Doctrines.* Rev. ed. New York: Harper Collins, 1978.

Kennedy, David. "Forgiveness." In *Encyclopedia of Christianity,* edited by John Bowden. New York: Oxford University Press, 2005.

Kimball, Heber C. In *Journal of Discourses.* 26 vols. Liverpool: F. D. Richards, 1855–886. 5:171–181.

———. In *Journal of Discourses.* 26 vols. Liverpool: F. D. Richards, 1855–886. 10:44.

Kreeft, Peter J. *Catholic Christianity: A Complete Catechism of Catholic Beliefs based on the Catechism of the Catholic Church.* San Francisco, Calif.: Ignatius Press, 2001.

Krieg, Robert A. "Creeds." In *The Harper Collins Encyclopedia of Catholicism,* edited by Richard P. McBrien. San Francisco, Calif.: HarperSanFrancisco, 1995.

Küng, Hans. *Signposts For The Future*. New York: Doubleday, 1978.

———. *Reforming the Church Today*. New York: Crossroad, 1990.

LaCugna, Catherine Mowry. *God For Us: The Trinity and Christian Life*. San Francisco, Calif.: HarperSanFrancisco, 1991.

———. "God." In *The Harper Collins Encyclopedia of Catholicism*, edited by Richard P. McBrien. San Francisco, Calif.: HarperSanFrancisco, 1995.

———. "Trinity, Doctrine of the." In *The Harper Collins Encyclopedia of Catholicism*, edited by Richard P. McBrien. San Francisco, Calif.: HarperSanFrancisco, 1995.

Lahey, John and Edward Scharfenberger. "Divorce." In *The Harper Collins Encyclopedia of Catholicism,* edited by Richard P. McBrien. San Francisco, Calif.: Harper, SanFrancisco, 1995.

Lawler, Michael G. "Marriage." In *The Harper Collins Encyclopedia of Catholicism*, edited by Richard P. McBrien. San Francisco, Calif.: HarperSanFrancisco, 1995.

LDS Bible Dictionary. Salt Lake City: The Church of Jesus Christ of Latter-day Saints, 1989.

Leader, Donal. "Judgement, General." In *The Harper Collins Encyclopedia of Catholicism,* edited by Richard P. McBrien. San Francisco, Calif.: HarperSanFrancisco, 1995.

Lectures on Faith. Kirtland, Ohio: The Church of Jesus Christ of Latter-day Saints, 1835.

Levada, William Cardinal. "Responses to Some Questions Regarding Certain Aspects of the Doctrine on the Church." Rome: Congregation for the Doctrine of the Faith, June 29, 2007.

"Limbo." In *The Harper Collins Encyclopedia of Catholicism*, edited by Richard P. McBrien. San Francisco, Calif.: HarperSanFrancisco, 1995.

Longenecker, Dwight, and David Gustafson. *Mary: A Catholic–Evangelical Debate*. Grand Rapids, Mich.: Brazos Press, 2003.

Ludlow, Daniel H. *A Companion to Your Study of the Doctrine and Covenants*. 2 vols. Salt Lake City: Deseret Book, 1978.

Ludlow, Daniel H., ed. *Encyclopedia of Mormonism*. 4 vols. New York: Macmillian, 1992.

Lukefahr, Oscar. *"We Believe . . ." A Survey of the Catholic Faith*. Rev. ed. Liguori, Mo.: Liguori Publications, 1995.

Lutzer, Erwin. *The Doctrines that Divide*. Grand Rapids, Mich.: Kregel Publications, 1998.

McBrien, Richard P. *Catholicism.* Rev. ed. San Francisco, Calif.: HarperSanFrancisco, 1994.

———. *The Harper Collins Encyclopedia of Catholicism.* San Francisco, Calif.: HarperSanFrancisco, 1995.

———. "Vatican Council II." In *The Harper Collins Encyclopedia of Catholicism,* edited by Richard P. McBrien. San Francisco, Calif.: HarperSanFrancisco, 1995.

———. *Lives of the Popes.* San Francisco, Calif.: HarperSanFrancisco, 1997.

———. *Lives of the Saints.* San Francisco, Calif.: HarperSanFrancisco, 2001.

McConkie, Bruce R. *Mormon Doctrine.* 1st ed. Salt Lake City: Bookcraft, 1958.

———. *Mormon Doctrine.* 2d ed. Salt Lake City: Bookcraft, 1979.

———. "Eve and the Fall." In *Woman.* Salt Lake City: Deseret Book, 1979.

———. *The Mortal Messiah.* 4 vols. Salt Lake City: Deseret Book, 1980–81.

———. *Doctrinal New Testament Commentary.* 3 vols. Salt Lake City: Bookcraft, 1987–88.

McConkie, Joseph Fielding. "Holy Ghost." In *Encyclopedia of Mormonism,* edited by Daniel H. Ludlow. 4 vols. New York: Macmillian, 1992.

———. *Witness of the Birth of Christ.* Salt Lake City: Bookcraft, 1998.

McDannell, Colleen, and Bernhard Lang. *Heaven: A History.* New Haven, Conn.: Yale University Press, 1988.

Mckay, David O. *Conference Report.* October 1968.

McKechnie, Jean L., ed. *Webster's New Twentieth Century Dictionary.* 2d ed. N.p.: Collins World, 1978. S.v. "Sacrament."

McLaughlin, R. Emmett. "Reformation, the." In *The Harper Collins Encyclopedia of Catholicism,* edited by Richard P. McBrien. San Francisco, Calif.: HarperSanFrancisco, 1995.

Mattox, Mickey L. "Reformation." In *Encyclopedia of Christianity,* edited by John Bowden. New York: Oxford University Press, 2005.

Millet, Robert L. "The Birth and Childhood of the Messiah" In *Studies in Scripture,* edited by Kent P. Jackson and Robert L. Millet. 5 vols. Salt Lake City: Deseret Book, 1986.

———. *Alive in Christ: The Miracle of Spiritual Rebirth.* Salt Lake City: Deseret Book, 1997.

———. "Where Did the Cross Go?" Presentation to the BYU Religious Education Faculty, September 16, 2005.

Monson, Thomas S. "Our Brother's Keepers." *Ensign* (June 1998): 32–39.

Morality. Various authors. Salt Lake City: Bookcraft, 1992.

Moran, Bob. *A Closer Look at Catholicism*. Waco, Tex.: Word Books, 1986.

"Mother of God." In *The Harper Collins Encyclopedia of Catholicism*, edited by Richard P. McBrien. San Francisco, Calif.: HarperSanFrancisco, 1995.

Murr, Andrew, Christopher Dickey, Eric Larson, Sarah Van Boven, and Hersch Doby. "Hail, Mary." *Newsweek*, August 25, 1997.

Nibley, Hugh. "Teachings of Brigham Young." In *Encyclopedia of Mormonism*, edited by Daniel H. Ludlow. 4 vols. New York: Macmillian, 1992.

O'Collins, Gerald. "Revelation." In *The Harper Collins Encyclopedia of Catholicism*, edited by Richard P. McBrien. San Francisco, Calif.: HarperSanFrancisco, 1995.

O'Gorman, Bob, and Mary Faulkner, *The Complete Idiot's Guide to Understanding Catholicism*. 2d ed. Indianapolis, Ind.: Alpha Books, 2003.

O'Meara, Thomas F. "Baroque Catholicism." In *The Harper Collins Encyclopedia of Catholicism*, edited by Richard P. McBrien. San Francisco, Calif.: HarperSanFrancisco, 1995.

Oaks, Dallin H. "The Aaronic Priesthood and the Sacrament." *Ensign* (November 1998): 37–40.

Ogden, D. Kelley, and Andrew C. Skinner. *Verse by Verse: The Four Gospels*. Salt Lake City: Deseret Book, 2006.

Osborne, Kenan. "Indulgences." In *The Harper Collins Encyclopedia of Catholicism*, edited by Richard P. McBrien. San Francisco, Calif.: HarperSanFrancisco, 1995.

———. "Reconciliation." In *The Harper Collins Encyclopedia of Catholicism*, edited by Richard P. McBrien. San Francisco, Calif.: HarperSanFrancisco, 1995.

Osiek, Carolyn. "Antichrist." In *The Harper Collins Encyclopedia of Catholicism*, edited by Richard P. McBrien. San Francisco, Calif.: HarperSanFrancisco, 1995.

Packer, Boyd K. "Washed Clean." *Ensign* (May 1997): 9–11.

Packer, J. I. "Foreword." In *Mary: A Catholic–Evangelical Debate*. Grand Rapids, Mich.: Brazos Press, 2003.

Palmer, Spencer W. "World Religions (Non-Christian) and Mormonism." In *Encyclopedia of Mormonism*, edited by Daniel H. Ludlow. 4 vols. New York: Macmillian, 1992.

"Patron Saint." In *The Harper Collins Encyclopedia of Catholicism*, edited by Richard P. McBrien. San Francisco, Calif.: HarperSanFrancisco, 1995.

"Penance." In *The Harper Collins Encyclopedia of Catholicism*, edited by Richard P. McBrien. San Francisco, Calif.: HarperSanFrancisco, 1995.

Perkins, Pheme. "The Gospel According to John." In *The New Jerome Biblical Commentary*. Englewood Cliffs, N.J.: Prentice Hall, 1990.

Peterson, Paul H. "Reformation (LDS) of 1856–1857." In *Encyclopedia of Mormonism*, edited by Daniel H. Ludlow. 4 vols. New York: Macmillan, 1992.

Peterson, Robert A. *Hell On Trial: The Case for Eternal Punishment*. Phillipsburg, N.J.: P & R Publishing, 1995.

Pfeiffer, Charles F., and Everett F. Harrison, eds. *The Wycliffe Bible Commentary*. Chicago, Ill.: Moody Press, 1975.

Pierce, Joanne M. "Vestments and Objects." In *The Oxford History of Christian Worship*, edited by Geoffrey Wainwright and Karen B. Westerfield Tucker. Oxford: Oxford University Press, 2006.

Piil, Mary, "Confirmation." In *The Harper Collins Encyclopedia of Catholicism*, edited by Richard P. McBrien. San Francisco, Calif.: HarperSanFrancisco, 1995.

Poelman, B. Lloyd. "Sunday School." In *Encyclopedia of Mormonism*, edited by Daniel H. Ludlow. 4 vols. New York: Macmillan, 1992.

Pollock, Robert. *The Everything World's Religions Book*. Avon, Mass.: Adams Media Corporation, 2002.

Poorman, Janice. "Modalism." In *The Harper Collins Encyclopedia of Catholicism*, edited by Richard P. McBrien. San Francisco, Calif.: HarperSanFrancisco, 1995.

Pottmeyer, Herman J. "Vatican Council I." In *The Harper Collins Encyclopedia of Catholicism*, edited by Richard P. McBrien. San Francisco, Calif.: HarperSanFrancisco, 1995.

Pratt, Orson. In *Journal of Discourses*. 26 vols. Liverpool: F.D. Richards, 1855–86. 2:334–347.

Rahner, Karl. "Anonymous Christianity and the Missionary Task of the Church." *IDOC Internazionale* 1 (April 4, 1970): 70–96.

Rahner, Karl. *The Trinity*. New York: Herder and Herder, 1970.

———. *Foundations of Christian Faith*. New York: Crossroads, 1993.

Reynolds, George and Janne M. Sjodahl. *Commentary on the Book of Mormon*, edited by Philip C. Reynolds. 7 vols. Salt Lake City: Deseret Book, 1955–61.

Roberts, Alexander, and James Donaldson, eds. *Ante-Nicene Fathers*. 10 vols. Peabody, Mass.: Hendrickson Publishers, 1994.

Robinson, Stephen E. "God the Father." In *Encyclopedia of Mormonism*, edited by Daniel H. Ludlow. 4 vols. New York: Macmillian, 1992.

Robinson, Stephen E. "Warning Against the Saints of God." *Ensign* (January 1988): 34–39.

Rusch, William G. *The Trinitarian Controversy*. Philadelphia, Pa.: Fortress Press, 1980.

Sachs, John R. "Resurrection of the Body." In *The Harper Collins Encyclopedia of Catholicism*, edited by Richard P. McBrien. San Francisco, Calif.: HarperSanFrancisco, 1995.

Seymour, Nicole. "Atmit to the Rescue." *Ensign* (January 2006): 74–75.

Sherman, Anthony. "Baptism." In *The Harper Collins Encyclopedia of Catholicism*, edited by Richard P. McBrien. San Francisco, Calif.: HarperSanFrancisco, 1995.

Shumway, Naomi M. "Primary." In *Encyclopedia of Mormonism*, edited by Daniel H. Ludlow. 4 vols. New York: Macmillan, 1992.

Smith, Hyrum G. *Conference Report*. October 1928.

Smith, Joseph. *History of the Church of Jesus Christ of Latter-day Saints*. Eight Volumes. B. H. Roberts, editor. Salt Lake City, UT: Deseret Book, 1978.

Smith, Joseph Fielding. *Origin of the Reorganized Church and the Question of Succession*. Salt Lake City: Deseret News, 1909.

———. *Church History and Modern Revelation*. 4 vols. Salt Lake City: The Church of Jesus Christ of Latter-day Saints, 1946–49.

———. *Doctrines of Salvation*. 3 vols. Salt Lake City: Bookcraft, 1998.

Smith, Joseph Fielding, comp. *Teachings of the Prophet Joseph Smith*. Salt Lake City: Deseret Book, 1976.

Smith, Thomas A. "Original Sin." In *The Harper Collins Encyclopedia of Catholicism*, edited by Richard P. McBrien. San Francisco, Calif.: HarperSanFrancisco, 1995.

Smith, Uriah. *Daniel and Revelation*. Mountain View, Calif.: Pacific Press, 1944.

Sorensen, David E. "Small Temples—Large Blessings." *Ensign* (November 1998): 65.

Strynkowski, John J. "Real Presence." In *The Harper Collins Encyclopedia of Catholicism*, edited by Richard P. McBrien. San Francisco, Calif.: HarperSanFrancisco, 1995.

"Subordinationism." In *The Harper Collins Encyclopedia of Catholicism*, edited by Richard P. McBrien. San Francisco, Calif.: HarperSanFrancisco, 1995.

Sullivan, Francis A. "Apostolic Succession." In *The Harper Collins Encyclopedia of Catholicism*, edited by Richard P. McBrien. San Francisco, Calif.: HarperSanFrancisco, 1995.

Talmage, James E. *The Articles of Faith*. Salt Lake City: The Church of Jesus Christ of Latter-day Saints, 1975.

Tanner, N. Eldon. "The Administration of the Church." In *Ensign (November 1979): 42–48.*

Taylor, John. *Mediation and Atonement.* Salt Lake City: Deseret News Company, 1882.

———. *The Gospel Kingdom: Selections from the Writings and Discourses of John Taylor.* Salt Lake City: Bookcraft, 1998.

Teachings of the Presidents of the Church: David O. McKay [Melchizedek Priesthood and Relief Society course of study]. Salt Lake City: The Church of Jesus Christ of Latter-day Saints, 2003.

"Theotokos." In *The Harper Collins Encyclopedia of Catholicism*, edited by Richard P. McBrien. San Francisco, Calif.: HarperSanFrancisco, 1995.

Tillard, Jean M. R. "Primacy, Papal." In *The Harper Collins Encyclopedia of Catholicism*, edited by Richard P. McBrien. San Francisco, Calif.: HarperSanFrancisco, 1995.

Tolson, Jay. "QA: Elder M. Russell Ballard on the Mormon Way." *US News and World Report.* November 12, 2007.

Toropov, Brandon. *The Complete Idiot's Guide to the Popes and the Papacy.* Indianapolis, Ind.: Alpha Books, 2002.

Tresidder, Jack. *Symbols and their Meanings.* London: Duncan Baird Publishers, 2000.

Turner, Rodney. "The Doctrine of the Firstborn and Only Begotten." In *The Pearl of Great Price: Revelations From God*, edited by H. Donl Peterson and Charles D. Tate Jr. Provo, Utah: Brigham Young University, Religious Studies Center, 1989.

Tvedtnes, John. "Priestly Clothing in Bible Times." In *Temples of the Ancient World*, edited by Donald W. Parry. Provo, Utah: Foundation for Ancient Research and Mormon Studies, 1994.

United States Catholic Catechism for Adults. Washington, D.C.: United States Conference of Catholic Bishops, 2006.

Van Biema, David. "Life After Limbo." *Time.* January 9, 2006.

"Veneration of the Cross." In *The Harper Collins Encyclopedia of Catholicism*, edited by Richard P. McBrien. San Francisco, Calif.: HarperSanFrancisco, 1995.

"Venial Sin." In *The Harper Collins Encyclopedia of Catholicism*, edited by Richard P. McBrien. San Francisco, Calif.: HarperSanFrancisco, 1995.

Voiss, James K. "Celibacy, Clerical." In *The Harper Collins Encyclopedia of Catholicism*, edited by Richard P. McBrien. San Francisco, Calif.: HarperSanFrancisco, 1995.

Von Wellnitz, Marcus. "The Catholic Liturgy and the Mormon Temple." *BYU Studies* 21, no. 1 (1981): 3–35.

Wainwright, Geoffrey, and Karen B. Westerfield Tucker, eds. *The Oxford History of Christian Worship.* Oxford: Oxford University Press, 2006.

Webb, Diana. "Pilgrimage." In *Encyclopedia of Christianity*, edited by John Bowden. New York: Oxford University Press, 2005.

Wells, Samuel. "Trinity." In *Encyclopedia of Christianity*, edited by John Bowden, New York: Oxford University Press, 2005.

White, Joseph M. "Seminary." In *The Harper Collins Encyclopedia of Catholicism*, edited by Richard P. McBrien. San Francisco, Calif.: HarperSanFrancisco, 1995.

Whitney, Orson F. *Conference Report*. April 3, 1921.

———. *Saturday Night Thoughts*. Salt Lake City: Deseret News, 1921.

Whittaker, David J. "Articles of Faith." In *Encyclopedia of Mormonism,* edited by Daniel H. Ludlow. 4 vols. New York: Macmillian, 1992.

Widtsoe, John A. *Gospel Interpretations*. Salt Lake City: Bookcraft, 1947.

Widtsoe, John A., comp. *Discourses of Brigham Young*. Salt Lake City: Bookcraft, 1998.

Williams, Paul L. *The Complete Idiot's Guide to the Lives of the Saints*. Indianapolis, Ind.: Alpha Books, 2001.

———. *The Complete Idiot's Guide to The Crusades*. Indianapolis, Ind.: Alpha Books, 2002.

Wirthlin, Joseph B. "Christians in Belief and Action." *Ensign* (November 1996): 70–73.

Wood, Susan K. "Tradition." In *The Harper Collins Encyclopedia of Catholicism*, edited by Richard P. McBrien. San Francisco, Calif.: HarperSanFrancisco, 1995.

Woodruff, Wilford. *Wilford Woodruff's Journal, 1833–1898, Typescript*, edited by Scott G. Kenney. 9 vols. Midvale, Utah: Signature Books, 1983–84.

———. In *Journal of Discourses*. 26 vols. Liverpool: F. D. Richards, 1855–86. 18:28–40.

———. *The Discourses of Wilford Woodruff*, edited by G. Homer Durham. Salt Lake City: Bookcraft, 1998.

Wright, Donald N. "Judgment Day, Final." In *Encyclopedia of Mormonism*, edited by Daniel H. Ludlow. 4 vols. New York: Macmillian, 1992.

Yarbro Collins, Adela. "The Apocalypse (Revelation)." In *The New Jerome Biblical Commentary*. Englewood Cliffs, N. J.: Prentice Hall, 1990.

Yarnold, Edward J. "Theology of Baptism." In *The New Dictionary of Sacramental Worship*, edited by Peter Fink. Collegeville, Minn.: Liturgical Press, 1990.

Young, Brigham. In *Journal of Discourses*. 26 vols. Liverpool: F. D. Richards, 1855–86. 7:147–49.

OTHER TITLES IN THE
KNOW YOUR RELIGIONS SERIES

❧

MORMONISM AND CATHOLICISM

MORMONISM AND ASIAN RELIGIONS

MORMONISM AND ISLAM

MORMONISM AND PROTESTANTISM

MORMONISM AND JUDAISM

MORMONISM AND JEHOVAH'S WITNESSES

MORMONISM AND THE COMMUNITY OF CHRIST

❧

LOOK FOR MORE TITLES IN THE KNOW YOUR RELIGIONS SERIES